"Melany Jackson is my hero! She is  be accomplished with God's guidance ; when I visited her ministry in 2015. No C-U at Home, but it's also an encoura_ .... to follow in Jesus' footsteps. You rock, Melany!"
    —**Bob Beeman**, author, musician, songwriter, founder and pastor of Sanctuary International Ministries.

"Melany Jackson is radical. Her powerful memoir, *More Than Enough*, the story of Melany's grit interwoven with God's grace, is a page-turner that is both uncompromising and unflinching. *More Than Enough* tells of God's faithfulness to society's most vulnerable through the eyes, heart, and hands of a champion committed to their protection and provision."
    —**Dr. Freddy Cardoza**, Talbot School of Theology, Biola University.

"One winter night, Melany Jackson went out onto the frozen streets with the goal of ministering to homeless people. Little did she know that a homeless man would minister to her, transforming her life in ways she never could have seen coming. Melany calls it her 'holy kick in the tail.'

More Than Enough is a wake-up call to anyone who has become complacent and comfortable worshiping on Sunday and then blending in with our culture six days of the week. As Melany makes so clear, Jesus is more than enough. In these pages, you will discover that stepping out in faith and giving beyond your means can produce fruit beyond your wildest dreams."
    —**Doug Peterson**, novelist and VeggieTales writer.

"*More Than Enough* is Melany Jackson's thoughtful journey of faith, looking through the lens of her call, love for others, and God's timing, to do what we each should do, 'seek first the kingdom of God.' Her stories, prayers and decisions weave the tapestry of God's leading that is sometimes confusing and uncertain, yet always deep and invigorating. As you read it, you, too, will find courage to trust the God who has more than enough for your own journey."
    —**Dr. Jimmy Dorrell**, author and founder of Mission Waco/Mission World, pastor of Church Under the Bridge.

"I've learned this over the years about leadership: There are LEADERS! And then there are actual, real-life, Jesus-shaped leaders. We don't need to listen to the former. We do need to listen to the latter type, and – I've known her for years – that's Melany. She's probably even embarrassed I'm writing this about her. (Too bad, Melany!) God is using her, and He'll use her book."

–**Brant Hansen**, Cure International, nationally syndicated radio host, and author of *Unoffendable* and *Blessed Are the Misfits*.

"I was raised on a healthy diet of Christian biographies from the nineteenth century. Reading the soul-stirring accounts of C.H. Spurgeon, D.L. Moody, George Müeller, and Charles Finney served as a reminder of God's gracious provision. In *More Than Enough*, this same divine provision is manifested through Melany Jackson. As the founder of C-U at Home, Melany's story is a refreshing account of surrender, obedience, struggle and success – only to be asked to surrender once again."

–**Dr. Rodney Harrison**, author and Dean at Midwestern Baptist Theological Seminary.

"Melany Jackson is a force of nature. I mean the passionate nature her Lord inspires, the One she has served by serving her 'friends without an address' for many years. Friend, advocate, and inspiration for myself and countless others, may her story compel us to serve 'the least of these' by the very example she has set: with kindness, with grace, and with practical help."

–**Glenn Kaiser**, musician, songwriter, founder of Resurrection Band and the Glenn Kaiser Band, and pastor at Jesus People USA.

"*More Than Enough* chronicles Melany Jackson's God-inspired journey to help those without an address find shelter, community, and hope. Written with uncommon transparency and vulnerability, Melany recounts both the elations and the heartaches of founding and shepherding a ministry that serves those who are too often relegated to society's margins. What emerges is a powerful testimony of God's providence and provision and a personal challenge to sacrificially live out our faith and values in a way that impacts others and brings God the glory."

–**Erika Harold**, J.D., Miss America 2003.

"In the early days of C-U at Home, Melany Jackson and I started meeting regularly. I saw how challenging it is to create a nonprofit ministry — building the infrastructure, finding donors, finding the right staff. Melany got a hold of a God idea, and she didn't let go. That's because she is a tenacious leader with a tender heart for those with no address."

—**Don Follis**, author and founder of Pastor-to-Pastor Initiatives.

"Innovative, cutting edge urban ministry seldom has the up-front financial underwriting for a comfortable launch. That's why it's called 'faith' ministry. Visionaries with a persistent passion are often called to venture out on risky, 'thin ice,' and trust that God will sustain them. That is Melany Jackson's experience in *More Than Enough*. Important reading for anyone who feels drawn to fashion new wine-skins."

—**Bob Lupton**, author of *Toxic Charity* and founder of FCS Urban Ministries.

"God's story of engaging with humanity is a story of grace, restoration, and purpose. *More Than Enough* is that kind of story. This book is an encouraging reminder of God's love for us, his redemptive work among us, and the purpose he gives us to serve others."

—**Micah Fries**, author and pastor of Brainerd Baptist Church.

MORE THAN ENOUGH:

MIRACULOUS PROVISION REVEALED THROUGH C-U AT HOME FOR OUR FRIENDS WITHOUT AN ADDRESS

Melany L. Jackson

Editor: JoAnn Shade

Proofreader: Cheryl Lehman

Cover: Matthew Rebel, Carly Conway, and Jay Schubert

More Than Enough:
Miraculous Provision Revealed Through C-U at Home
for Our Friends Without an Address

Printed in the United States

ISBN-13: 978-1979586153
ISBN-10: 1979586152

CONTENTS

INTRODUCTION

Thank you for your interest in seeing God's glory revealed through His miraculous provision for one of His daughters. What God did in and through me to develop a new ministry for our friends without an address is truly nothing short of miraculous. My faith was stretched beyond the point of no return and my life will never be the same.

This book is written largely in chronological order from 2010-2017. I used a combination of daily journal entries, meeting notes, phone records, email, and a schedule calendar to piece together what happened when. So, that's how I decided to tell the story.

I was born and raised in the small town of Centralia, in Southern Illinois. My early years were spent going to church every single week at the little Southern Baptist Church less than a block from our home. Though I was presented over and over with clear renderings of the Gospel of Jesus Christ, its Truth only became real to me as an adult.

I went through marriage and divorce before I was twenty-five. Eventually, I moved to Central Illinois, and God finally got my attention. It was only after fully surrendering my life to Him as an adult that I started down various paths of ministry as a vocation. Once I became a Jesus-follower, my faith in Him has become the driving force in my life.

As you will see in this book, God has blessed my gifts of administration, passion, and compassion, a rabid work ethic, and entrepreneurship. Like all humans, one of my greatest strengths has a dark side to it. The dark side of my leadership and passion is that of performance orientation, being demanding, offending others, and expecting perfection from myself and others. In the book, I refer to this as my "flat side." We are all in process. We all have a flat side.

1

That doesn't mean God loves you or me any less. It just means that He longs to redeem us, one conversation or instance at a time.

The prevailing theme throughout the book is one of provision — financial, housing, volunteers, staff, and more, both for me personally and for the ministry of C-U at Home (CUH). Also included are the themes of dealing with my flat side, being overwhelmed, hi/lo days, God-incidences (rather than coincidences), and prayer and fasting (particularly on Thursdays).

I hope you will see yourself on these pages, relating to the struggles and victories of launching a new ministry and learning from my mistakes. Above all, I pray you will see that God IS faithful. That He is ready to welcome you home even after you've blown it once again. That He can and will bless what we do, sometimes in spite of ourselves. Often, that's when His grace is really alive and we can see His glory most clearly revealed.

The events chronicled on these pages are depicted as best as I can remember them. And several names have been changed to protect the identity of those who were a part of this journey with me.

1

Talking to Jesus on My Behalf

It was a dark and stormy night . . . well, more like a cold and blustery night, in Central Illinois. On that Monday night in December 2010, with snow on the ground, snow falling from the sky, and a brisk north wind howling, the Canteen Run's mobile ministry truck pulled into the parking lot of the iHop on Urbana's Green Street in campus town. Three men slowly made their way up to the back of the truck. They were cold, really cold, and their unkempt appearance and stale odor were indicative of a rough life. Several of the volunteers in the truck already knew the men by name and they started talking with them. I noticed that one of the men wasn't wearing gloves. His fingertips were starting to get dark.

Frostbite.

A disconnect. That simply shouldn't be happening here in this affluent and educated community. We're literally standing on the campus of the University of Illinois.

Pastor Steve had told me about the Canteen Run. It's a volunteer-led mobile ministry that takes donated materials to people right where they are, many of them having no permanent home. They distribute shirts, coats, blankets, socks, underwear, hygiene packets, sack lunches, and water to folks at the public libraries, bus terminal, parks, and on campus. Steve and I first went out together on the Canteen Run on that snowy December night. It was quite a God-incidence that Steve told me about this ministry, as this divine interruption became the adventure that led to the birth of C-U at Home, a ministry for our friends without an address.

We served some hot coffee to the men and provided them with blankets. They said they would be spending the night in an underground parking garage, out of the wind and snow, but with little

3

protection from the bitter cold. One of the volunteers on the truck asked if we could pray for them, and they agreed. Everyone piled out of the truck and we joined hands in a circle. The prayer was simple: for God to take care of these guys tonight, to protect them from the elements and to watch over them until morning.

Amen.

And then one of those guys started praying for us. He thanked Jesus for bringing people to care about them, and he prayed that we would be safe and we would be warm that night.

Amen.

That prayer was the game-changer for me. When I climbed into the Canteen Run's truck for the first time that evening, I had no idea that one of the guys from the street would be talking to Jesus on my behalf. God now had my full attention.

The prayer of the man who had no home resonated with me, as I was being called to live out my faith in Christ in a more radical way. Following an intense time of personal struggle just a couple of weeks earlier, I'd read David Platt's book, *Radical: Taking Back Your Faith from the American Dream*. Platt's premise in the book is that many people who consider themselves to be Christ followers in America don't look much different from their neighbors. Same houses, cars, bikes, boats, vacations, jobs, all striving daily for the coveted American dream. Many churches in the United States have similar goals, putting their focus on top-notch programs, well-trained staff, and state-of-the-art facilities. Platt's book calls us to a very different type of life. If we, as believers, are to emulate Christ as our model, we should be living a life of intentional sacrifice, including the sacrifice of our time, our finances, and our possessions. True sacrifice, not just a donation or an offering, but sacrifice, giving away something that you really love to someone, with nothing expected or accepted in return. Giving until it hurts. Giving beyond your means.

At the end of *Radical*, Platt challenges the reader to take the "Radical Experiment" for one year, to live an intentionally sacrificial life in five different areas. This personal challenge was just the holy kick in the tail that I needed, and became the catalyst for me to do something about the guys I had just met who were living on the streets. When something like reading this book and the Canteen Run experience happen at the same time, I don't call it a coincidence, but rather a God-incidence, a divine interruption.

Years before, I had learned this truth through Henry Blackaby's *Experiencing God* Bible study: God is ALWAYS at work around us. He offers us an invitation to join Him in that work. Then it's up to us to respond, either to accept or to deny His invitation. God was clearly inviting me to join Him in His work, helping the most desperate, chronic, street homeless guys in Champaign.

Not long after that frigid night, just a few days before Christmas, I received an email shared through the Canteen Run ministry that included a *New York Times* article about a nationwide movement, a three-year plan to house the most vulnerable homeless, called 100,000 Homes. I was more than intrigued by this, for here was a plan, a project, an established movement to tangibly help people like the three guys I had just met on Green Street. God was indeed inviting me to join Him in His work.

Needing to find out more about the ministries and organizations in our area that were already involved in helping the homeless, I attended a meeting of the county-wide Council of Service Providers to the Homeless (CSPH), comprised of more than twenty-five different homeless organizations. I also attended a meeting of Partnering Against Homelessness, the parent organization for the Canteen Run. At their January meetings, I shared about the national 100,000 Homes project to generate interest in developing a Champaign County chapter to help the most vulnerable folks living on our streets.

I discovered that a group was working to develop an emergency shelter in the Oscar Romero Center at St. Mary's Catholic Church that would be open during the brutal winter months. They were able to provide sixteen beds to the most vulnerable homeless during the month of February, which was a huge blessing. The shelter was organized and staffed entirely by volunteers. This was good. But was more needed?

I gathered a few people from my church to dive deeper into the concepts of *Radical* and into the scriptures about a more radical walk with Jesus. As we did so, the Lord began to solidify my call to devote myself to the cause of the people dying on our community's streets. Convinced of the power of Platt's writing, over the next seven years I was inspired to give away more than 2500 copies of the book *Radical* to people I met. I was quite passionate about getting the message of *Radical* into the hands of folks who might be deeply impacted by its message, to sacrificially follow after Christ.

As spring approached, I was leading the *Radical* home Bible study, planning and leading weekly worship at my church, and working in a variety of part-time jobs. I was also leading the effort for our church to develop a new English as a Second Language (ESL) ministry called USA Café. Through it, we taught idioms to international students at the University of Illinois, encouraging church members to build relationships with them and invite them into their homes. I've never been one to let the grass grow under my feet, so I continued searching out more information about homelessness, going out on the Canteen Run each week, and learning more about the 100,000 Homes national campaign.

I was privileged to meet with two local leaders of homeless organizations, Barb Davies and Jason Greenly. Barb and her husband Dan had started the Canteen Run mobile ministry several years earlier, and Jason was the director for the TIMES Center, a men's transitional shelter/housing program. As I shared my desire to launch a local 100,000 Homes campaign here in Champaign, they were gracious and encouraging. We realized that to start something like this, it would take buy-in from local stakeholders and that it would take a leader, someone to develop and to be the face of the project. It was my hope to get the Council of Service Providers to the Homeless behind this effort. Jason was resigning as chair of the CSPH, and the group would be electing a new chairperson at the next meeting, on April 5. Both Jason and Barb encouraged me to submit my name to potentially be chosen as the next chair for the group. I was very new to everything about homelessness and I had only been to two of their meetings, but if this was the Lord's leading, I was willing.

I was prayed up and prepared to submit my name for nomination as chair for the Council of Service Providers to the Homeless. When it came time for new business, electing a new chair was first on the agenda. My name was the only one nominated, and I was voted in unanimously as the new chair. Later, I realized no one else really wanted the job, but at that time, I was on cloud nine. I received that vote as a green light from God to proceed with plans to develop a local chapter of the three-year 100,000 Homes national campaign.

During this time, I was renting a room from a church friend, Marie Davis. Her family would be moving back to Illinois from California in the summer, and she said I was more than welcome to stay, that there would still be room for me. But I knew she needed space to be able to minister to her own family. I remember thinking, "Okay God, here you've got me starting a homeless ministry, and now I don't have a place to live. You've got a great sense of humor!"

Often God speaks to us through other people – our pastor, a friend, a family member, a singer, a co-worker, someone from our neighborhood, or even someone we randomly meet. God used two of my friends, just a couple of days apart, who had the same message for me: "Maybe you should go talk with Ervin at Restoration Urban Ministries." Once the second friend said that to me, it dawned on me. A year and a half earlier, I had been headed back to Illinois with no job, no money, and no place to live, with two ministries on my mind: Salt & Light and Restoration Urban Ministries (RUM). When I got to Champaign, I started volunteering at Salt & Light right away and was hired on staff there a couple of weeks later. However, I never even made it over to RUM to say hello to Ervin. Now God was making it clear that it was time to visit.

Ervin Williams is the founder and the director of Restoration Urban Ministries, a ministry that took over an old two-building, two-story hotel in 1997. It's a place where those without an address can get a new start at life. They offer Restoration Church, as well as a wide variety of classes for GED, anger management, substance abuse, parenting, and other life skills. Folks who live there go to chapel in the morning and then have classes until lunch. After lunchtime, they spend four hours each weekday afternoon working somewhere on the ministry property. Those who have outside employment work either second or third shift.

In my meeting with brother Ervin at RUM, he shared about many aspects of their ministry and listened intently to how God was prompting me to get a chapter of the 100,000 Homes campaign started in Champaign. Might it be possible for me to move into Restoration? Doing so would provide a safe place for me to live without rent or the cost of utilities, and I would be able to live in community with folks who have been in homeless situations. This would give me the opportunity to build relationships with them, to get to know them, to laugh together, and to cry together. I would live with a few slight inconveniences and get just a small taste of what it might be like to actually be homeless.

Ervin explained that over the years, a few people had come to live intentionally at Restoration. Sometimes it worked, sometimes it didn't. The only way to know was for me to try it out myself. He suggested I come to a church service and a staff meeting, plan an overnight stay, and then, if everything pointed in that direction, I could move into a room sometime in the next couple of months. I could launch this new ministry effort while living as part of the Restoration community.

On that first visit to Restoration, I reconnected with a friend named Rita, who used to be a part of my church. Her husband had abandoned her and her two children and she had no place to live. Rita was to become an incredible prayer partner and encourager for me throughout the next eighteen months.

As for what to call the ministry God was drawing me to? I am a swimmer for exercise, doing laps on a regular basis since about 1998. In the pool, underwater, and riding down the road on a motorcycle are two places that God frequently inspires me. While I was swimming laps one morning, the idea to call the ministry C-U at Home and to use a house in the logo came to me all at once. The twin cities of Champaign and Urbana are often referred to as "C-U," and several events and businesses have C-U in their titles. The play on words for "see you at home" was intentional. The whole idea behind C-U at Home (CUH) was to help those folks who are closest to dying on the streets have the dignity of a home of their own.

To get this started would take some money and LOTS of time and energy. At this time, I didn't really have much of either. So, the best way I knew to get money was by selling some of my belongings. I had a pretty nice motorcycle and the nicest vehicle I had ever owned, an SUV. I still had quite a few seminary books that might be worth some money. I was praying, "Lord, I'm somewhat anxious about going through my stuff. What stays? What goes? I want to be faithful, but not stupid. If I trust You totally and You lead me, C-U at Home will be huge in spite of me. Please keep me humble. Help me be kind to those who are helping me. I want to be Your obedient servant. Amen."

I listed my Honda Magna motorcycle and my Mazda Tribute SUV for sale on craigslist in mid-April. My bike sold for my asking price of $3800. I purchased a Geo Prizm for $1650 on May 18, and I got my asking price of $8800 for my Tribute on May 25. God was providing seed money for the start-up of C-U at Home.

Then I reconnected with an old friend, John Smith, and I shared a copy of the book *Radical* with him, as well as the idea of C-U at Home, finding places to live for the guys who are dying on the streets. He was interested and soon became a valuable partner with me to launch the ministry. A Canteen Run volunteer, Elaine Harper, was also quite instrumental in the start of what would become C-U at Home, introducing a day of prayer and fasting for the ministry each week on Thursdays. In support of that effort, we also started sending out a weekly prayer email on Wednesday evenings to keep everyone updated on our prayer needs in time for Thursdays.

By Memorial Day of 2011, I had finished the last of my five part-time jobs, and things were falling into place to build the foundation of C-U at Home. My prayer journal recorded my concerns: "Afraid of failing God. I can't do this alone. I will fail if I don't put God in control. I want a tender, compassionate spirit, but fail every day. Am I being obedient or strangely selfish? I want to know You more in an intimate, personal way. Help me open my mouth and share my faith."

During this time, another homeless organization in our town, the Center for Women in Transition, offered space in the attic of one of their homes for us to set up a small starter office for C-U at Home. This was a HUGE blessing. It was so exciting, moving in our small stash of office supplies and getting the phone and computer all set up to use.

A yard sale to sell my seminary books and other items was also successful, netting the ministry over a thousand dollars. The following day, I spent my first morning at Restoration Church and my first night sleeping in room #284 at Restoration Urban Ministries, which was to be my home for the next eighteen months.

2

The Path Begins

How did I get to room #284? The journey began when I was eight years old, when I went home after church one Sunday and knelt by my bed to ask Jesus to come into my heart. I knew that's what I was supposed to do, as I was raised in a little Southern Baptist Church, one-half block from our home. I attended Sunday School literally every Sunday of my life until I was nineteen years old. I think I still hold the all-time record for that church! I knew Jesus was the Son of God and that He lived a sinless life, paid the price for my sin with His own blood on the cross, and rose again on the third day. Death could not hold Him in the grave. And when my Sunday School teacher told us we needed to ask Jesus into our hearts, that's what I did.

I enjoyed diagramming scripture on big pieces of poster board for the congregation, grammar geek that I am. My dad was a deacon and my mom was the church secretary. But it was empty. I don't ever remember them reading scripture or praying at home. Not one time. Theirs was a very rocky, unhealthy marriage. Many, many nights I went to sleep crying, trying to drown out the sounds of their screams at one other. I came to realize that I modeled my Christianity like them – on Sunday morning I put on the mask; the rest of the week, I lived like the rest of the world. Thank God that He got my attention one day in 1995 and drew me into right relationship with His Son and subsequently, into a life of ministry.

I was working the sound booth in the loft at the back of the sanctuary at Christmas Tree Road Baptist Church in Decatur, IL. Lanny Faulkner was preaching, serving as our interim pastor, when something happened to me. I had made friends with two young families in that church, the Conways and the Whitneys. Watching them as they interacted with each other and observing how they were raising their kids, I realized they had something I did not have. I wanted what they had. I fell on my face, prostrate, and surrendered my life to Christ. I confessed my sin and inadequacy and asked Him to take control of my life. That was the true beginning of my life as a Christ-follower. From that day on, my life did look different. I had a desire to follow Him.

A few months later, I was riding through the country with John, my ex-husband, channel surfing on the radio, and stopped the dial for this catchy folksy story song called, "Two Sets of Jones'." I kept listening and discovered that the station name was WBGL in Champaign, IL, and that it played what they called "Contemporary Christian" music. I was hooked. I couldn't get enough of this type of music. Music with a theme of Christian faith that sounded like other bands on top 40 radio. How cool was that!

A young Canadian artist, Carolyn Arends, sang a song, "Seize the Day," that especially spoke into a recent tragedy in my life. I had lost a friend and co-worker at *The Herald & Review* in Decatur, IL, Karyn Hearn Slover. She was heinously murdered and dismembered by her ex-husband and his parents. Karyn was only twenty-three years old, and left behind a precious three-year-old son named Kolten. Through my grief, God was calling me to be much more intentional, to suck the marrow out of life, to live each day to the fullest, to seize the day. Carpe Diem.

WBGL announced that Carolyn Arends would be coming to Heartland Church in Decatur. I didn't quite catch all the details, so I called the DJ to find out how to get tickets to her show. When Tim Nelson answered the phone, I mentioned how much I had loved my time working in radio in college, learning to blade edit 8-track reels, spin programs on vinyl, and play spots on carts at Real Rock Radio, WTAO, in Carbondale. Tim suggested I get in touch with Steve Young, the station manager, as they were looking for a part-time announcer.

And the rest, as they say, is history.

I was hired to do the weekend overnights at WBGL in December of 1996. I spent the next year living in Mt. Zion, teaching at Richland College, working at *The Herald & Review* in Decatur, and driving to Champaign each weekend. The Lord blessed me with a full-time position at WBGL in December of 1997, when I bought a house and moved to Urbana. I continued to work at WBGL in a combination of on-air and other secondary roles until 2004. I absolutely loved being a part of Christian radio – the music, praying with listeners, attending live concerts, and connecting with others involved in Christian radio.

I joined Garden Hills Baptist Church, a Southern Baptist Church on the west side of Champaign. They welcomed me in and over the years, I developed close friendships. One of my closest friends, Tim Hendrix, was the worship leader. At that time, we projected words for the music using an overhead projector. A visiting evangelist referred to me as the "ministress of transparencies." I loved being Tim's assistant, helping him by making copies of choir music, organizing the files, and doing the transparencies.

In the spring of 2002, Tim graduated with his Ph.D. and accepted a teaching position in another state. With his departure, the church needed to find someone else to lead worship. After a friend encouraged me to consider the possibility, I got in touch with Pastor Steve Diehl and asked if I could be the interim worship leader until we found someone permanent for the position.

I served in that position at Garden Hills for two years, thematically planning the flow of worship songs to go with the sermon each week. I was privileged to lead the congregation to the throne of grace each Sunday morning. I don't have an excellent singing voice and I only play a bit of basic guitar and no keyboard. But the Lord did bless me with a gift to connect with people during worship, to tear through the veil between heaven and earth in order to help others experience God's presence. More times than I can count, I have had someone from the congregation come up to me after I have been in the choir or part of the worship team or serving as the worship leader and say something like this: "I just love to watch you worship! There's something special about the way that you connect with God when you sing." I am blessed to use this gift for God's glory.

In January 2004, God turned my life completely upside down. I took a trip to visit a dear friend and knew we were going to have a difficult conversation. That trip ended with the abrupt severing of our close friendship. Even before I was back home, I had communicated with Pastor Steve about our church doing 40 Days of Purpose, based on the book *The Purpose Driven Life* by Rick Warren, starting in February, and for me to be the lead organizer for that. It was good for me to have something important to focus my attention at that point and to get my mind off the pain of losing the relationship.

I'd had a copy of the book in my possession for a few weeks, but I waited to read it until I could go through it with the rest of my church family during the 40 Days campaign and study groups. Somehow, I sensed this book would have a powerful impact on me at this particular time in my life.

We launched our 40 Days of Purpose campaign in February 2004, the same month the new Mel Gibson film, *The Passion of the Christ*, was to be released. The film faced criticism that it was anti-Semitic, that it depicted unnecessary extreme violence, and that Gibson took too much artistic license with the theology of the film, rendering it inaccurate.

Pastor Steve and another pastor friend had joined 4,000 other pastors at a special preview screening of the film at Willow Creek Church. We discussed how lots of churches and religious groups across the country were planning to use the film as an evangelistic tool in a variety of ways. Some planned to buy all the tickets for showings and to give the tickets away in their neighborhoods. Others planned to host public discussions about the film so that people could get their questions answered. Steve and I brainstormed about how we could use this film to reach people in our community for Christ, advertising it on our sign and promoting the film at the Beverly Theatre, a few blocks to our north. Perhaps they would let us have some of the gospel materials from the film there at the theatre for moviegoers to take home.

I will never forget that conversation. When he said that, I looked him in the eyes and said, "Yeah, right," thinking to myself, of course a secular multi-plex movie theatre is going to let us set up a table in their lobby and hand out gospel materials! Still, Steve offered to contact the Beverly to see about getting permission. What I did not know was that God was at work here, allowing Steve to see the preview and then have this idea about partnering with the theatre. This was a real God-incidence, a divine interruption in my life.

Just two days later, he received permission from the theatre to set up the table with materials that covered half of the theatre lobby! Not only that, but theatre manager Rebekah Brumleve gave us permission to have volunteers at the table the entire time the film was showing, twelve hours a day, to pray with moviegoers, listen to them, and offer Kleenex for their tears.

I was off to the races. Not only was I working full-time at WBGL, working part-time at my church, and leading our 40 Days of Purpose campaign, but now I would also be leading a major community-wide Passion Outreach at the Beverly (POB). We started getting the word out left and right, collecting funds for donated materials and recruiting volunteers to spend time at the Passion table at the theatre. We set up a website with all kinds of resources, and Great News Radio, the Moody affiliate station in our area, came alongside us, a huge blessing to help recruit volunteers for the table and donations for the gospel materials. Mark Burns, the station manager, became my right-hand man for the outreach.

We also held a major community-wide event at the Virginia Theatre, a locally owned downtown venue, called "Passion Answers: A Community Dialogue," where an Evangelical Pastor, a Catholic Priest, and a Jewish Rabbi led a panel to answer questions from the community, emceed by a local TV news anchor.

The Passion of the Christ ran at the Beverly for seventy-nine days in a row, and our outreach was supported by three hundred volunteers from more than seventy-two churches and at least twenty-three denominations. God provided the funds to purchase and distribute over 11,000 pieces of gospel literature associated with the film. I lost count of how many boxes of Kleenex we used. This particular God-incidence resulted in a tremendous evangelism opportunity in our community through the POB, and provided valuable ministry organizational experience for me. I was humbled and grateful that the Lord used me to coordinate this Gospel effort in our community.

During that spring, God also used two books to powerfully impact my life. *The Purpose Driven Life* by Rick Warren helped me realize that God does indeed have a particular purpose and plan for my life. It would be up to me to have an open heart to see what that purpose was. For those three months, I knew that my purpose was to orchestrate the community-wide Passion Outreach at the Beverly.

I learned of the second book through *Focus on the Family*, listening to an interview with Bruce Wilkinson on the radio about his new book. I had read his previous book, *The Prayer of Jabez,* several years earlier, and it had a pretty strong impact on me. I even bought a couple cases of books and gave them to family and friends. This new book, *The Dream Giver*, began with an allegory, much like *Pilgrim's Progress*, and then Wilkinson applied the allegory to our lives. The crazy thing about this is when I read the book, literally every character and event in the allegory was being lived out in my own life right at that time.

Through the 40 Days of Purpose at my church, the POB, my work at WBGL radio, and planning and leading worship at my church, I was living out the life of the main character in this book. Wilkinson writes, "He thought about how wonderful it would be to do what he loved to do instead of just dreaming about it." I wrote in the margin,

"What is this for me? Is it really leading worship or is it leading/planning/organizing a ministry?" I was excited. I was confused. I wanted God to show me more of how His story for my life would go. He used this God-incidence as confirmation that I should get prepared for something new.

In April, I had my annual employee review meeting at WBGL, and as I walked into the room, I had the distinct sense that one of two things was going to happen: either I would be promoted or let go. And even stranger is that the Lord gave me His peace with either outcome. That was pretty crazy since I LOVED working at the station and being a part of Christian radio. And previously, I had assumed I would work there my whole life. I was right about the meeting: they were letting me go. The official word was that they were "outsourcing their IT needs," which was the only area I had been working in for the previous few months. I had been taken off the air permanently in January, after having had a regular on-air shift there since December of 1996. I was disappointed and hurt when I was removed from being on the air. But by the grace of God, a short four months later when they told me I would no longer be working at WBGL, I was able to remain peaceful and actually say "thank you." I was being released for a new ministry position. No real idea what or where, but full-time ministry somewhere.

The loss of my position at WBGL was counter-balanced by an unexpected gift. I learned from Pastor Steve that some of the folks involved with the POB wanted to thank me for getting it organized. They were giving me a ten-day pilgrimage to Israel. WOW! To say I was surprised is an understatement.

So in June, I found myself boarding an EL AL airlines plane for the Ben Gurion International Airport in Tel Aviv. It was incredible to be in the Holy Land, to literally walk on the same streets where Jesus walked. Once we made it by bus to our hotel in the Old City of Jerusalem, I made my way up to our room. My roommate Brenda was helping Mark and Carrie organize the trip, so she was downstairs working with them and I had a few moments to myself. We were on an upper floor with a nice view of the Old City.

I wanted to go out on the balcony for a few minutes and relax, spend a few minutes alone with the Lord. Pausing in the threshold of the sliding glass door, I looked down and saw four perfect feathers at my feet. I dropped to my knees and started to cry. I knew without a doubt that it was a visit from the Lord and an encouragement to me that yes, He did have a new dream waiting for me and that He would

16

reveal it to me in His time. In *The Dream Giver*, a feather is the symbol of God's dream for you, and while I had no idea what four feathers might mean, I knew this was my Abba Father speaking to me. No coincidence here, only a God-incidence, once again confirming I would be doing something new to serve Him.

All throughout the trip, as we visited one holy site after another, were taught from the Bible, and sang worship songs together, my Abba continued to send me feathers. One landing softly on the shoulder of the speaker and then floating my direction. Another landing on my own shoe. On and on, throughout the whole trip. No one else was seeing these feathers. It was INCREDIBLE. I returned home with eighteen feathers from nine different locations in Israel. These feathers are matted in a frame with a photo of my baptism in the Jordan River, one of my most treasured possessions.

Our trip included a visit to the Yad Vashem Holocaust Museum in Jerusalem. The exhibit was striking, completely dark except for a single lit candle, which was reflected in a series of mirrors from floor to ceiling throughout the building. There was a winding path to walk through, surrounded by what seemed like a million points of light. Silence enveloped us, except for the somber announcer who continuously spoke the name and age of each child murdered in the Holocaust. It was absolutely haunting. I began to weep. I couldn't stop weeping once we left the exhibit. I asked myself, what does this mean, Lord? Why are You breaking my heart in this way? I don't even like kids! Through the feathers and the experience at Yad Vashem, I knew the Lord was speaking to me, but I didn't really know what He was saying. I sensed He wanted me in full-time ministry, that it was going to use my administrative and organizational gifts, and that it was going to have impact on many people. That's all I had.

3

Ready to "Go"

So, to get ready for this new adventure, I figured I had better get ready to go, whatever "go" meant for me! I owned a small home that needed some work, so I spent the summer of 2004 painting, repairing, and replacing items at the house, hoping to get it sold that fall.

Several thousand dollars on the credit card later, I put the house on the market, for sale by owner. Newspaper ad after newspaper ad, flyer after flyer, open house after open house, with no offers at all. I was discouraged. Now with no job, no source of income, several thousand dollars of debt, and a house to sell, I began to wonder what God was up to.

I needed to find some way to make money while I waited for the house to sell and the Lord to give me some ministry direction, so I ended up with a couple of seasonal kiosk jobs at the mall. The kiosk jobs were just exactly what I needed. They were cash jobs and I got between 50-60 hours/week doing something I enjoyed, as well as time off for Illini basketball games and choir rehearsals. By the way, God really does have a sense of humor. Back when I had first been learning to write, I was doing everything in my life that I could to emulate my older brother, Mike Shaw. And I succeeded in developing penmanship that is almost identical to his, to this day. What no one bothered to tell me at the time was that Mike had lousy handwriting. This kiosk job at the mall involved making customized Christmas ornaments, writing names on them by hand! And the crazy thing is, I did a pretty good job at it. Sticks and curves and dots. Not really writing, but drawing each tiny letter on the ornaments.

Meanwhile, God was providing me with some much-needed direction. Sometimes God's provision comes through other believers.

Three different friends from church all came to me within a few days of each other and mentioned seminary. Had I ever considered going to seminary? Well, no, not really, not until that moment. But I have always loved school and even got my Bachelor's Degree in English, along with a teaching certificate. So, I looked into it a bit. I looked online to find the Southern Baptist seminaries, since I knew that by being a part of the denomination, I could attend for 50% of the regular tuition. The two closest seminaries were in Kansas City, MO, and Louisville, KY. As I looked at their websites, I saw that Midwestern (MBTS) in Kansas City was launching a new Master of Divinity (M.Div.) with an emphasis on worship leadership. That seemed like a pretty interesting direction for me to go.

After the holiday kiosk jobs ended, I decided to take a road trip. When I visited the seminary in Kansas City, everything just started to click. As my excitement grew, I really thought that my house would sell in the next two weeks and I could enroll in the spring semester, but that didn't happen.

On that same trip, I also felt led to go to Colorado Springs. I spent some time with friends out there and investigated the possibility of working for one of the many national and international ministries in the area. There was one job that I was very interested in and seemed to match closely my qualifications and the direction I felt God leading me in. But after a month of waiting, I found out that job was not meant for me. I also had a very meaningful experience at a Woodmen Valley Chapel worship service while I was in Colorado Springs. I was overwhelmed by the Holy Spirit throughout the service – during the times of prayer, music, singing and the sermon. I wasn't sure exactly what was happening, but when I left, I had the distinct impression I was to be a worship leader and that God was calling me to serve Him in the Springs.

Upon returning to Illinois, I was quickly running out of money and needed to find a job right away when I did start looking again in late February. Prospects looked very good. I had several interviews and I figured I would be putting two or three part-time jobs together to make ends meet; I didn't want to make a long-term commitment because I was pointing toward moving to KC for seminary in the fall.

Little did I know what wonderful things the Lord had in store for me, including an incredible NCAA basketball tournament run for the Illini. I even got to attend each of the tournament games in person! I know that God cares, even about our simple pleasures.

Without a doubt, the Lord worked out circumstances such that I got two jobs on back-to-back days in March of 2005, and I know that they were both specifically for me and for this five month transitional period in my life. One was as an administrative assistant for a professor in the College of Veterinary Medicine at the University of Illinois. It was a temporary job through the university's pool of extra help workers. I would be working a total of twenty-three weeks AND making more per hour at that job than I had been making after seven years at the radio station. I was grateful.

The other job is hard to even call a job. It was really my next call to ministry. Central Christian Church in Danville, IL, needed someone to help them launch a new Sunday morning contemporary worship service at their church. They already had a core band and worship leader for this new service, but they needed someone to mentor this new worship leader and pull all the details together, both of which were my strengths. I went for the interview on a Wednesday afternoon.

That evening, while I was sitting in silence at our church's weekly prayer meeting, I heard God say to me, "take good notes." I felt that meant I'd be filling this specific role as interim again, helping a church get something set up so they could get to the next step. I took this as a call to transitional worship ministry. What a God-incidence, that He would solidify this new call on my life right in the middle of what I thought was a 'dead' prayer meeting. Thank you, Lord, for the divine interruption. We had a very powerful summer together at Central, as God healed the new worship leader from throat cancer, allowing him to take over leading when my five months were up at the end of July.

And then as August came around and the summer was winding down, my house FINALLY sold! God's timing and provision were just right. I was offered the full asking price for the house, just two weeks before heading to Kansas City for my fall seminary classes. During that summer, the Lord gave me a verse that I have come to call my life verse, and it's about His constant provision. This version is from the Message: *The One who called you is completely dependable. If he said it, he'll do it!* (1 Thessalonians 5:24).

I journaled, "I believe that my Danville interim worship assignment, in conjunction with seminary and all of my experiences there, will be key in what the Lord would have me do next. I believe that I have been called to help churches start new worship ministries. Maybe I will stay in one place for four or six or nine months, maybe even a year and help that church get established in a new service under their own leadership. And then I will move on to another church that needs what I have to offer. My vision is clear, though I do not yet know the details. And I know that my seminary experience will help me prepare for this role."

Some people have a relationship with the Lord where He calls them in a specific direction that's pretty much for the rest of their lives. Mine has been more segmented – I don't know how long one thing will last until God wants something different. This has already happened to me several times over the last few years and I don't ever know what the next position or location will be. I wouldn't by any means say I'm a great listener to God, but I have a lot of help, lots of friends walking with the Lord, and each time some new direction has happened for me, God has used my pastor, friends, a worship lyric, a feather, or some other means to affirm it.

I have never held too tightly to locations. I don't really have a home and it's not that important to me. This is something God put in my heart so that I would be able to be more mobile and be content being mobile, even seeking that to some degree. If you told me I'd be in this house for twenty years, I'd probably cringe, because I don't really want that. Maybe it's because of my past. The amount of time I've spent in ministry and working with churches and hearing other peoples' stories gives me tangible evidence that God works in different people's lives in very different ways.

This type of transient ministry has given me a HUGE appreciation for the Lord's provision in my life. He ALWAYS provides for me – through my finances, employment, a place to live, transportation, health insurance . . . and the list goes on and on. First Thessalonians 5:24 has been made real in my life so many times, I can't even count them!

I drove to Kansas City for seminary, and I arrived with a plan. I had calculated out the amount for tuition, books, rent, and other expenses needed for two years of seminary. The profit I made from selling the house after paying off the credit card would be just the right amount to provide for me during those two years. God's provision once again!

Just two weeks after I arrived on my seminary campus, Hurricane Katrina hit New Orleans. It was Monday, August 29, 2005. Not by coincidence at all, but once again, by God-incidence, I had already met with the Dean of Students to talk about getting a group of students to go through Southern Baptist Disaster Relief (DR) Training and take a group of students on a DR trip during our fall break in October. As we started organizing for the trip, the dean gave me the nickname "Action Jackson." On October 15, our team of seminary students left for New Orleans to do everything we could to help the folks there, just eight weeks post-Katrina.

Later that semester, when I went to register for spring 2006 classes, I got some crushing news. The way the seminary classes for my degree were organized, I would not be able to take all the classes that I needed, in the sequence required, in a two-year period. I had been planning to complete my 92 hour M.Div. in two years, but the classes were set up on a three-year rotation, with the plan that students would take three years to earn the degree. I did have the option of taking about twenty-five of my ninety-two hours either as online classes, via correspondence, or by independent study, but that would mean cheating myself out of all that valuable classroom experience. There was only one logical thing to do: I would be at Midwestern for three years instead of two. That meant I would have to work and earn enough money to pay for another whole year of room and board and tuition and books. NOT what I had planned!

In August of 2006, I sent out an email update: "I still have some of my house money left, but at this rate, I will be out of money sometime next summer. And I had hoped that with what I made this summer and next, that would be enough to get me through my time at seminary. I will be somewhere between $8000 and $10,000 short, and that is with no savings and no emergencies. Thank you for praying that I will have peace, not be anxious or worry about this, and that I will have faith that the Lord will provide for me financially. And that I will be patient and obedient as I wait."

God does answer prayer, sometimes in an overwhelming and mighty way. With no foreseeable avenue for me to raise or earn $8-10k, God saw fit to provide for me fully, and in advance of my need. When my dad became ill in 2002, he was misdiagnosed by the VA and once they realized it was cancer, he did not have much time left. After his death, my stepmother, Lori, decided to pursue legal action against the VA to help cover the huge medical bills. My brothers and I had waived our rights to any financial awards from the lawsuit. Lori, as his wife, would be the sole beneficiary.

On Wednesday, September 13th, I came back to my apartment unexpectedly before praise team rehearsal to get some cold medicine. As I pulled up, the mail truck was pulling away from my apartment. He drove around the cul-de-sac, pulled back up, and said, "You're

Melany, aren't you?" And I said yes. He told me he had just left a notice on my door that I had a certified letter to sign for, so he could just give it to me now. I had no idea why I might be getting a certified letter. Then I saw the address – from Lori in Winter Park, FL. I figured it must be a letter about the court case, probably another form to sign or something like that.

Then I opened it. Inside was a simple card saying that this was in honor of the memory of my dad. And the card had a cashier's check for $10,000 in it! I was OVERWHELMED, as you might imagine. All glory be to God! I have no idea why He chose this method to take care of my financial need or why He chose to do it at that time, but I know that I know that I know I was at that seminary at that time because it was His will. And for whatever reason, He chose to give me peace and assurance ahead of time, months before I needed the money. What a powerful God-incidence of His provision, that the check was just the amount I had estimated I would need to finish seminary. What a powerful divine interruption. Thank you, Jesus!

I was quickly reminded of the verse the Lord had given me soon after my call to ministry, which is on the bottom of all my email messages: *The One who has called you is completely dependable. If he said it, he'll do it!*--I Thessalonians 5:24 (The Message). This was never more true and more real in my life than after receiving that significant financial gift. Please, if you hear nothing else that I say in this book, know that our God is completely dependable. He IS FAITHFUL! If He has said it, He WILL do it!

Through God's provision, I was able to finish my seminary degree in those three years. During the time I lived on campus, I served in a variety of churches in transitional roles of worship and evangelism. Another constant during my three years of seminary was being a leader for the Midwestern Evangelism Teams. We went to various areas of the city for about ninety minutes at a time and offered to pray with folks and handed out pieces of gospel literature. For almost three years, once a week, I was either a member or a leader of a team that went into the streets in the heart of Kansas City's downtown financial district. It was interesting to see how the homeless and prostitutes reacted to us, compared to the "suits." The suits would almost always completely ignore us, even walk on the other side of the street. These experiences with folks on the street foreshadowed what would later become the homeless ministry of C-U at Home.

During the summer of 2009, the Lord began to speak to me once again, calling me in a new direction for ministry. He used two very different settings with a similar experience to get my attention.

In July of 2009, the National Worship Leader Conference was held in the Kansas City area, and St. Luke Church, where I was serving as the worship and evangelism leader, arranged for me to attend. One of the speakers, David Nasser, told of the number of orphans in the world and then reported the number of people in the United States who claim to be Christ followers. Then he said it: "If every Christian in the U.S. adopted one orphan, problem solved. No more orphans in the WORLD." For some reason that struck a chord in my heart. I began weeping and could not stop, just like what had happened to me at Yad Vashem in Israel. I even had to leave the auditorium. And, again, I don't even like children! What was God up to? Breaking my heart for orphans across the world? I wasn't sure if it was just hearing some emotional statistics and stories that got to me or if it was the Lord speaking to my heart.

A couple of weeks later I took a motorcycle trip to do evangelism at the big Sturgis bike rally with a group of riders from the seminary. Many people came to Christ right there in the tent where we were raffling off a new Harley. The price for a raffle ticket was to come into the tent for three minutes, while one of us shared our story of coming to faith in Jesus. We also spent some time riding in the Black Hills, some of the nicest motorcycle roads in the country.

After Sturgis, we headed to the Pine Ridge Native American Reservation in South Dakota, which was quite an emotional and impactful experience for me. It was the beginning of August, and it was VERY hot, triple digits! I was riding in full gear with a full-face helmet. Sitting on my bike with the others in our group outside of the little church waiting for the pastor to arrive, I took a look at my surroundings. I saw a baby without a diaper and a very skinny dog, and I smelled squalor. It was much like what I imagined it would be like in a third-world country, right here in the middle of the U.S. I began to weep uncontrollably inside of my helmet, keeping it to myself as best I could.

Now this had happened three times. Uncontrolled weeping. All three times had to be a God-incidence. All were related to the most vulnerable, to poverty and death. Then I realized that through this divine interruption, God was calling me to some sort of compassion ministry, to help people in need. But I had no idea what that was supposed to look like. As my time was wrapping up at St. Luke, I began applying for positions all across the country. I interviewed for church positions in two places where I would really like to live – Arizona and Colorado. But God wouldn't let me take either job.

In August, while I was at work in Lexington, MO, I was listening to K-Love national Christian radio. They told the story of the TV show *Extreme Home Makeover* working with a family from Philo, IL, which is just outside of Champaign. Then they mentioned that they also helped with a ministry in Champaign called Salt & Light, a food pantry and clothes closet. The man whose family they had built the home for was Nathan Montgomery, the founder of Salt & Light. I had a connection to Nathan and this ministry. In 2004, during the period after WBGL and before the mall kiosk jobs, I had spent a few days volunteering with Nathan there, just as he was getting started. I thought it was very cool that the TV show had decided to help his family and that ministry for those in poverty. Was God speaking to me through the radio?

By the time October rolled around, I had no job, no money, and no place to live. On October 20, 2009, the day before I turned forty, my default was to go back home, back to Champaign, IL. I had friends there who were willing to let me stay with them for a while. I planned to re-connect with two local compassion ministries I had helped out before seminary: Salt & Light and Restoration Urban Ministries.

As I packed up my Jordan River baptism picture surrounded by the Israel feathers, I looked at those first four feathers that I had found outside of the hotel room in Jerusalem, and I wondered if just maybe "four" meant the four years I spent in Kansas City? Still not sure, but that's the only thing that makes sense to me.

Back in Champaign, I was able to pick up two small temp jobs quickly. I started as a fill-in teacher for an eight-week GED class at Parkland College. And I went to work doing odd jobs for Dave Jansen at his home. Dave was a friend from years of playing together in the church softball league. I also made my re-connection with Salt & Light that week and started volunteering for them. They were planning a big public watch party for the *Extreme Home Makeover* program airing on TV that Sunday night. Everything took off once the show aired. We had people calling and emailing us from all over the country, wanting to know more about the ministry. Two weeks later, I was on payroll at Salt & Light as their administrative assistant.

Just like that, God had given me the opportunity to serve in a compassion ministry focused on helping those who were living in poverty. While serving at Salt & Light, the Lord also gave me a vision and idea for fundraising that was very successful. I was on the phone with a restaurant and we were talking about the big restaurant-size cans, a little bigger than a coffee can, when the idea came to me: we could have a "Canless Food Drive." Get a bunch of those cans, put our own labels on them, and ask businesses to put them on the counter near their cash register. It was a lot of hard work getting everything coordinated, but at the end of the campaign, we had raised just over $30,000. God had blessed our obedience to follow through with the vision He had given me.

At Salt & Light, I focused on offering prayer and encouragement for people who were longing for acceptance and love. Nathan shared with me that he and others recognized my excellence in showing compassion and praying with those coming to our ministry for assistance.

But a few months into my new position at this ministry, my "flat side" reared its ugly head. Being demanding, controlling, and expecting perfection from myself and others are all aspects of my dark side, or flat side. As long as I can remember, I've tended toward being bossy at times. My drive to be in control had left carnage in my wake, and I was largely oblivious to it. As I grew to adulthood, that affected the way I interacted with co-workers and volunteers. My internal drive for perfection damaged my relationship with the volunteers who were helping us in the office at Salt & Light.

Nathan asked to meet with me, and he shared that they had decided to let me go because of my unacceptable behavior. But they were willing to give me one more chance, on a zero-tolerance basis, with the added requirement for me to seek Christian counseling.

I spent that afternoon out at Homer Lake, one of my favorite places to meet with God. This would be a day of wrestling with God. What did He want me to do? Was I even supposed to be in ministry? God had my attention through this painful divine interruption. I could not face the idea of continuing to hurt people, most of the time without even knowing it. I was broken. Maybe I should just find a place and make widgets, I thought. I'm a very good widget maker. Without any clear direction, I decided to show up at work the next day and to seek counseling.

A few months later, I was let go from the ministry, asked to clean out my desk, turn in my keys, and leave.

That was a very low point in my life.

It brought me face-to-face with my flat side, with my signature sin of performance orientation and perfectionism. I could be humble, gracious, patient, and compassionate with someone in need, someone I was assisting. But with one of my peers – a co-worker or volunteer – I set a very high standard for tasks to be done in a specific way on a specific timeline. And there were times when I would be short or rude with my replies or instructions. Too demanding. Not enough compassion and understanding.

The Wednesday they let me go was a day I will never forget. At 4:45pm, I was given the news. I drove across town with tears in my eyes and an ache in my heart to meet with folks from my church. Ironically, at 5:30pm that very day, I had an interview to be their new minister of worship and evangelism. Being hired part-time by my church had been months in the making. It's pretty incredible the way the timing of this worked out. What in the world was God up to? I shared with the search team what had just happened, and they were gracious.

The next day was beautiful, especially for November, so I took off on a motorcycle ride. I was riding by Parkland College and decided to stop in and let them know I once again had daytime availability for teaching. I walked into the Adult Ed office and the director looked at me and said, "Melany Jackson. We were just talking about you thirty minutes ago." They had a teacher who was injured, and they were in a tough spot. She asked if I had ever taught English as a Second Language (ESL). I hadn't, but I was willing to give it my best shot. So, twenty-two hours after being released from Salt & Light, God gave me a great four-week job, teaching ESL to adults.

But I was still struggling with whether I should I remain as a candidate for the church position. Did I need to step away from ministry for now? Forever? I realized that I simply couldn't do more people damage, yet I was specifically equipped (gifts, education, and experience) for the position, as well as by my thirteen years of history with this particular church. It was my home church, my family. What was I supposed to do?

I led worship that week, while continuing to pray regarding my decision whether or not to remain as a candidate for the paid position at my church. At 5pm, one hour before the business meeting started, I did decide to remain as a candidate. At the business meeting, I shared with my church what I had been going through and asked for their help identifying when I'm getting into the mode of being demanding and offensive, so they could help me change. The church voted with confidence to hire me as their new part-time minister of worship and evangelism. God had given me job number two, a new ministry position.

The next day brought even more new employment opportunities. I started the afternoon on Monday by teaching ESL for the first time ever, and it went VERY well. After class, the director asked to speak with me. She said that they would be adding a new GED night class in Rantoul (a town fifteen miles away) in the spring. Would I like to teach it? And, by the way, the daytime instructor there was due to deliver in March. Would I like to take the class over when she had her baby?

So much for no spring opportunities. Isn't that just like God? He gave me some financial security even beyond the end of the year, teaching adults, which is something I love to do! More of His miraculous provision.

4

C-U at Home

Fast-forward back to my move into Restoration Urban Ministries (RUM) in June 2011, where I set up camp at 1213 Parkland Court, room #284.

One decision I had to make early on was how much of the required resident programming I would participate in on a weekly basis. RUM residents must go to chapel at 9am each weekday morning. 10am to noon, time is spent in classes five days a week. Lunch time. Then from 1pm to 5pm, there is a requirement to spend time working somewhere on the property. Participation at Wednesday night service and Sunday morning church is also mandatory.

To both integrate my life with others living at RUM and to allow the time and energy needed to launch a new ministry, I decided to participate in chapel each weekday morning and begin attending Restoration Church on Sunday mornings. This allowed me to start each day with a focus on scripture and to begin to build relationships with my new neighbors.

That first night, I prayed in my journal: "God, help me adjust to my new life. Please help me learn names and get used to everything new. I want to be your holy witness here at RUM and through C-U at Home. Please guide and mold me, Lord. Amen."

During my very first week at Restoration, I saw the Lord's provision for this new ministry God had led me to start, C-U at Home, in three powerful ways. First, on Wednesday morning at devotions, I met Les Gioja, who spent time talking with me and praying for me. He was a strong encourager, and a few years later, God would use his son Phil to impact our ministry in an incredibly powerful way through film. Second, God provided again, when later that day, we moved into our new office location, with donated space and the use of furniture, a computer, and a phone. Thanks to the Center for Women in Transition, we were blessed to have devoted office space to launch this new ministry! And third, on Friday, I met with Stacey Krejci about developing a website for C-U at Home. Stacey had helped with web work when I was at WBGL, and he offered to set up our new ministry website as well as CUH emails at no charge. You can see our website, designed and maintained by Stacey, at **www.cuathome.us**.

Based on the agreement I had made with Nathan at Salt & Light to get help with my performance orientation, I enrolled in a year of monthly prayer counseling classes through Freedom House in Chicago. The Lord brought much wisdom and healing through those classes, and at the final session in the spring of 2011, one of the leaders, Mike Wilson, felt led to do something very special for me as I launched deep into this new area of compassion ministry. Mike called me to the center of the room and asked me to sit in a chair. He sat down across from me and gently took my sandals off. He began to wash my feet and then anointed my feet with oil, while others in my class laid hands on me and prayed. Afterward, he wiped my feet with a dry towel and put a new pair of white socks on them. To this day, I think of these as my anointed socks, and I only wear them at very special times. The Freedom House family took the time to commission me to this new way of life and ministry, helping the homeless. What a blessing!

The Lord was also at work providing for my mental health through a relaxing day of sailing on Clinton Lake with my friend Bill Lawless. He invited me to join him and he brought along another friend, Kim Simpson. I was able to share with both of them about the new ministry the Lord was prompting me to develop and both were very receptive and interested. Kim was to become one of my closest friends and a long-time supporter and board member for C-U at Home. This was also the first of my intentional Sabbath days on Sunday, which I have continued up until today. No email on Sunday, and sometimes I turn the phone off too. That night I journaled, "Thank you Lord for this first day of rest and recalibration. Help me follow through in my regular, intentional time with you. I love you Lord. Help me be more like you. Amen."

Business cards might seem like something small and insignificant, but it was a very big deal for me at the time. God used Paul Conforti, owner of the local Minuteman Press, to provide that first set of two hundred business cards for free. He has continued to print every business card C-U at Home has ever had at no charge and has been a strong supporter of our ministry with discounted printing services.

Sadly, early death is sometimes the end result of chronic homelessness. On July 7, we found out through the Canteen Run that our friend Nate had lost the battle. He had been found dead in the heat and his body was already badly decomposed. This was a tangible loss for us and a poignant reminder of why God was calling us to launch C-U at Home, to prevent others in our community from suffering the same fate. This was my prayer that night: "Lord, let me NEVER forget how I feel right now. Let me channel this anger and frustration into help for the homeless. I need You and I love You. Amen."

I was first interviewed about C-U at Home during a television news story about Nate's death. Our local CBS affiliate, WCIA, has stood behind our ministry, featuring it several times each year. They, along with other media, have come to respect C-U at Home as a local authority on issues related to homelessness. The local newspaper, The News-Gazette, has also run many articles related to C-U at Home. I have kept one copy of each newspaper in a large tub, and the tub finally ran out of space in 2016.

WGNN, Great News Radio, the Moody affiliate in our area, has been another key media supporter. Station Manager Mark Burns was my partner in leading the Passion Outreach at the Beverly in 2004. And in 2011, he invited me to come and record a program about Radical and how the book was impacting my life. Mark has continued to be a strong supporter, allowing us to use air time to share about the ministry of C-U at Home. God's provision and favor through local media has been a key factor in the strong community support for our ministry over the years.

Not long after Nate's death, I received my first invitation to speak about C-U at Home at a small church in Monticello, as God began to provide support through local congregations. They graciously donated $375 to help with our ministry start-up.

God provided both warehouse storage space and a much-needed brand new printer on the same day. Jeff Ross agreed to allow us to use a portion of his garage for our donated appliances and furniture. What a blessing! That same afternoon, an adult Sunday School class from my former church, now called Cornerstone Baptist Church, agreed to collect funds and buy C-U at Home a new printer. Yet two days later, Elaine told me she would be leaving the ministry because of a number of family and other issues in her life. What was God doing? Now I had no ministry partner for C-U at Home. And it meant that I would be going to the 100,000 Homes training in Richmond alone. I was greatly disappointed and felt alone. I prayed, "Lord, help me be strong and stop counting so much on individuals who keep letting me down. Show me Your ways. Give me Your peace. I love You. Amen."

This was the first of several times that God would bring someone in to play a key role in the ministry, only to have them leave abruptly. Sometimes it was mainly because of something I did or did not do and sometimes it was for other reasons. Each time this happened, God found various ways to fill the gap, to provide for me and for the ministry.

It was not until early September that another young woman came along to partner with me and support the development of this ministry. She was a social work student at the University of Illinois. We did many things together during that month. And then, three weeks later, she got in touch with me and said that she had to step away from C-U at Home, as school was demanding too much of her time and energy. Another ministry partner come and gone. I wasn't sure how much more of this I could take!

I had a really GREAT day at the end of July, meetings with two different pastors, both very interested in helping us out with the ministry. One of these churches, Stratford Park Bible Chapel, eventually supported us in two powerful ways, through board membership and weekly involvement in our ministry. The other church was willing to serve as our fiscal agent and overseer for donations. University of Illinois School of Social Work staff were interested in getting their students involved with our upcoming survey, providing much appreciated manpower. I also met with Donna Camp, founder of the Wesley evening food pantry, and found her to be a wonderful kindred spirit. And that same night, I coordinated and led a very successful street outreach with Meadowbrook Church. I prayed, "THANK YOU LORD! What a great day of watching You at work. Please keep me humble and thankful. Open the doors and make the connections You want me to have. I love You Lord. Thank you. Amen."

A few days later, I flew to Richmond, VA, to attend a training weekend with leaders from the 100,000 Homes campaign. They were already one year into the campaign, with two years remaining. My plan was to bring a chapter of this movement to Champaign and to lead it for the next two years. The day before leaving, I found out that a church cannot be the financial umbrella organization for a ministry such as ours any longer. This was a huge blow, and without a fiscal agent, we had no idea how God would provide a way for us to raise the funds needed to do our fall survey and to get the ministry off the ground.

While in Richmond, my brother, Steve Shaw, called from Lakeland, FL. He had just been evicted and spent the night sleeping in his car. What was God up to? My big brother was now officially homeless for the first time in his life. That night, I prayed, "Lord, I need You. I really need You. Please reveal Yourself in Steve's life. Protect his body, mind, and heart. Lord, show me what to do. Do you have a plan for C-U at Home or not? Was it really all just me? Please show me through the CSPH meeting on Tuesday. Help me be Your witness here in Richmond. Thank you for sweet salvation, grace, and faith, Jesus. Amen."

As summer drew to a close in the midst of all this planning and prayer, an international trip was looming on my horizon. In the book *Radical*, Platt offers a one year challenge to the reader: to engage in five different powerful activities in the course of one year. One of these activities is to sacrifice yourself for a gospel ministry in a context other than your own. As I had agreed to this one year challenge in December of 2010, I fulfilled this part of the challenge by joining the first mission trip ever planned by WBGL Radio, a trip to Peru, South America, in early September of 2011. God had several powerful lessons for me on this, my first international mission trip.

Upon arrival in Peru, I was soon disillusioned as to the stated purpose of the trip. The group sponsoring the trip had advertised they were providing new shoes for poor orphan children who had no shoes at all. Yet as we went from one orphanage to another, many of the children already had shoes that were quite new. We were, in fact, taking nice shoes off their feet and replacing them with new shoes. What a waste of resources! It is likely that the children had been given new shoes from this very organization only a few months before. Things are not always as they seem.

Another lesson came from a very unfortunate experience at our hotel. When we were at dinner that evening in a crowded restaurant, a man knocked my bag off my chair, falling to the floor with my bag underneath him. After a few seconds, he got up and apologized and returned the bag to me. This seemed like no big deal. Then as we walked back to the hotel, I couldn't find our room key. We got another one at the desk, and my roommate and I entered to find that our room had been broken into and ransacked. That man had unzipped my bag, stolen the key, and re-zipped it in a matter of seconds. And unfortunately, in that Lima hotel, the key was on a keychain that included both the hotel name and the room number!

Things went from bad to worse. Police investigators came to the hotel and questioned both me and my roommate. They only spoke Spanish and had to use a translator. The tone was one of accusation. They thought we were making this whole episode up when we claimed an iPad and several hundred dollars had been stolen from the room. This went on for several hours, and I was even asked to board a bus and to go downtown to the police station for further investigation and fingerprints in the middle of the night.

That night/morning, when I finally got back to the hotel, I prayed, "God, please help me understand and process this. I want to see You in this. As I've been teaching all week, I know You are at work for my good even when bad things happen. Thank you for being here even now. I love You. Amen."

The next day as our mission team boarded the bus, one of the folks from our group made a presentation to me. They had collected money for me. They handed me a stack of cash that amounted to a little more than the amount stolen: God's provision for me, redeeming a very dark situation.

5

To Fast and Pray

As Elaine and I had considered the scope of the ministry, she suggested we spend regular time each week fasting and praying for C-U at Home. We decided that we would do that on Thursdays. Then each Wednesday evening, I sent out a prayer email to our friends and asked them to join us by fasting in some way on Thursdays and praying for C-U at Home. I am grateful that even though Elaine stepped away from this ministry, she helped build this legacy of continuing prayer into C-U at Home very early on.

Another prayer strength for me was spending prayer time with my friend Rita at Restoration. Rita had been a member at my previous church, a dear sister in Christ who prays with great faith and conviction, often praying words of encouragement through her tears. Her prayer for C-U at Home was often seeing it as a little seed in the ground that would one day grow into a mighty plant with branches reaching far and wide. That image has remained with me. Rita had more power and faith in her prayer than I will ever have.

My prayer that summer was specific: "Lord, I need to know Your voice. Please let me hear You and follow You. What do You intend for C-U at Home? Do You want me to keep going like I have been or change direction? How do You want us to receive donations? How much 100k Homes involvement? Survey or not? October or not? HMIS [homeless management information service] or another database? So many questions, not many answers. I do love and trust You God. Guide me. Amen."

Not being able to use a church or ministry as our umbrella organization so that we could receive tax-deductible donations was a huge roadblock. I was quite concerned because we needed several thousand dollars to execute the large-scale registry survey of the homeless in October. One friend who I had worked with at WBGL, Meridith Foster, invited me over for dinner with her family. She handed me $100 to help with the survey, encouraging me to continue the effort to develop C-U at Home. God used Meridith to provide for us and to bring me hope, right when I needed it most.

Following that generous gift, I prayed in my journal: "Lord, I'm totally dependent on You for my provision. Jehovah Jireh, I trust You. Help me draw closer to You. I want to know You more. Draw me deeper into You. I want Your strength in my weakness. Show me Your ways. I love You, Lord. Amen."

Just one week later, on August 25, 2011, I had an appointment with Joan Dixon at the Community Foundation, which serves as an incubator for new organizations. They were happy to help with the development of C-U at Home, and in just a couple of days, the paperwork was in place and we could begin to take tax-deductible donations, with the Community Foundation serving as our fiscal agent. Once again, God's provision for C-U at Home had come just in time.

I prayed that night, "Lord, thank you for this next phase in this homeless ministry. I can now raise funds freely. I love You and I am grateful. Thank you. Draw me closer to You, Lord, closer every day. Keep me faithful and obedient. Amen."

We did our first public marketing of the name "C-U at Home" in August and September of 2011. Back when I had been working at Salt & Light, I had met a very talented graphic artist named Jill Kirby, who worked at a billboard company. She designed both our C-U at Home logo and our One Winter Night logo. When I approached her about doing billboards for us at a discount price, she was able to give me a quotation to do two different billboards for two months for just over $1100. But in order to get that price, we needed a registered non-profit to pay for them on our behalf. I was blessed when New Horizon United Methodist Church offered to do that for us. One of the billboards was a play on the "got milk?" advertising campaign. It said, "got property? Help the homeless," and it had our logo and web address in the corner, as well as a photo of a house cupped in a person's hands. It was our hope that these billboards would get property owners interested in allowing us to use their property to house and support the most vulnerable homeless.

By the end of the month, we had taken two more steps towards becoming a bona fide organization; opening a checking account at

Busey Bank with $2,000 of my vehicle money, and applying for and receiving a federal EIN number.

As the fall semester began, we were privileged to get some University of Illinois social work students involved through a brown bag lunch where students could come hear about C-U at Home, and I was also invited to guest lecture for a policy class. I met a young woman named Gabriella Sorich. She signed up for our email list and asked me about how she could get involved with our upcoming survey. Gabby did so much to help our ministry over the next two years. Looking back, I can see how that brown bag opportunity was really a divine appointment. My prayer that week was: "Lord, please keep my eyes on You. Help to open my heart to Your will. I want to see You in new ways. I ask for a miracle with C-U at Home. Lord, do what ONLY YOU can do so that everyone will know it's You. Amen."

During 2011, from about April through October, I personally met with more than sixty churches in the Champaign-Urbana area to talk about C-U at Home. Sometimes I met with the pastor, other times the mission leader, and a few meetings were with the entire group of church leaders. I presented the plan we'd devised, "Each One, Reach One." We asked each church to make a minimum one year commitment to adopt one of the most vulnerable homeless people in our community by providing housing either at the church or parsonage or possibly an apartment owned by someone in the church. The second part of the plan involved a support system for the resident, maybe a small group teaming together to offer life skills, help with medical needs, and offer assistance with applications. The final component of "Each One, Reach One," was to assist with an employment opportunity for the resident, either small jobs at the church or simple employment arranged through a church member.

My first church contact to meet with was Lisa Sheltra, the outreach minister from Windsor Road Christian Church. I took out a copy of *Radical* to give to her and she said her church would be studying it later that year, which I thought was pretty cool. Church meeting after church meeting went something like this: "Wow, Melany! It's really great that you are working to help the people living on the streets. We will pray for you." Sometimes they prayed with me right then. Yet,

Not one single dollar donated.

Not one single volunteer.

Not one single apartment offered.

Not one single job opportunity.

One pastor shook my hand and said, "We'll do our part." That night, I was on cloud nine. We had our first official church partner, and I journaled: "Lord, thank you for opening the door with this church. You are SO good! Please let me follow You as we go along on this journey together. I love You, Lord. Amen and Amen!"

Over the next two months I called and emailed that pastor, with no response. I even showed up at the church to see him and he refused to meet with me. It appeared as though his "yes" had really been a "no." Through all this rejection, I guess I was either foolish or stubborn to keep on going. But I did continue. If God was calling me to do this, He would provide. He would make a way where there seemed to be no way.

Late summer and early fall saw the development of an Advisory Team (A-Team) to help build C-U at Home. Even though we did not need an official board of directors, I wanted to get a team behind me to help guide the direction and decisions for developing this ministry effort. For a few weeks, we met for dinner in the back room at The Urbana Garden Family Restaurant and ate, planned, and prayed together. The A-Team eventually morphed into our board of directors.

In September, I met with the missions pastor from First Christian Church, Don Orr. I shared with him how God had used that first Canteen Run and the book *Radical* to point me in the direction of starting C-U at Home. And I shared with him our "Each One, Reach One" plan for folks in the church to connect with one of our town's most vulnerable homeless people. As our conversation continued, he called and canceled his next meeting so that we could keep talking. He told me about two men in the church, Jeff and Michael, who had also been influenced by reading *Radical* and had just started a new ministry where they hosted Agape Feasts with folks in poverty, eating a meal and sharing fellowship with people from a variety of churches. He wanted to put me in touch with Jeff and Michael so that we could meet. God would use that first meeting with Pastor Don to impact our ministry in many powerful ways over the next six years.

That night, I prayed, "Lord, thank you for another encouraging day. Please help the churches understand this ministry opportunity and not be afraid to take a chance. It's up to YOU and NOT ME! I love You, Lord. Please let me always give You the glory and not accept praise myself. Amen." I cried out in my prayer journal: "Lord, make me a blank check, willing to say 'yes' before You ask. Help me yield control to You. I love You, Lord. Change me, break me. Provide for those in need. Break my pride and break my heart for what breaks Yours. Amen."

At the beginning of October, we received a donation check for $1,000. I was blown away. Our plan was to do the community-wide registration survey during the last week of October. This survey process was designed to identify the most vulnerable homeless people in our community. We wanted to give those who responded a $5 gift card for a restaurant meal, and this donation provided about 1/3 of the amount needed for those cards. John Van Es agreed to help lead the survey training for us. We also needed t-shirts for the volunteers, and Gabby, the social work student I had met at the brown bag event, stepped up to the plate and secured seventy-five donated shirts from her hometown of Joliet. God was indeed providing again in a wide variety of ways.

I prayed, "God, thank you for being so good to me. I know that You will provide my every need and more if I will only let go of control and put my faith in You. Thank you for providing enough volunteers. I love You, Lord. Amen."

During the second week of October, I became overwhelmed. We did not have anywhere near enough volunteers to do the survey. We didn't have a headquarters location. We didn't have enough money to buy the gift cards, and our database wasn't ready. The list went on and on. I had been invited to speak to the women of Stone Creek Church at their Wednesday evening gathering, and as I was introduced to speak, I started crying out of my brokenness. I didn't even know what to say.

A few days later I was invited to borrow a friend's motorcycle and go with them to the Beef House near Danville for dinner. I was excited to get my mind off all things C-U at Home. During dinner, my friend Miriam started choking. She could not breathe. Her husband, John, quickly wrapped his arms around her and performed the Heimlich maneuver, saving her life. We were all affected by this and deeply grateful to God for saving her life. Somehow, a database didn't seem quite as important after that experience.

Two days before the survey, I prayed: "Lord, my life is in Your hands. Please be in control of this survey. Help me remain calm when I would normally be stressed. Volunteers are here to HELP. Help me love them! Understand them. I know that I will be tested. Lord, please help me pass the tests. I love You and need You now more than ever. Amen."

41

I had asked a university database specialist to help us develop the database for the survey. He was more than capable of doing this, but problems arose, and the database was not ready to use until part-way through the second day of the survey. Following the survey, there were issues regarding access to the data, which added to my frustration. Now, more than ever, I needed the peace of God.

Overall, however, the survey week was a success. First Presbyterian Church in downtown Champaign agreed to host the survey headquarters for us. We did more than three hundred surveys and identified sixteen people in the highest category of vulnerability: two females and fourteen males. Two of those sixteen said that they did not want assistance with housing. That left us with fourteen people identified in desperate need of housing and support. Who would we help first and who would come to the forefront to help that person?

On October 29, the day after the press conference sharing the survey results, I was totally wiped out, having hit the wall of exhaustion. I was dizzy, fuzzy-headed, woozy, and weak. I couldn't even keep my cereal down. That night I prayed, "Lord, show me Your ways. I know I am weak and need Your help. Please guide and direct C-U at Home next week. Help us make good decisions. Show me Your ways. I love You, Lord. Amen."

The survey had yielded only $100 in donations for our ministry. Even though it was not a fundraising event, I had hoped that some of the volunteers who helped would make donations to our ministry. We still had not yet heard from the pastor who had shaken my hand and said, "We'll do our part" in regard to "Each One, Reach One." That night I prayed: "Lord, I am in a dark place. I want to trust You, but I don't know what for. Please help me. Show me the way. Is it C-U at Home or something else? I am ready to walk away right now or to keep on. Whatever You want, Lord. Please direct me. Thank you. I love You. Amen."

It was not until November that I had a real hope this plan might actually succeed. Barb and Dan from the Canteen Run invited me to a secret church prayer gathering of their small group that was studying *Radical*. We met on the living room floor with only our Bibles. We spent time reading scripture and praying together. I really needed some encouragement. The group prayed for me and for the development of C-U at Home. When the meeting was over, the host walked me out to my car. His name was John Hancock (really, it was!). He had just retired from the Post Office and he was looking for

42

ways God could use him to help others. He offered to help someone get an ID and to provide transportation to medical appointments. I was thrilled to have our first advocate!

That night I prayed, "God, thank you for bringing me encouragers. Do I move someone into an apartment with the money that I have left, with John Hancock as the advocate? What are You up to, Lord? Show me Your will and Your way. Less of me, more of You. I want to walk in Your purpose, not mine. Thank you. I love You now and forever. Amen."

By Thursday, a day with focused prayer and fasting, I sensed a breakthrough. Our survey data had finally been emailed to us, and I met with an engineering student interested in assisting our folks with getting a job. It felt incredible to be going through surveys, sorting them and potentially beginning to help some of the most vulnerable. Bits and pieces were coming together. A friend from Gifford called us with a donated bed and night stand. Another friend emailed that he would like to host a few of our friends without an address on Thanksgiving. Professor Min Park from the School of Social Work offered to help in any way possible. And that evening I shared with a local church outreach team who had several professionals very interested in getting involved with us. All in one day! "God, what a great day. Today I really felt You in control. Please lead me each moment and be glorified. I want to know You more. Amen."

For Thanksgiving, I secured a ticket to fly my brother Steve from Lakeland, FL, to Illinois, and I drove to Chicago to pick him up. My good friend Jason Frericks was away for the holiday, so he let me use his house to prepare and host Thanksgiving dinner with both of my brothers, as Mike and Donna drove up from Salem, IL, for the day. It was the first time the three of us had been together since my seminary graduation in 2008 in Kansas City and the first Thanksgiving we had been together since the late 80s. What a blessing to hear about their lives, and to show my brothers around Restoration, describing how God was at work in developing C-U at Home. The best part was sharing memories, as we talked about our momma and daddy, remembering what Thanksgiving was like growing up, with dinner at our cousins, the Rollinsons, and the annual Turkey Bowl football games. It was good to be together with Steve and Mike, even if only for a few hours.

During the next few weeks, one of the men the survey identified as the "most vulnerable" kept crossing my path, even as God was bringing him to the top of the list to be housed first by C-U at Home.

Vernon (Vern) Chounard would be the first person moved into a home, and we had an advocate, John, ready to help him along the way to a new life. What we did NOT have was a house or an apartment for him to move into. My heart hurt. I cried and I prayed, "Lord, who are You going to use to provide housing for Vern?"

In early December, I had a dinner meeting with Deana and Luke Hammock who had contacted me because they had heard we were looking for houses to help people get off the streets. It was quite a humbling conversation. Deana had previously worked at the TIMES Center, one of the local homeless shelters, and she and her husband were used to helping out folks in need. They explained that they had a small house across the street from their own. Her mom had lived in it for a while, and a missionary had stayed there for a few months. But now it was vacant.

Luke had replaced the plumbing in the little house that summer, but they didn't have the money to keep the power on and keep the house heated through the winter. Deana said if we could help them by paying the power bill to keep the pipes from possibly busting, they would make a way to get one of the men off the streets for the winter. I knew that C-U at Home would only have about $1,000 total left by the end of December, as my SUV and motorcycle money was almost gone. That's enough to pay three months of utilities, but not rent and utilities. And the really remarkable part of this is that Luke and Deana had only part time jobs and got most of their own food from pantries. They were barely getting by themselves. Humble means of provision for Vern, and just in time for Christmas!

The next couple of weeks went by like a whirlwind. There was the house to get ready, all kinds of things to do for Vern, as well as introducing John to Vern so that they could start building a relationship with one another.

In the middle of all this, I was trying to work my way through writing a very detailed and complicated grant application for getting vital United Way funding support for the next two years. I was in over my head, as I had never written narrative, charts, or metrics for a grant application. The deadline for the application was December 15. Once again, God came through just in the nick of time when he brought Jennifer Williams, an experienced and successful grant writer, to the rescue! Our grant application was submitted just minutes before the deadline. I prayed, "Lord, give me the strength to get it all done. I am so overwhelmed and weary. Please help me be strong and faithful. Amen."

That Saturday, I completely lost my voice. Over the years, even several times while working in radio, I experienced stress-induced (think – extremely low resistance, lack of sleep, and exhaustion) laryngitis. Why now Lord? This story MUST be told! We would be handing Vern a key and welcoming him into his new home in just three days. The whole community was watching us. I prayed, "Lord, help me be obedient. I'm really not sure what losing my voice means right now. Reveal Your Truth and direction to me. Thank you. Amen."

Sunday was an emotional day. I went to a special Christmas Agape Feast at the Douglass Community Center. Vern was there, the Hammocks were there, and John Smith was there. And I had no voice. I tried to write everything down, as I was so excited to introduce many friends to Deana and Luke and to Vern. While I was wallowing in my self-pity about not being able to talk, Don Orr, the Missions Pastor from First Christian Church (FCC) caught up with me. FCC would be donating $200/month to C-U at Home through their missions fund in 2012. This was the first monthly donation commitment to the ministry, a powerful vote of confidence. He also had personal provision news for me as well that made me cry. The church had extra mission funds at the end of the year, and they would be cutting me a check for $2500 to help meet my personal needs. WOW!!!! What a blessing! A few months later, a friend contacted me with a commitment to pay for my health insurance for the year. Praise the Lord! Tangible personal provision for me again.

"Lord, give me Your strength and wisdom. Keep me close to You. Help me put You first and put people second and put tasks last. Give me a sweet and humble spirit, Lord. Show me Your glory." And a second prayer: "Lord, please help me be strong. I have no voice, so please use Yours – for Your glory. Thank you for housing, provision, and hope. Amen."

Tuesday, December 20, 2011, is a day I will never forget. It started with a front-page article in *The News-Gazette* that chronicled Vern's story and C-U at Home's commitment to providing him with a key and a bed of his own that afternoon. In the morning, we were able to get the lease signed and had more radio and television interviews. The van pulled up on Elm Street, John Hancock arrived with Vern, and the C-U at Home team was waiting inside the house with several of Vern's friends, and even the mayor. A cake was waiting for him, iced with the message, "Hope and a future." It was almost surreal when he walked through that door for the first time. The big reveal included a stuffed bear on his bed that he named Yogi, new boots, jeans and other clothes, a fridge, and cabinets already stocked with food. I was so grateful. Success. Relief. Still no voice. But God had this story told through the voices of others. He is faithful.

And then, just six days later, tragedy struck. Shelly, one of our friends living on the streets, had lost her battle to pneumonia at the hospital. Her death deepened my passion and drive to serve the most vulnerable homeless in our community, to advocate for them. We would be a voice for the voiceless. C-U at Home would make a difference. I prayed, "Lord, please bring more workers to help the homeless. Open some hearts and unlock some pocketbooks and wallets. Please help us save some. Amen."

6

One Winter Night

In the first part of November, a friend and I had discussed the idea of a winter event that would raise funds for the ministry. My original idea was to ask people to spend the night camping outside in their front or back yards in January and then donate the amount of their January power bill to C-U at Home. I wanted to do this through WBGL, but they were not able to do the promotion. So, instead, we talked about getting celebrities and local government leaders to spend the night in tents in West Side Park. We would call it C-U at Home One Winter Night (OWN). It was a bold idea to involve the community as well as to raise awareness for our friends with no place to go in the winter. I'm good at planning events and I couldn't wait to get started.

Unfortunately, and rather ironically, the park district had an ordinance that prohibits people from sleeping outside on any of its properties. Any exemption to the ordinance would have to be approved by the park district board of directors. Their next board meeting would not be until January 11, and our event date of Friday, February 3, was too close for us to wait for that permission, so we had to switch gears once again.

Laura Huth, a local non-profit consultant, joined me to meet the mayor. She suggested we switch to downtown Champaign, use cardboard boxes, and focus on getting twenty of the right people to raise money for us, such as the mayor, other elected officials, and community and business leaders. And the rest, as they say, is history!

Over the next month, I worked feverishly to recruit box dwellers to spend the night outside in a cardboard box on the sidewalk and raise $1,000 each, for C-U at Home. There was lots to get done – an event permit from the city, a personal web page for each box dweller, and a process for donations to be worked out with the Community Foundation, not to mention the task of finding twenty or thirty cardboard refrigerator boxes!

As the next Thursday approached, we prepared a prayer email to send to a several hundred people who prayed and fasted for the needs of C-U at Home. As so often happened on Thursdays, God provided – not as a simple coincidence, but as a God-incidence. A couple had reached out to meet with us. That morning when we met with Rick and Debbie Cruse, it led to them assisting with our ministry. Rick gave many, many hours of blood, sweat, and tears to help John and me with C-U at Home, as our volunteer coordinator. My afternoon meeting with Bob Kirby, one of the lay leaders at First Presbyterian Church in Champaign, led to the offer of office space. We had already outgrown the donated space in the attic at the Center for Women in Transition. We moved into the new ministry incubator space at the church, rent-free, for the next two-plus years. Thank you, Jesus!

On that very same day, we had a very challenging interchange with our fiscal agent. We had set up individual PayPal links on our One Winter Night box dweller web pages to process credit card donations. Once they saw that, we were told that if we did not take the PayPal links down immediately, we would lose them as our fiscal agent. That would be an absolute disaster for OWN and for our ministry because we could no longer receive tax deductible donations. But if we used our fiscal agent's credit card company, there would be no way to track credit card donations throughout the event, hour by hour, making it impossible for box dwellers to know how much money they had raised. We were in a catch-22 situation.

During this same time, we went through a HUGE learning curve with Vern, including visits to the Emergency Department, continued alcohol use, and evidence of demonic interference, along with several other shocking adventures. At times, Vern seemed to forget he had a house and ended up staying outside. On January 20th, Eddie, who was living with Vern, called before 6am to say that Vern was passed out in the living room and he had to leave for work. He was quite concerned for him. So John Hancock and I went to check on him. When I saw Vern passed out on the living room floor, soaked in his own vomit and urine, I honestly thought he was dead. Dan and Barb came over to try to help him, and that afternoon we had a team of believers come in and attempt an intervention with Vern. It was an utter failure. What was I doing? How were the other communities involved in 100,000 Homes achieving such success with this most vulnerable population? What should we do differently?

Yet what was success? As the weeks progressed and I learned more about the 100,000 Homes campaign, I saw that much of what they were touting as success was really smoke and mirrors. Out of 186 communities who were participating in the 100,000 Homes campaign, we were literally the ONLY one not using federal housing vouchers to pay for the housing or using government-paid caseworkers. C-U at Home was launched as a ministry, to engage and mobilize our community to house and support the most vulnerable homeless on their journey of healing and restoration. Our ministry had the vision to be the hands and feet of Jesus, to collaborate to bring a new opportunity for change to those living on the streets who were closest to dying. We were not and will never be dependent on government funding for our ministry.

The smoke and mirrors? Most of the housing in other communities was in efficiency apartments in segments of an apartment building, or even an entire apartment building. On one level, that could be positive, allowing the folks who didn't have a place to live to move into an apartment and become neighbors with their friends from the street, to remain in community with one another. But the flipside was often very, very detrimental. Many of the host cities had a disengaged government-funded case manager visiting the property only once or twice a month. As part of the harm reduction housing model, residents were allowed to continue drinking and/or using drugs, and they were not required to take meds or receive treatment for severe mental illnesses. In some communities, the apartments turned into crime infested party houses where vodka and heroin were pervasive and prostitutes were frequent guests.

Their yardstick for success was one person being given a home for one day. End of story. Nothing beyond that first day was counted towards success or failure in the program. Still, while I may not agree with the efforts of other communities, there would likely never have been a C-U at Home if there had not been a 100,000 Homes campaign. I probably would have continued to be involved with the Canteen Run and gone back to some type of regular full-time employment. So, I am grateful for the role that 100,000 Homes played in my life and in the lives of so many others.

By the middle of January, the pace was picking up. Just two weeks before OWN, I had one of what would be many difficult hi/lo days. Joel confirmed that we could move our C-U at Home office into their space at First Presbyterian Church without cost, we got confirmation to use a vacant building as our headquarters for OWN, we received over $3,000 in the mail, and Sergeant Anthony Cobb, soon to be named the Police Chief of Champaign, confirmed he would be a box dweller. On the flip side, Eddie called for help with Vern, who was drunk, angry, and threatening. And then, the woman who had been organizing all the OWN volunteers resigned on the spot (and took all of the volunteer contact information with her!!!). Gabby Sorich saved the day once again. She stepped up right away and offered to organize all the volunteer information for us. On another positive note, we were finally able to get event liability insurance purchased and bonded for OWN. And we reserved the large meeting room at the Champaign Public Library for a "Get to Know C-U at Home" event following One Winter Night. That all happened in one day.

We all experience days when very, very good things happen and very, very bad things happen almost simultaneously, a hi/lo kind of day. The human psyche is not equipped to easily navigate such a situation. Should I be happy? Should I be angry or sad? How can I be both? Throughout the course of developing C-U at Home, I experienced many days with both extreme joy and extreme sadness or anger. I didn't really have anyone coaching me along for the early part of that journey, to help me process what was happening and provide insight into how I should be reacting or how I should be dealing with everything.

Sometimes I managed it fairly well, relying on my ability to compartmentalize the positive from the negative and to deal with them separately. Other times, it was a disaster, as I either reveled in the joy and ignored the pain or wallowed in the suffering and dismissed the blessings. Starting this new and very challenging ministry gave me lots of practice. And by God's grace, He eventually provided me with several friends and mentors along the way to help me deal with hi/lo weeks, days, hours, and even moments. Thank you to John, Rick, Eric, Don, Tony, Seth, and Mike, for being there when I needed you most.

A few days before that first One Winter Night, I was feeling lots of stress about Vern, event details and finances, and more. I prayed, "Lord, please help me keep my focus on You. Help me be humble and patient, not controlling. I love You Lord. Thank you for being who

You are and for loving and forgiving me. You are my Savior. Thank you for the cross and for sweet salvation. Amen."

C-U at Home One Winter Night 2012 began early that morning with doing TV interviews and reserving our load-in parking spots. My adrenaline was cranking. It seemed like everything took longer than it was supposed to – the boxes, the signs, the accounting computers.

The afternoon high was a balmy 54° and I was doing event set up outside without a jacket. The evening was not so friendly. The low only got down to 32°, about 15° above normal, but there was rain, combined with high winds, for about eight of the twelve hours we spent in the cardboard boxes. Wet and cold. Absolutely miserable!

We had twenty-six box dwellers spend the night on our behalf, including a surprise box dweller named Nathan Scheelhaase, quarterback for the Fighting Illini. My dear friends, Chuck and Cheryl Conway, and some other friends from Hands of Jesus in Decatur came over with their instruments, and I had my djembe with me, so we had an impromptu worship time together in the entryway to the city building. This was the highlight of the night for me. Before that night, we really had no idea what to expect. Over 130 volunteers showed up to help with the event. There were more than enough folks to take care of everything, and I was grateful.

There are several bars in the area of town where OWN was held, and we knew that closing time could lead to some challenges, so, John, Rick, and I worked together with Sgt. Cobb, and several others who stayed awake and alert during that 2am time period. We had the donations tallied by about 3am, so I was able to climb into my own cardboard box around 3:15. My feet had gotten wet and cold in the wind and rain, so it wasn't long before I was shivering violently. I fought the cold and lay in the box until about 5:45am. Breakfast would be served at 7am at the TIMES Center, a local transitional housing shelter for men. One thing that I hadn't anticipated was all the noise. People walking by talking. Garbage trucks. The wind. Music. Cars going by. The combination of the miserable weather and all that noise gave us box dwellers just a small taste of what it might be like to live on the streets every day.

Most people bailed on breakfast and went on home. They were cold, tired, wet, and grumpy. I was so proud of our mayor. Don came to the TIMES Center and enjoyed breakfast with the guys who were staying there at the shelter. Clean up took a lot longer than we anticipated. I didn't get to my own bed at Restoration until about 10am, after being awake for about twenty-eight intense hours straight, and I hit the wall. Complete exhaustion. When I pulled back the blankets, crawled in, and laid my head on the pillow, the tears came. I was different: so grateful for the bed and so sad for my friends without a place to live.

A few days later, once all the donations were processed, One Winter Night had raised over $26,000 for C-U at Home. Jehovah Jireh, my Provider, thank you for using this event to provide for our ministry throughout the next year.

The week after One Winter Night, my flat side reared its ugly head with a key volunteer who was trying to help us. Deana was not only a volunteer, but also a key donor, letting us use her house for Vern to live in. She was at the office trying to help me with some paperwork and I snapped at her. Lord, why do I keep biting the hand that feeds me? Why do I hurt those who are working hard to help me? I did apologize and wrote this in my journal that night, "Lord, please kill my arrogance and perfectionism. Show me Your heart for others and Your love. Help me be more like You and less like me. Amen."

At the end of February, we had another great instance of provision for our ministry. Dan got in touch with us just after Christmas, as he had seen a story on the news about housing Vern and heard we were looking for additional houses to help folks get off the streets. He took John and me to look at two properties that he owned. The first was a beautiful two-story house that would require at least $700 in monthly rent. Very, very nice, but not right for our population. Stairs just wouldn't work for most of our guys, and the cost was way out of our budget. Then he took us to a second house, a three bedroom one-story that was quite a bit more humble. Yes! This looked like a place we could use.

Dan told us the story of what had happened here. He had allowed a ministry to use the property to help folks get back on their feet. They did not take care of the property. In fact, they did damage and even stole the stove when they left. And then he said, "I could let you use this house for a year." I asked how much rent would be. And he said, "How about a dollar a month?" You could have picked my jaw up off the floor. After all someone else had done to his property, and in the name of Jesus? How could he turn around and show so much grace and favor to us?

Another example of a hi/lo day happened on a Saturday. I drove to Decatur to help with kids' church at Hands of Jesus and saw my friend Lisa who I knew from when I had worked at the newspaper. She was there taking photos of the ministry to do a story on them.

Later in the afternoon, Vern called me and he was lucid. Not only lucid, but sober and had been reading the Bible. As he read some scripture to me over the phone, I was deeply touched, crying in response. Two hours later, Eddie called to report that Vern was very drunk and was yelling at him. Sometimes when Vern was very, very inebriated, he would do some things that appeared to be demonic.

I struggled with my own reaction. In one moment, he's reading scripture to me and in another moment, he is acting like a crazed man, quite possibly being influenced by Satan. My journal prayer that night went like this: "Lord, thank you for Eddie and for Ann. Please keep growing this ministry Your way. Show me Your love and how we should care for Vern. You are amazing. Keep me simple and humble, Lord. I love You. Amen."

On March 16, I recorded a tough prayer in my journal. "God, this is so hard to say, but You already know my heart. There is a part of me that wants to stop doing what I am doing, get a 'normal' job and a 'normal' place to live. I am tired of not having a kitchen, of not having all my things in one place. I really want a motorcycle again. A part of me just wants to be anonymous, another worker bee, only known for working hard. I don't want to be popular. I want a regular paycheck, money for tires and dental insurance. I know that I am being selfish, but it's how I feel. Please help me, Lord. Amen."

The next day I met a young woman named Jessica. She spent time talking with me and praying for me. I was encouraged and wrote this in my journal: "Lord, You are so good. You knew just the encouragement I needed and You brought it to me through Jessica. Thank you. Help me not doubt Your provision. Keep me faithful. Help me be more balanced. Build C-U at Home Your way, Lord. I love You. Amen."

The very next day, the Lord worked His provision in the life of my brother Steve. His disability application was approved AND he received several thousand dollars in back pay that he put in the bank. He would no longer be homeless and now he would have basic financial provision for the rest of his life. I was grateful.

One lesson in the *Radical* Bible study focuses on faith. Each time I taught this lesson, I talked about the acronym F.R.O.G., fully rely on God. When I asked to see if anyone had a frog I could borrow, Cheryl, a fellow RUM resident, brought me the cutest little ceramic frog standing on his back legs, with the message "be happy" below. I put a sticky note on his belly that said, "F.R.O.G." and used him as an example to teach the lesson. God has used that simple image of a frog to bring my faith to the forefront time and time again. It's NOT up to me! If I have faith and walk in obedience, He WILL provide.

Vern had previously been a sous-chef, as he really loved to cook, and he was good at it! Several times, while he was in the house he invited both Johns, Luke and Deana, me, and others to join him for dinner. One of those evenings, he cooked a fine meal with spaghetti, salad, and fresh baked bread. We ate together and told stories and teased one another, just like any group of friends would do. Those times with Vern breathed new life into me and gave me hope, both for his future and for the future of C-U at Home.

In early March, we brainstormed as a staff to come up with a summer companion event to One Winter Night. After a couple of meetings, we settled on the name, "One Summer Day," a grocery cart walk through the park. Walkers would be asked to raise at least $100 each for the homeless, wearing a pedometer and soliciting pledges based on the number of steps taken. We would invite several other service providers to set up tables and have their information at the event. We would share 50% of the funds raised and divide that evenly among the participating service providers. We would also ask the walkers to donate razors, fresh produce, socks, deodorant, and laundry detergent to fill their grocery carts. These supplies would then be donated to the other participating organizations.

To promote the event, the manager of the Country Market, a local grocery store, allowed us to borrow a shopping cart for a couple of hours. We used it in a promotional video that Phil Gioja had offered to record for us. I had first met Phil many years ago when I worked at WBGL. He was a radio intern, studying Radio & TV at SIU-Carbondale. Now he had his own business making videos. Phil is also the son of Les Gioja, who I had met that first week living at Restoration. A couple of years later, Phil got involved once again with C-U at Home through video, in an even bigger way.

We continued to have challenging days. Our external hard drive with ALL of the C-U at Home, One Winter Night, and survey information was not working. I was concerned about Vern, as well as housing our next resident, and we had started looking at getting our 501(c)(3) for our tax-exempt status. At the same time, my personal money was running out, and I asked myself, "Are we doing what God wants?" A big question. That night I prayed, "Lord, thank you for everything. I owe You everything and know I can count on You when it comes to Vern, the next person, and me. Be glorified. Amen." That evening Rita came over to my room and spent time praying over me and crying with me. She reminded me that C-U at Home is like a little seed in the ground. God planted it and we would have to water it to help it grow, in time.

I continued to struggle with worry about my personal provision. I had a hard talk with John Smith, my partner in leading the ministry, about my own finances. Later I prayed, "Lord, please speak clearly to me. I do not want to be confused about what You want me to do, especially regarding my personal provision. Give me peace in the right decision and not to second guess. Lord, please bring healing to Vern's life. I love You, Jesus. Amen."

At the end of March, Don Orr called me from First Christian and said they would be giving me a $2,000 check for my personal support the next week. I cried on the phone with him. That evening, I met with Joel and Rachel Williams who were serving the Lord as a young couple and living at Restoration Urban Ministries also. They brought me $200 cash in a beautiful card and they spent time praying with and for me. God was making it clear that even without any employment source of income, He was continuing to be my Provider. Jehovah Jireh. More than enough.

We didn't know how to respond to Vern's behavior. One evening, as I was relaxing with friends, I got two phone calls. One let me know that Vern was out of jail. Later that evening I got a call from Eddie about Vern. I went by to see him and left after just a few minutes. He was drunk and lying. "Lord, what do you want me to do? How do you want me to feel?" I prayed.

That same night, I found out that one of the sixteen most vulnerable who we were trying to help with housing had lost her seven-year-old son in an accident. Such sorrow. Then a few days later we found out that she had actually made up the story of her son's death. He was fine. It was amazing to see the lengths that some people will go through to try to get assistance.

I'd been serving with the Canteen Run throughout this season and was ready to move into a new role there. The process to become a driver for the Canteen Run is rather arduous. The application booklet takes awhile to get filled out, and then the wait time for The Salvation Army to process an application takes anywhere from several months to a year or more. My application was finally approved in March. I went out with Dan to do some practice driving, and then I was ready to drive on my own. I began driving the Canteen truck on a regular basis, once a week for most of the next two years.

We developed an Organizational Development and Planning Team during this period to work with Joan Dixon from the Community Foundation, exploring what it would look like to incorporate as a 501(c)(3) non-profit organization.

On April 1, my journal prayer was no joke. "Lord, please show me the way. I feel so far from You. Do You really want me to be leading this ministry or just be the marketing director and event coordinator? I feel so overwhelmed. Help me keep my focus on You and not everything that is not done yet – everything out of my control. Help me let You lead me and C-U at Home. Keep me humble and transparent, giving You alone the glory. Thank you. Amen."

The hi/lo days continued. Vern was released from detox in Decatur and refused the two rehab programs offered to him. Eddie moved out permanently, as living with Vern was too taxing on him. That same afternoon, I met with a friend at the University of Illinois School of Veterinary Medicine, where I had previously worked the temp job, who said that he and his wife would like to help me financially when I needed it, which was very humbling. More provision on the way. And that evening one of our key volunteers was pushing hard for us to house a particular homeless family. We had previously discussed it and determined they were not a good fit for our ministry. This type of pressure from someone who was helping us was very stressful. It was a day with back and forth, good and bad once again. On top of it all, I was sick and losing my voice again, just feeling lousy.

The ups and downs continued the next day. Rick helped me with a game plan for organizing our warehouse. Vern went MIA once again. I met with the director of the Champaign Park District about One Summer Day and she was very encouraging.

Pretty soon, it was Good Friday. I have kept a Good Friday tradition since 2004, watching *The Passion of the Christ* in the still of the evening. But I was disappointed to discover that night, the laptop I had would not play the DVD. Fortunately, I was able to get a different laptop the next day and watch the film on Holy Saturday instead, reminding me once again of Jesus' life-giving sacrifice.

We continued to develop a housing agreement for Vern, our new resident Bruce, and future C-U at Home residents, based on a three-strike system. That day I wrote, "God is able: to heal Vern with or without me, to provide an advocate for Bruce and a support team for him, to build C-U at Home His way, in His time, and to bring salvation to our friends who do not yet know Him."

7

Listen and Time

In April 2012, God provided education and encouragement for me during a powerful weeklong experience in the inner city of Chicago called Immersion. Immersion is a training experience offered by the Christian Community Development Association (CCDA) for churches and ministries interested in poverty alleviation through long-term investment in developing neighborhoods and communities. There were seventy-plus students in our Immersion cohort. We had class from morning until night, long days with shared meals, stretching our hearts and minds, and developing new life-long relationships with others who have a similar heartbeat. During the week, we also had the privilege of visiting fourteen different CCDA locations in metro Chicago. The experience deeply impacted me both personally and with what God was doing through C-U at Home.

Two overarching themes from the week were "listen" and "time." To lead effective community development work, it is absolutely necessary to listen, REALLY listen, both to what others are saying and to what they are not saying. We need to allow them to identify their own challenges and solutions rather than figuring it out and trying to solve their problems for them – problems that they might not want you to solve and problems that they might not even be seeing as problems! Time is also needed. Time to learn. Time to wait. Time to become a part of their community. CCDA encourages us to commit at least fifteen years to the community the Lord is calling us to serve, with a guideline of at least two years living in the community and just being, before we do any particular ministry or mission actions. Simply live with them and begin to identify with them, so that "they," in time, becomes "we."

A very powerful exercise at Immersion was personal asset mapping, helping the people we are serving actually write out their areas of gifting and strength using three categories: head, heart, and hands. We did an asset mapping exercise with the seventy-two people in our cohort, people from all across the country dedicating their lives to Christian community development. We were each given a marker and nine sheets of colored paper – three blue, three pink, and three yellow. On each blue paper, we wrote one gift, skill, or talent that comes from the head, the intellect. One thing I wrote on mine was administration, as I'm a natural organizer. On the pink sheets, we focused on heart gifts or passions. For me, first was worship music and the second was advocating for those in need – standing in the gap. The last three sheets, the yellow pages, were for talents that we do with our hands, physical abilities. This one was harder for me. One that I came up with was endurance. I can be tenacious and work at something for what seems like forever in order to accomplish the task.

We then taped all our nine pages on the wall, in random order. Those colorful representations of just a snippet of the gifts, the assets, held by our cohort filled a wall that was 8' x 24' from top to bottom. What a powerful image! As we discussed how these gifts could be used in a system of barter to mutually help one another, we recognized that I can fix your lawn mower if you can watch my children over the weekend. If you are able to teach me to play the guitar, I will help your son build a soapbox derby car. Or maybe I can help you navigate the process to apply for Social Security disability and you could help my spouse learn to cook authentic Indian food.

Every single person we meet is imago Dei, made in the image of God. Each of our friends living on the street has many skills, gifts, passions, and dreams. Focusing on the positives the community brings to the table BEFORE looking at areas that need work can be very beneficial to all. Hope is born from despair when we start with what they know and build on what they already have. Begin with the individual, then map assets of the entire community. This yields a sense of abundance, versus a needs map that focuses on scarcity and lack of resources, which is the way we typically approach poverty using our American mindset.

We talked about biblical principles for helping the poor, brought to life using the "teach a man to fish" premise. A person has to work to eat, to get the food and cook it, NOT expect it as an entitlement. This requires listening, time, and using existing assets to create empowerment. It involves work and money or barter, and it brings dignity to the poor. Christian development ministry teaches principles to live by—not only how to fish, but also how to buy the pond, and beyond that, how to effectively manage and maintain the pond.

We heard a true story about missionaries to Mexico in a community where babies were dying from lack of sanitation and clean water. Rather than immediately digging a well that may not even be used by the community, only to fall into disrepair in a few months, they asked the community what they most wanted help with. The answer was a soccer field for the men. So the missionaries helped them build a soccer field. In time, the men saw the ladies crying together week after week on the sidelines of the field. They found out that the sadness stemmed from the loss of their babies. At that point, they begged the missionaries to help them find a solution. The clean water well and latrines were THEIR idea, and that sense of ownership generates staying power. As my Immersion experience came to a close, I asked myself, "Do I have the kind of faith it takes to watch babies continue to die while I build a soccer field?"

God used many simple conversations, as well as some powerful experiences, to mold and shape me during the first eighteen months of C-U at Home, while I lived at Restoration Urban Ministries. My prayer warrior friend Rita continued to pray with me and for me several times a week. I love Rita for the woman of God she is and for the ways He used her in my life during those early years when I was so often discouraged and couldn't see a way out.

I learned of the day-to-day challenges of poverty, including dental care. I remember having simple meals with other folks in our little rooms. That's when I realized that most folks on the street are not able to have regular dental care. Many people who are chronically homeless have lots of problems with their teeth. Sometimes they only have a few teeth left, or even no teeth at all. So, eating anything that you have to bite into or anything that is tough to chew is out of the question.

Violence is another challenge of poverty. One afternoon, my friend Judy got a phone call that changed her life forever. She was on the phone with her sister from Texas. They were talking, and then Judy heard gunshots, screaming, and the phone went silent. She had just heard her sister being shot. Judy was hysterical. I was able to cry with her and pray with her. Just be with her.

Because a third challenge of poverty is transportation, I briefly considered using public transportation and a bicycle after I sold the motorcycle and SUV. But when I thought about the number of meetings I would be having to get things off the ground, I decided to purchase a well-running, economical used car; a little 1995 Geo Prizm. As it turned out, a working vehicle with valid tags quickly proved to be a hot commodity at RUM. God used my little Prizm as a platform to build relationships by offering rides to friends who did not have a vehicle.

Joel and Rachel, the young missionary couple living and serving at Restoration, had an impact on me as well. We had talks about our fears and God's faithfulness. We prayed together, me for them and them for me. They are now serving the Lord in Kenya, and it is a privilege to continue to pray for them and their ministry as they prayed for me and C-U at Home.

God used the example of Pastor Ervin Williams and many others through our daily devotions at RUM to teach me about listening to God, waiting on Him, and being faithful. There are so many times it would have been easy to quit, to simply walk away. But the Lord used many faithful believers at Restoration to encourage me to stay the course and trust in God.

At the end of April, we finally heard from The United Way about the grant funds we had applied for back in December. The answer was "no." They would not be funding us for the next two years. This was a HUGE disappointment. I had been praying for and counting on those funds to be our financial foundation. That night in my journal I wrote, "No grant $ – anger, disappointment, injustice – fear. Will I have to work elsewhere for the rest of the year? Lord, help me, please. I need You to encourage and guide me. I want to trust You. Help my unbelief. I must decrease . . . You must increase. Amen."

On the first day of May, God provided a wonderful experienced volunteer bookkeeper for our ministry. Bill Newell agreed to come in on a regular basis and take care of processing our bills, writing checks, developing our monthly disbursement requests for the Community Foundation, filing receipts, and balancing the checkbook. It was a pleasure working with Bill, as he was a natural born encourager, in addition to being God's provision of a bookkeeper for our ministry. This was especially exciting for me because working with finances and spreadsheets is NOT my forte. A few months later, when Bill had to step away, the Lord brought along Claudia, a University of Illinois accounting student from China. Bill took several weeks to train Claudia on all of our processes.

Early that month, we entered into a creative partnership to house and support a man with mental illness who also struggled with alcoholism. Pastor Janet Guthrie from First Mennonite Church had contacted me about his situation. He had been in public housing and hoped to get back into a Housing Authority apartment soon. He received disability payments from the government each month. The idea was for the resident to pay a portion of his rent and utilities, for the church to pay a portion, and for C-U at Home to pay a portion. Since Vern would be in Springfield at The Salvation Army Adult Rehabilitation Center (ARC) for six months to a year, we asked for his permission to use his house to help this man for a few months. He gave us permission, allowing us to move the new resident into the house where Vern had been living.

Later in May, I was contacted by the friend who was paying for my personal health insurance. Though he had previously promised to provide this benefit for me for the entire year, he now said he could no longer afford it. So, starting in June, I needed to find a way to pay for my own health insurance. I sent out an email to three friends about two specific needs: new tires for my car and health insurance. My friend from the University of Illinois Vet Med contacted me and said that he and his wife wanted to give me the funds to pay for my health insurance for twelve months. Hallelujah!!! A few days, later a friend from church invited me to share about C-U at Home at her small group. On Sunday after church, she placed a $500 check in my hand for a new set of tires. More tears. I thought, "Once again, Lord, Your provision, right on time!"

More support came in the form of almost $1500 in cash from a university journalism student. Emily Cleary and some friends with Her Campus had hosted a fashion show, and all the funds raised were donated to help us. When she delivered the money, she said that they wanted it to be used to help me as I led the ministry for things like gas in my car and for my cell phone bill. I could never have imagined that students doing a fashion show would help take care of my personal needs for another couple of months. What a blessing!

Lunch with a friend from church softball provided additional financial support. In taking early retirement from the university, he wanted to give a portion to God's work, and he handed me a $2,000 check for my personal provision. Once again, God doing what He does, bringing me the funds I needed to keep going. That same day, one of my prayer warrior friends, Melody, filled my tank with gas. Even more tangible provision.

In the midst of all the challenges of our ministry, I had started doing a bit of house sitting, staying in someone's home while they were away for a weekend or an entire week. I could take care of a pet, water the plants, get the mail, etc. And it gave me a mental health respite from life at Restoration, as well as a place to cook and do laundry. I was grateful for each opportunity given to me to house sit. This would become more important down the road.

I started attending Steve and Kathie Cole's small group during the week and teaching the *Radical* Bible study class at First Christian Church on Sunday mornings, allowing me to build a few more deep relationships with folks there. I was grateful. God was providing a support team to help keep me healthy, as I poured myself into others and into building C-U at Home. I also got to house and dog sit for seven days in a mansion. Wow! God's provision that time around came in a particularly luxurious setting.

Near the end of May, we had the first official meeting of our C-U at Home board of directors. Our founding board members were Mike Kessel, Eric Kraft, Phil McGarvey, John Smith, and Michelle Grindley. We discussed and adopted by-laws, and as a formality, I was "hired" to be the executive director of C-U at Home (without a salary, of course). God continued to build the foundation for the ministry. This was a huge step toward becoming an actual organization, rather than simply a loose affiliate of a two-year national movement.

We were able to go to Springfield and visit with David, another man who was at the ARC with Vern. He was doing so well! Really incredible. He looked and sounded like a new man. David was one of the hardcore street homeless in Champaign and the folks from the Canteen Run and those of us at C-U at Home had grown to love him. We were all praying for his success in breaking the chains of alcoholism and accepting a new way of life.

In June, I was able to attend the Cornerstone Music Festival, hosted by Jesus People USA (JPUSA), on Cornerstone Farm in remote Bushnell, IL. I had been to this week of renewal and encouragement through community every year for sixteen years, beginning in 1996. Chuck and Cheryl Conway had told me about it soon after they experienced it themselves in 1995, knowing it would be a good place for me as a new true believer with a passion for Christian music. We camped together that week, and it didn't take long for me to see just how special this place was. There were between 20,000 and 30,000 men, women, and kids from every race and from all over the world, many of them tatted and pierced. It wasn't my normal crowd to hang out with, but I soon found more authentic Christianity in some of these strange looking people than I had ever seen inside the church walls. Cornerstone was kind of like a Christian Woodstock, with lots of music, art, teaching, worship, campfires, swimming, canoeing, food, sweat, dirt, mud, and more. So, for seventeen years straight, regardless of what else was happening in my life, I made the pilgrimage to that remote farm on the west side of Illinois and set up camp with the Conways. "The mother country," I called it. And in 2012, it all came to an end.

The economy had taken its toll on the music festival. Numbers had started dwindling, especially since the recession of 2008, and the price to book musical acts was steeply rising. Those two realities were a toxic mix for the future of the Fest. JPUSA had announced that 2012 would be the final Cornerstone Music Festival. There was a sadness in the air when I arrived. Many of us felt it was kind of like losing a family member. We were grieving together. The final night of the final Fest, we walked from one end of the grounds all the way to the lake, carrying a Viking boat on our shoulders, led by headlights rigged up on a couple of golf carts. The boat was launched into the lake and once it reached the middle, a man shot a flaming arrow into it. Soon the entire boat was engulfed. We watched as if it was a dream or a movie. We prayed. We cried. We remembered. We grieved. We stayed on the beach late, until the flame was completely extinguished, the boat no longer in sight. It must have sunk. Good-bye Cornerstone.

The next morning, I couldn't believe my eyes. There, on the far shore sat the boat. Tattered and torn, she was still floating! What did this mean? Would God somehow preserve Cornerstone and bring it back to life, against all odds, and against several million dollars in debt? Several folks formed a group called Occupy Cornerstone, with the idea of resurrecting the Fest in 2013 there at Cornerstone Farm. Only time would tell. But one thing was for sure, Cornerstone had changed my life and the lives of thousands of others across the country and the world, opening my heart to see people who looked very different from me as being loved by God, made in His image. This annual experience had helped to open and prepare my heart for leading C-U at Home.

When I met next with Joan Dixon, she made it clear that the Community Foundation was unable to accept tax deductible donations to go towards my personal support. This was very disappointing and frustrating. There were people asking for their donations to go towards my personal financial needs. In my journal that night I wrote, "Lord, what are You trying to tell me? How do You want me to live? I am broken and discouraged. I want to make a difference. Show me how to follow You. Break my heart for what breaks Yours. Amen."

Preparing documents and getting everything lined up for our 501(c)(3) incorporation (c3, for short) application was a high priority. We had a board of directors and by-laws in place, but that was only the beginning. The IRS application process was a daunting one. We asked a local non-profit legal organization for assistance, but they were not familiar enough with the non-profit incorporation process to help us. So, I was doing the best I could with what I had, developing financial reports and writing lots and lots of narrative.

Finally, Mike, Eric, and I drove to Springfield to meet with an attorney about helping us with this application. She had quite a bit of experience with successful applications and she was a Christ follower. It would cost us probably between $1500 and $2000 for her to help us, but it was so very worth it! She could walk us through each step of the way and help us if anything went awry. The completed 501(c)(3) application was finally mailed to the IRS in mid-July. Now for the waiting game . . .

Cash flow for C-U at Home continued to be a challenge. In September of 2012, we needed several more thousand dollars than we had in the bank because of the delay in getting our reimbursements from the Community Foundation. A couple of us in the ministry fronted $1,000 each to pay for what we needed. And a generous couple donated $1,000 directly to us (not funneling it through the tax-deductible cycle of the Community Foundation). He WILL make a way where there seems to be no way.

Friends organized a Sunday afternoon event at First Christian Church to invite people to join them in regular, monthly financial support for my personal living expenses. While it was sparsely attended and very little response came from the event, I was so grateful that these two couples were doing what they could to help. Though we were all somewhat disappointed, we had faith because God had already miraculously provided for me throughout the previous sixteen months. He would continue to sustain me as long I was walking according to His will.

When the Lord led me to start C-U at Home as a part of the remaining two years left in the 100,000 Homes campaign, I felt clearly that He would provide both for me personally and for the ministry. To be more specific, that He would provide *financially* for me and for C-U at Home, however He saw fit. So, I had done my part by selling the motorcycle, SUV, seminary books, and a few other belongings in April and May of 2011. That had yielded several thousand dollars of seed money to start the initiative. At no point along the way did I consider sending out a "missionary letter," asking friends to support me financially. I also didn't consider doing church presentations asking for funds to provide for me personally. On the contrary, I went the route of prayer.

In seminary, I learned about a faithful servant in nineteenth century England named George Müeller. His total faith in God to provide was inspirational to me. He came to faith while in college, and time after time, he prayed for God's provision for him personally, and later for the orphans God called him to help. When he took a job as a pastor at a church, he refused to receive a salary. He trusted God to meet all his needs, and God did so. George's family never missed a meal and was always able to pay their rent. His heart began to break for all the hungry orphans in his area of the city.

Each day, as George walked the streets, he saw children everywhere who had no mom or dad. They lived on the streets or in state-run poorhouses, where they were treated badly. George felt God calling him to open an orphanage to take care of the children. George asked God to provide everything needed – a building, furniture, staff, and the money needed for food and clothing for the children. God answered George's prayers time after time. God was faithful. Donations, large and small, came, often just in time. But God faithfully provided every single time without George telling a single person about their needs. He prayed and he waited for God to provide. Over the years, more than 10,000 orphans lived in the orphanage that God had built through George.

I'm certainly no George Müeller, but I did believe that if God wanted C-U at Home to develop and grow, He would provide everything that we needed, and He would provide everything I needed personally. So, I followed the example of George Müeller. I fasted and prayed. We formed a prayer support team to be the foundation for the ministry. I went a total of twenty-six months without any means of personal financial support or income. And that entire time, I had a cell phone with service, gas in the car, a Y membership for my lap swimming, and health insurance. My bank account never went below $500, and it only went below $1,000 twice. Without asking one person for help or writing one single missionary letter for support, Jehovah Jireh has been MY Provider. He is more than enough for me.

Some might call that a miracle.

I call it God doing what He does.

Providing for His kids.

Philippians 4:19 states, *And my God will meet all your needs according to his glorious riches in Christ Jesus.* He promised that he will "meet all your needs." In Matthew 6:31-33, He says, *"So don't worry about these things, saying, 'What will we eat? What will we drink? What will we wear?' These things dominate the thoughts of unbelievers, but your heavenly Father already knows all your needs. Seek the Kingdom of God above all else, and live righteously, and he will give you everything you need."* If we are obedient in seeking His Kingdom, He will give us what we need—what we NEED, NOT necessarily what we want. When you follow after God and join Him in His Kingdom purposes here on earth, He IS faithful. He will provide for you. As my life verse, 1 Thessalonians 5:24, states, *The One who called you is completely dependable. If he said it, he'll do it!* (The Message).

One day, while walking back from lunch at the Daily Bread Soup Kitchen, I got a crazy idea. Vern had left the ARC without completing the program and returned to the streets of Champaign. What if we housed Norm and Vern together? They were best friends, street brothers. What would they think of the idea? How would they do together? What would John and Rick and the others in our ministry think? We continued to ponder this possibility and discuss what it might look like for the next few weeks.

We decided to talk first with Vern about coming back into a house with us. Once he said yes, we asked him if he would like Norm to live with him. He was ecstatic! Then came the next conversation, asking Norm if he would like to live with Vern in our house. That answer was also yes. We were all very excited about this. The only problem was at that moment, we did not have a house for them to move into.

An old friend from Garden Hills Baptist Church contacted me. Kevin Coey had heard about the ministry and knew we needed houses for folks to stay in as their lives were being transformed. He met me for dinner and told me about a vacant property that he owned, and he offered it to our ministry to use at no charge! In fact, Kevin even donated $100 per month to help with the utility costs. The place did need a bit of work and cleaning before anyone could move in, which would take some time. But this was good news. Now we would have a place for Norm and Vern to live, even if the other man living on Elm Street (Vern's former home) didn't get into an apartment soon. Our timeline was to have the Hedge Road house ready by September 1.

Then the unthinkable happened. We received word that Vern was in the hospital in intensive care. He had suffered blunt force trauma on Saturday from hitting his head on a table, resulting in severe bleeding on the brain. Part of his skull had to be cut away to relieve the pressure. This happened on Saturday, but we didn't find out about it until Sunday afternoon. His family had already been contacted and were there with him at the hospital.

On Monday, they had a family conference, as he had been shown to be brain dead. They had a brother coming in from Missouri, to arrive at about 8pm, and my softball team was scheduled to play in the championship game at 8pm. They all encouraged me to go play. I decided to. It was the wrong decision. I played terrible. I was up to bat with a chance to tie in the last inning and I struck out, something I almost never do. When I arrived back at the hospital after the game, Vern had died twenty minutes earlier. After praying and crying with the family, we went out to look for his street brother, Norm. Richard and I both looked, but we could not find him.

We were able to find Norm the next day, and he was with Richard. John picked them up together and got them into a hotel. This was no time for either of them to be alone on the streets. On Wednesday I spent time with Penny, Vern's sister, and helped with the arrangements. We contacted New Covenant Fellowship, Vern's church, and arranged to have his memorial service there on Saturday. We helped Penny write the obituary and get it to the newspaper.

That Friday afternoon we were attacked, slandered publicly. Someone was blaming us for Vern's death. That cut me to the quick. How could someone be so hurtful? We had done everything we could to love Vernon and to help him. My prayer that evening was, "Lord, please help me. Calm me. Keep my eyes and my heart on You alone. Give me Your peace and compassion in the morning. I need You. I love You. Amen."

When I went to seminary, I never really thought about organizing and leading a funeral. I had assisted with a couple of funerals while still in Missouri, but this time the family was looking to me to put everything together. It was quite the celebration of life, with about 275 friends and family in attendance. Lots of pictures of Vern from all throughout his life. Friends from his childhood telling stories about him as a kid. Friends from the street sharing their adventures with Vern. No more pain. No more fear. We laughed. We cried. We said good-bye. Vernon loved Jesus. We will see him again.

After the funeral, we moved the guys (Norm and Richard) to a different hotel with a better weekly rate, praying the new house would be ready for them to move into on September 1.

8

Fragile Days

The Community Foundation provided our funding on a reimbursement basis. That meant that we had to have the funds up front to pay for anything we needed for the ministry. Once a month we submitted an expense spreadsheet and receipts to them to be approved by their board of directors. At that point, a check would be requested and it could take up to another week for us to have the funds deposited into our bank. This method was quite frustrating, especially for a grassroots ministry that was initially funded with a few thousand dollars from selling some of my belonging in the spring of 2011.

With Vern's death, we missed getting our request to their board on time in August, so we would not receive any funds for at least six weeks. We needed to purchase $3,000 in liability insurance, and we had $10,000 in reimbursements to request. In the meantime, we learned that our resident in the little house on Elm Street had been having a woman stay with him. We quickly discerned that there was nothing inappropriate between them: he was sleeping on the couch and she was sleeping in the bed. We had a tough intervention, and he told us that he was not going to sleep in that house while a woman was living outside. He was only trying to help her like we were helping him. Wow! We decided to place the woman in a hotel and pay for her to stay there for a week. More expense. I prayed, "Lord, I am so low and downtrodden. I am weak and overwhelmed. Please help C-U at Home keep our focus and resources on the most vulnerable. I need You, Lord. Your way, not mine. Thank you. Amen."

Monday, August 27, was a joyous yet somber day. We were all still grieving Vern's death and asking questions, but the new house was decorated and ready. We celebrated with cake and handed the guys each a house key. They now had a home. Rick took Norm and Richard shopping at Target to get personal things they needed and supplies for the house.

The ministry rollercoaster continued in these fragile days, as Bruce, one of our other transitional housing residents, had a meltdown and decided to move out of the house. He was in a manic state with lots of tension. He had already gotten one frenzied load of stuff and was coming back for the rest the next day. Bruce was in a battle for his soul. He had done so well, applying for a grant and enrolling to go to Parkland College. But there was a woman who had his heart, and she was like poison to him. He knew she was not good for him, but he couldn't resist. He self-sabotaged and lost everything he had gained. Two steps forward and three steps back. Two men housed and one man leaving, going back into his mess.

Another accusation was thrown our way, this time from someone who had been a part of our inner circle. The insinuation was that I had made Vern's memorial service all about me and about C-U at Home – that it was disgraceful and that we were trying to capitalize on publicity about his death. I was crushed. Another accusation that couldn't be farther from the motive of my heart. I prayed, "Lord, please help me. This is so hurtful. I only want to serve You. I need You. Please, less of me, more of You. Show me the way to lead as a humble servant. Thank you. Amen."

A few days later, it was David's fiftieth birthday and he was celebrating it while still living at the Adult Rehabilitation Center (ARC) in Springfield. I got a birthday cake for him and picked up both Norm and Richard that morning. They went with me to worship at First Christian Church. Somewhat to my surprise, they both really liked the music. Then we made our way to Springfield. We picked up David and we all went to the Golden Corral buffet for lunch. We ate until we were stuffed, and then we had birthday cake! Next stop was Wal-Mart to pick up a few things for David. After that, we spent a couple of hours together at the Abraham Lincoln museum in downtown Springfield. For just a few hours, the guys and I got to just be friends doing normal things together – eating, shopping, enjoying a museum together. That night I prayed, "Lord, thank you for a great day with three sober alcoholics today. This is what C-U at Home is about. Please help us find more ways to get the guys together more often. Thank you for encouragement. I love You, Lord. Amen."

As for our summer event, C-U at Home One Summer Day was held on the morning of Saturday, May 30, at Hessel Park in

Champaign. We were very excited to get the event off the ground, even if liftoff was a bit bumpy. The Lord provided enough volunteers and we had 107 walkers signed up, though our goal had been to have at least 200. We raised just over $12,000, having hoped to raise at least $20,000. The pedometers to measure each walkers' steps didn't work right, so that was frustrating. Even more disappointing was that two of the six participating organizations did not even show up to display their information, and they were splitting 50% of the money raised!

Soon after the event, we were contacted by a young woman who had recently moved to the area after working full-time for a national ministry. She had heard me give a presentation at church about C-U at Home One Summer Day and wanted to help with the ministry, especially with administrative support and event planning. Hallelujah! Unfortunately, her offer only lasted one week because she got a full-time job. I was so disappointed. Once again, it seemed like God had dangled a carrot in front of me and then abruptly taken it away. How many more times would this happen to me? A couple of years later, however, God did allow this young woman to join our board of directors, which was a wonderful way of redeeming this situation that had caused me so much angst.

There was a new couple who got involved with helping our ministry in a variety of ways throughout 2012. They had lots of ideas and at different points had people in need that they wanted C-U at Home to assist in specific ways. They eventually stepped away, apparently because we were not assisting people in the way they wanted us to help them. This was disappointing and frustrating. Yet again, key volunteers had stepped away from our ministry.

In these difficult days, while we continued to grieve the loss of Vern, my flat side became evident again. Rick and John met with me at the office, and they both told me they had been hurt by me. It was more of the same, control and perfectionism. I asked myself, "Will this ever change?" It is my problem. It is my sin. Once again, I was hurting those closest to me, those trying to help me help others. I prayed that evening, "Lord, please do not let me destroy C-U at Home from the inside. Help me see what I am doing to hurt others before I do it. Humility instead of pride. Servant leadership. More time with You. More focus on You, Lord. Less flesh. More Spirit. Thank you. Amen."

In July, I had the privilege of guest lecturing for two Master of Social Work classes at the invitation of Professor Min Park. He and a colleague were doing a research project focused on the homeless through the Emergency Department at Carle Hospital. It was designed to expose the high cost of repeatedly treating a small number of individuals and even doing so inadequately, without the ability to medically detox them from alcohol or drugs. Dr. Park gave me the entire class period for both sections, so I shared my personal story of starting up C-U at Home, the survey, housing Vern, One Winter Night, the next house, One Summer Day, and more. Many of the students asked good questions and signed up on our email list. Several came up to me about getting more involved. One of those students, Kelly-Jane, would become a key person in helping our ministry, first as a volunteer, then later as an employee.

C-U at Home was beginning to get a few new volunteers interested in helping us on a regular basis. Two of these were Kelly-Jane (KJ) and Geri. They were both at the office to help me with administrative tasks one afternoon, and my flat side came out again. I was agitated and frustrated with them. The stress and pressures were getting to me and I took it out on them. I knew that I must be calm, gentle, and encouraging with volunteers. They were there to help us! Was I ever going to get better at letting go of control and no longer be so demanding of others?

That summer, Terry Hickman, a friend from the Canteen Run, provided an answer to prayer. We desperately needed additional warehouse space to store donated furniture and appliances. Terry's employer, The International Society of Arboriculture, had a huge empty warehouse. John and I went to look at it. They said they would let us use it for FREE! Warehouse provision. Thank you Jesus.

During this time, the Lord brought a very important person into my life. Don Follis had retired from pastoring and saw the need for someone to be a pastor for pastors. So many pastors carry such heavy loads and feel like there is no one in whom they can confide or receive practical encouragement and spiritual advice from. He started a new ministry called Pastor-to-Pastor Initiatives and began meeting with me on a monthly basis early in 2013. His listening ear and heart have been used by the Lord to encourage and guide me on this crazy C-U at Home journey. Over the years, he has seen me "lower than a snake's belly," bursting with joy and excitement, and everything in between.

During the last week of October in 2012, we once again did a community-wide survey to identify the most vulnerable homeless. This year there were eighteen people identified as most vulnerable –

sixteen men and two women. We still had so much work to do to try to find housing for the most vulnerable. Slowly and steadily, the Lord was providing for our needs. We prayed that He would continue to guide us on this journey.

Sometimes, that guidance came through the provision of time away. In the middle of November, I took a four-day silent retreat (at least mostly silent) to Southern Illinois. I stayed in a little cabin in the Shawnee National Forest near Alto Pass, IL. Lots of sleep and long walks in the forest helped me decompress from the stress and challenges of ministry. No phone, no internet, and no television were a big help.

When I hit Carbondale on my way to the retreat, I had a meal at my favorite college pizza place, Quatro's. It helped me be reflective, with a good dose of nostalgia. My husband John and I had spent many Friday nights together at Quatro's. On the first day of the retreat, I made notes of things I wanted to implement in my life. One thing was to restrict checking my email to a maximum of five times a day, at regular four-hour intervals – 6am, 10am, 2pm, 6pm, and 10pm. Email had a way of often taking on a life of its own, so this seemed to be one way to limit my time on email. I decided to continue journaling daily and spending more time with God throughout each day in prayer, being silent (listening), reading or listening to scripture, and singing or playing worship music. I also laid out what a typical work day might look like for me, with specified time for swimming, devotions, work, meals, journaling, and prayer. I needed a template to keep my focus and my sanity, as I wanted to gain balance in the various areas of my life. In particular, I wanted to focus on interweaving my faith more into the fabric of each day.

On the second day of my retreat, I wrote, "Stop trying so hard and let God be in control – NOT ME! Love our volunteers like the residents. Slow down – think before speaking and doing. Stop being so selfish. The order must be 1) God, 2) others, 3) me." I also made a list of things to do weekly: Daily Bread Soup Kitchen, the Canteen Run, devotions, cook for the week, and laundry. My life often got so out of kilter that I didn't eat some meals, and many of the meals I did eat were a quick fix and not very nutritious.

That night I made a list titled: Am I grateful? And on that list, I wrote the following: positive attitude, aware of God's presence, humble spirit, peacefulness, thoughtful of others, generous (share with joy), unselfish, friendly, contagious, motivated, a servant's spirit, high level of faith, fruitful, and joyful. I made a long list of goals to shoot for and boiled it down to five priorities: 1) daily God time, 2) recognizing that God is in control, NOT ME!, 3) less pressure/more peace, 4) prayer before each meeting (of any type), and 5) read a random verse from the Bible (from an app I downloaded on my phone) before reading or sending a text, making a phone call, reading or writing email, or accessing Facebook. Certainly, powerful goals to shoot for.

On Sunday morning, I got to attend Lakeland Baptist Church to hear Phil Nelson preach. Phil and his family had lived in Champaign for several years, while he did campus ministry at the University of Illinois. Phil is the one person God has used more than anyone else in my life to show me what an evangelistic lifestyle looks like. It's in his DNA. He's so good at turning conversations in a spiritual direction and being led by the Spirit to pray with others. Sitting under Phil's preaching breathed new life into my dry bones.

On Sunday afternoon, I wrote, "Work in each area, each day: people — short-term and long-term, places — short-term and long-term, and events — short-term and long-term. Find my identity in Christ, NOT C-U at Home or success or failure." The Lord also brought to mind the image of Team Hoyt, a father/son triathlon team in which the adult son is a spastic quadriplegic with cerebral palsy. Rick, the son, asked Dick, his father, if he could be in a five-mile race to raise funds for a lacrosse player at his school who had been in an accident and was paralyzed. Dick was thirty-six years old at that time and had never been a runner, but he would have done anything for his son. So, he became the legs and feet for Rick and ran the race, pushing his son the entire five miles in his wheelchair. Rick said, "Dad, when I'm running, it feels like I'm not handicapped." They went on to complete in many grueling Ironman Triathlons as Team Hoyt.

There is an image that has been seared in my mind of Dick pushing his son in a race. Rick's arms are flung open wide, and he has a big grin of contentment on his face. The Lord had used that image a year earlier during a powerful time of prayer counseling I had experienced. It's a beautiful picture of God's sovereignty and His love for us. He loves us because of who we are, NOT because of anything we can do. We are designed to find joy in being led by our Daddy, relinquishing control and resting confidently in His arms. This picture of Team Hoyt continues to be the lock screen image on my cell phone to this day.

My prayer that last night in the cabin was, "Lord, please help me keep my focus on You and off email and Facebook, anxiety and stress. I want to walk closer and closer with You. Reveal more of Your Truth and Your Word to me. Please show me Your ways. Lord, help me let go of control and give it to You. Please help me leave pride behind and instead embrace humility. Thank you. I love You. Amen."

When I returned to the office, I faced a day that was both hi/lo and overwhelming for me. So much for the retreat! I found that I would not be able to have any contact with John Smith, my right hand man, until the next week, as he was completely unavailable. Then came the spectacular part of the day. Two friends who were College of Law instructors at the University of Illinois would be teaching at Brigham Young for the spring semester. They invited me to house sit and care for their pets for five months, beginning just after Christmas. I made the decision to move out of Restoration and put my belongings into storage.

Next, I went to visit Norm. He had been hospitalized for several days, and the medical team was unable to figure out why he couldn't walk. He was not doing well at all. Finally, Norman was diagnosed with a large tumor on his lower spine, advanced stage cancer. Palliative care was the only option. He died on the first Sunday in December. Richard attended the funeral with John and me, and then he began to slide into a deep depression. He felt like he had a target on his back. First Vern, then Norm. He believed that he would be the next one to die.

We had also been working with Brandon, helping him get a mental health assessment, partnering with the State's Attorney, and preparing to offer him housing. We had arranged with the court to release him into our custody. The cake was on the table at the house and his key was in my pocket. The plan was to go straight from the courthouse to his new home. Just to be sure, we called him around 7:30am, but there was no answer and his phone was off. Several of us scoured the town, looking for him in every place we could imagine. We kept calling the phone and prayed that he would make it to the courthouse, but he never showed up. We found him later that day. He said he had lost the phone and that he was asleep at 9am. So, rather than moving into his new home, he went back to jail. Unbelievably frustrating and disappointing: another guy self-sabotaging.

A few days later I went to First Christian to print our OWN 2013 signs to go inside of all the public buses in town. I was feeling quite discouraged because of both Norm and Brandon. One of the pastors there, Jason Epperson, came into the office area where I was working. He said that they had done an outreach event earlier and had some Wal-Mart gift cards left over. He handed them to me and said they were for me—for gas in the car, food, whatever I needed. I was blown away by this gracious gift for my personal provision.

A couple of days after Christmas, I was able to move out of Restoration and into the house where I would be pet-sitting. It was a bittersweet time of saying good-bye to all my friends at Restoration and saying hello to an elegant house in Southwest Champaign that I would call home for the next five months, a real culture shock for me. Once again, God provided a home for me while I was leading C-U at Home.

I seem to be wired to be somewhat transient, not tied to a particular home. I connect with folks without an address as a kindred spirit. Moving from place to place is comfortable for me, and God used that part of who I am to fit right in with what He had called me to do to serve Him. In fact, over the next four and a half years, I would move eight more times. Time after time, the Lord provided housing for me, sometimes just in the nick of time. Most often I was living in an empty house while the owners were away for a few weeks or a season. They trusted me to take care of their pets, their plants and their yards. I learned to trust in God's provision for my own living arrangements and to see Him come through over and over again. What a blessing to know that I can trust Him to always care for my physical needs.

Having completed my move, I was ready to dedicate January 2013 to One Winter Night preparation, in addition to taking care of the folks in our houses and continuing to tell our story. One way that we spread the word about C-U at Home One Winter Night was by sharing about the event during all the services at First Christian Church on Sunday morning, with a table display just outside of the sanctuary. As we were packing up to leave, I felt pretty disappointed that we had garnered only a couple of small donations and a handful of volunteers for OWN. Little did I know that this disappointment would be turned on its head in just three short days, when I received an email from Don, the Missions Pastor at First Christian Church who had already provided essential personal support to me. Someone from the church who had heard about our ministry and our need for property had contacted him with a small two-bedroom house that they were interested in DONATING to our ministry! I was beyond excited. We would have to find out what all it would take to get the house in our name, and we knew it would take assistance from an attorney and some leg work, but we couldn't wait to make this offer a reality and have a house of our very own to use to get folks off the streets and back on their feet. Praise the Lord!

A local attorney was willing to help us through the process of transferring the title to our name. But there was one problem: we were not yet a legal entity. Only a legal entity can receive and own property, but we were still waiting on our 501(c)(3) non-profit application to be approved. We contacted our U.S. Congressman to advocate on our behalf, as it seemed that religious organizations were being scrutinized by the IRS at that time. I had the distinct feeling that our application was being unduly delayed.

At the end of the month, David graduated from the ARC in Springfield. Several of us drove together to celebrate that day with him and then bring him home to his new place, while a whole crew of friends waited for us at the house, complete with a decorated cake on the table. David had been through very, very tough times on the street with severe alcoholism, and now he had been delivered. We were so excited to offer him a chance at a new life.

With all this excitement, there was still a huge community awareness event to get organized in the next three weeks. And this year, against all odds, we had received permission from the University of Illinois to hold OWN in a second location, on their main Quad. This was quite a challenging accomplishment, as the University, much like the city park where we had originally tried to hold our first One Winter Night, had an ordinance preventing anyone from sleeping outside on campus property. Permission had finally been granted in early November, and a small group of students who wanted to help us had developed an official Registered Student Organization (RSO) for C-U at Home. We were counting on this group of students to plan and organize the OWN Campus location, while we focused on everything for OWN Downtown.

But in December, the RSO started to fall apart. The students were weighed down by busy schedules followed by finals, and then they all went home to other cities and states for an entire month between semesters. All this, during the critical OWN planning period between mid-December and the last part of January.

No students, no help.

Gabby to the rescue once again! This is the same Gabby who had done so much to help us get t-shirts for the survey and had stepped in at the last minute to organize One Winter Night volunteers the previous year. She started working with the OWN Campus information just three and a half weeks before OWN 2013. And she got everything organized – box dwellers, volunteers, a headquarters location, marketing, and more. This wonder woman student stepped up to the plate for us yet again, and in a HUGE way. We simply did not have the staff to manage two separate locations for OWN simultaneously.

We actually had 125 students, faculty, and staff (mostly students) sign up to be box dwellers on the Quad, and we had asked each student to set a goal to raise at least $50 for us. The night of OWN turned out to be quite cold, and only about forty people showed up on campus. While the university OWN location didn't come anywhere near raising the funds we had hoped, we were grateful for the exposure, both to the frigid air and to the University of Illinois community at large.

OWN Downtown 2013 raised over $40,000, and we kept the books open for two more weeks to try to make up the difference in what we had hoped OWN Campus would raise. Through His faithfulness, the Lord did provide. We were able to bring in just over $57,000 for One Winter Night 2013. I was so grateful. His financial provision once again.

Within the ten days following One Winter Night, our volunteer staff of four went down to two. One was Kelly-Jane, who had been helping us with administrative tasks and had helped with lots of OWN needs. KJ had been pregnant the entire time she was helping us, and her first child, baby Aili, was born on February 7. We also lost Rick Cruse, who had been serving as our volunteer coordinator for more than a year, but needed to step away from our ministry for family reasons. He and his wife soon moved to Indianapolis to be close to their grandkids. Losing half of our team was devastating, as I was already feeling overwhelmed. What would God do to help us?

With Kelly-Jane and Rick gone, I was getting buried in details. Though we could not legally hire any employees until our 501(c)(3) status was granted, we desperately needed help. We developed a job description for a part-time administrative assistant and distributed it far and wide. It would initially be a volunteer position, transitioning to a paid position once we gained our incorporation status. We had quite a few applicants, which was encouraging.

During this overwhelming time, Don Follis reached out to me and offered to meet with me and coach me on a regular basis. Our friendship continued to grow over the years, as Don was often my closest confidante and strong encourager throughout this C-U at Home adventure.

God was at work in another area of my heart that February, as well. I had developed a burning desire to once again own a motorcycle and to launch a new bike ministry with Blake, one of my friends from church. So, I asked a few local friends as well as some motorcycle-riding friends around the country if they would contribute to my "bike fund." I was hoping to get about $3,000 to purchase a cruiser-style motorcycle, much like the Magna I had sold to help start C-U at Home.

I collected $2183 for the purchase of a motorcycle. I searched on craigslist for the motorcycle God wanted me to have, and a bike listed in Urbana immediately caught my eye, a red 1996 Honda Magna with 5,000 miles on it. The price was way MORE money than I had to offer, but I called to come see the bike that afternoon. He let me take the beautiful Magna for a test ride. It was just like having my old bike back! It felt and ran just the same, so smooth. It was just a different color, red instead of yellow.

I didn't dare dream that it could be mine. After I got back from the test ride, I told him how much I loved the bike. I told him about the '96 Magna I had sold and the homeless ministry the Lord had led me to start, and how several biker friends across the country had donated to my bike fund. I also shared about the motorcycle ministry we wanted to start. He told me to go get my money and when I came back with the cash in a bank envelope, he asked me how much I had. I told him I had $2183. He said, "OK, it's a deal," and handed me the title to the bike. He said, "I believe God wants you to have this motorcycle."

Wow! I was in disbelief that God cared enough about my heart's desire to give me this very special motorcycle for this very special price. Thank you, Jesus. I was excited to start planning our new bike ministry with Blake and to make plans for a Memorial Day bike trip with the IBSA (Illinois Baptist State Association) crew to Ridgecrest in North Carolina. I couldn't wait to finally get two wheels on my favorite road in the entire country, the Blue Ridge Parkway.

February ended with the completion of repairs on a new property for us to use as transitional supportive housing. The previous December, we had been contacted by property owners who were interested in allowing us to rent their three-bedroom home. We kept in touch with them as they worked on repairs, and so by February, the house was ready. We had been working with Mitch, one of the men we'd identified as most vulnerable, whose cousin Jeff was also living on the street. After interviewing both Jeff and Mitch, we decided to move them both into a hotel for a couple of weeks. Once we had seen they could live together well at the hotel, we moved them into the house together on March 8. Two more guys off the streets.

Two weeks later, I invited our residents to go to the big Winter Jam concert at University of Illinois Assembly Hall. Three of them took me up on it. It was so fun taking them to see the great live music. And just like that afternoon at the Lincoln Museum, it was great for me to get to spend time with the guys doing something "normal."

Soon, it was Good Friday once again, and I got up early and joined my friends Steve and Kathie Cole on a powerful walk through the city. Steve was dressed as Jesus, complete with a crown of thorns and theatre blood, carrying a full-sized wooden cross on his shoulders. Several years before this, God had convicted Steve and challenged him to be a visual witness on the day that we remember His crucifixion. It was a moving experience. And that evening, I followed my tradition of watching *The Passion of the Christ.*

A few days later, I took a few hours to reflect on how I was doing both personally and professionally, and to review the list of priorities I had made at the beginning of the year. I was doing OK on some of them and lousy with others. I also made a list of the positives and negatives in my personal life at that point. Positives: housing that was very nice, education, a small group, good health, bills paid by God's grace, motorcycle, and administration and leadership gifts. The negatives included: a dead car, being alone in this ministry, little joy, professional failure, little prayer, being overwhelmed, constantly falling behind on email, and personal failure.

The list of positives and negatives for C-U at Home was perplexing. In the positive column: favor from the media, three churches that were all monthly donors, OWN – good annual event, raising awareness, helping a few people, donated office space, favor from a few businesses, and donated warehouse space. The negatives included: no 501(c)(3), a lack of policies, virtually no staff, useless database, an inactive board, failing the most vulnerable, and insufficient male mentors for our residents.

On April 25, the City of Champaign held their annual ceremony where they present STAR Awards (Service Together Achieves Results) to community leaders in various categories. I knew I had been nominated in the Difference Maker category, but I was caught off guard when they announced my name as the winner. What an honor. I was humbled by what God was doing through C-U at Home. God had once again done something very special for us on a Thursday, our weekly day of prayer and fasting. The award affirmed the positive strides we were making.

At this point, we had five different houses that we were using to transition folks from being the most vulnerable on the streets to restoration. This is the maximum number of homes that we would see through April 2017. It's our hope to continue to use single family homes and hopefully eventually apartments or even an entire apartment building to help our friends transition off the streets.

In May, my church served as a satellite host site for the national Chick-fil-A Leadercast conference. I was excited to attend and learn from the top-notch slate of presenters as well as network with local Christian leaders. The host of our conference site, Stephan Seyfert, unexpectedly called me up on stage and introduced me as the leader of C-U at Home. I shared our vision with the audience, one of healing and restoration for our most vulnerable friends on the street. A challenge during the simulcast asked attendees to financially support local missions, and Stephan received an offering for several $500 move-in kits for C-U at Home. What an unexpected way for God to bless our ministry!

After many hardy miles, my car had died on the University of Illinois Quad during OWN. It was completely dead, and wouldn't even turn over. The quest to fix it lasted more than four months with various mechanics and diagnoses, and six different friends who loaned me a vehicle to use (more provision). Finally, on a two-hour phone call with my ex-husband, John, in Sacramento, he figured out the problem: two blown fuses and a cracked ignition coil. Simple fix, and I had my car back on the road again.

On Thursday, June 13, 2013, I went to the post office to check our mail. My anticipation was heightened as we had been waiting on pins and needles for our letter from the IRS, verifying C-U at Home as an official, legal non-profit. Sitting in the car, I shuffled through the stack of letters I had taken from our mailbox, stopping when I came across one from the IRS. I sliced the envelope open, and THERE IT WAS – our IRS determination letter, approving our official status as a tax exempt non-profit. Hallelujah!!! I literally cried tears of joy. Then I sent a text to our board and key volunteers, posted it on Facebook, and said a prayer of thanks. Of course, God would arrange to have this important event take place on a Thursday. With all of those who were fasting and praying for our ministry on that day each week, why would He do it at any other time? We could finally take receipt of the donated house, hire Kim as our administrative assistant, and hopefully hire a case manager soon. What a relief!

9

Growing Pains

On the day of our 2013 July board meeting, John Smith came into the office, handed me his C-U at Home paperwork, and walked out. He said that he would not be back, as he was resigning from his volunteer staff position and from our board of directors. I was devastated. He didn't have to say it – I knew that my performance orientation had been a big part of why he was walking away. I had been too demanding with him, asking for too much of his time and energy. "Lord, what do I do now?," I prayed. "My partner through thick and thin, gone. I DO NOT want to do this alone. I can't. Will this flat side of mine ever go away? Why can't I stop it? Please help me. Amen." I cried and prayed and asked others to pray.

And later that day, God answered my prayer. That very day. It was almost unbelievable. Tony Comtois had been around our ministry a few times off and on over the previous year. He came into the office and said that he wanted to start volunteering more regularly with us. One chapter painfully closed, and another joyously opened. Only God could orchestrate a course of events like this. It was yet another hi/lo day.

Kim Ormsby had been "hired" and had been serving as our volunteer administrative assistant since the beginning of May. Now with our non-profit status approved, we officially hired her as our first paid staff member for C-U at Home at fifteen hours a week, a big step forward for our ministry.

Our One Summer Day 2013 fundraising goal was $20,000, funds that would be used to hire a part-time professional case manager for the residents in our houses. On a beautiful Saturday morning, lots of friends walked on our behalf. We collected several tubs of donated items for area shelters – laundry detergent, fresh produce, razors, socks, and deodorant. But our goal fell short by about half. We raised almost $10,000. I was grateful and disappointed at the same time that we only got halfway to our goal. How would we pay for our new case manager?

The next day I was invited to a house church with friends from the prayer counseling ministry and classes I'd attended over the last two years. As I pulled into the driveway, I was both anxious and excited. After a powerful worship experience of sharing God's word, fellowship, song and prayer, I spent precious time with Mari Anne Andersen, one of the leaders of Freedom House. During our conversation, she said, "I'd like you to do this thing that sounds kind of crazy. Get a container of Miracle Gro and have it with you during your prayer times. Let it be a tangible reminder that our Daddy can and will provide, that He is still in the business of miracles today for you and for C-U at Home."

I stopped at a store on the way home and purchased a container of Miracle Gro, placing it in the chair at the foot of my bed where I kneel and pray each morning and evening. Ever since that day, I have knelt with my knees on the floor and my forehead on that box of Miracle Gro as I cry out and rejoice with God through prayer. I believe in tangible, physical markers that remind us of God's provision. We find such examples throughout scripture, such as the Passover meal, the twelve stones from the Jordan River memorial, and the Lord's Supper. God used Mari Anne that day to speak hope into my life, reminding me about our faithful, miracle-producing God.

That summer, I was privileged to work the front admissions gate for the first ever AudioFeed Music Festival. It was almost surreal, getting to welcome so many Cornerstone friends from all across the country and even from a few other countries! The remnant of our Cornerstone family was intact and we had come together once again. Now our annual gathering would be in my very own backyard, at the Champaign County Fairgrounds, and God was making it happen through my friends Jim and Jenny Eisenmenger. Fifty bands on four stages, arts, teaching, food, prayer, music and craft vendors, camping, porta potties, and more made this feel so much like Cornerstone, it brought tears to my eyes.

The first full day, it was so exciting to see our friend Harry Gore lead a set with musician friends. Harry had been a staple for many years at Cornerstone, playing in the food court, with his guitar and a small amp, his guitar case open for donations. Such talent. And a couple of times he was able to make it on the stage to join another artist for a song or two, but this was his moment to lead his own set. It was beautiful. The next day I got to sing and play my djembe with Cornerstone friends and a new AudioFeed friend on the front porch stage (much like the Impromptu stage from Cornerstone). Harry played the set with us, which was fun. In the afternoon, some of the younger folks got together a game of buck-buck out in the grass, another Cornerstone tradition. It was beautiful to have the family together once again. Rising up out of the ashes, the spirit of Cornerstone lived on!

Later in July, board member Kim Simpson and I spent the entire day at Home Sweet Home ministries in Bloomington, IL. It was a wonderful experience to learn from the staff, volunteers, and guests at a ninety-five-year-old homeless shelter ministry. We experienced an intake interview, had lunch with staff and guests, spent time with the ministry leaders, and toured the property. A strong theme throughout the day was grace and truth – walking on that fine line of love: God's unmerited, undeserved favor vs. personal accountability, rules, and consequences. They demonstrated that it is OK to live in the gray area, as not everything is black and white. In fact, most of the time, when you're dealing with people, things tend to be gray.

Kim and I also visited Outreach, Inc., in Indianapolis, IN, to observe that ministry, which focuses on youth across the metro area who have no place to live. They offer gender specific, in-school case management in many high schools in Indianapolis. They shared a powerful diagram with us about the various types of assistance offered to the youth through their ministry. On the left is the ocean with rough seas (outreach), next is the island (drop-in center), then a bridge (trusting relationships built through GED classes and other opportunities) to the mountain (case management), and finally leading to stable housing in the community. They described the stages of their guests: street, browser, subscriber. Their core values are relationship, sustainability, and advocacy. The faith aspect of their ministry is individualized and developed through relationships, with no spiritual hoops required for their guests to jump through.

Outreach's executive director challenged me right out of the gate. He saw it in my eyes. How did I expect to keep up the pace at which I was working? He said that it's absolutely necessary for leaders to take regular time completely away from the ministry and to do something fun, as well as to spend time alone with the Lord. Their staff has four weeks of annual paid vacation and four paid spiritual formation days. He explained the burnout he experienced and saw me headed the same direction at breakneck speed.

As soon as I got back, I looked at the calendar and planned a time for a spiritual retreat in the beginning of October. I also scheduled an entire afternoon of "God vision time" each week to include me, the Bible, and a notebook. Sometimes worship music was incorporated, but the computer and phone were both literally turned off and I went to a location where I would not be disturbed.

I was feeling the weight of C-U at Home on my shoulders. Things were not working as I had hoped and as other 100,000 Homes communities seemed to be doing. We had people who were dying and people who were returning to the streets. We did not have nearly enough volunteers to spend time with our residents to build trusting relationships. I was asking hard questions, like – "God, do You want us to end C-U at Home and give all of our resources to another ministry? Or, do You want us to continue, but go in a new direction?"

During this time period, the Lord began to pry my clenched fists from C-U at Home as my main identity. I had poured so much blood, sweat, and tears into this ministry for the last two years that it had indeed become how I saw myself. I was C-U at Home and C-U at Home was me. There was no separating the two. This call to repentance, my surrender to God being in control of C-U at Home rather than me, was a painful process. Over the next three months, the Lord helped me realize that I was first and foremost His child, and my identity was as a daughter of the King. C-U at Home was not who I was, but rather what I did to serve the Lord. This was a very important realization for me, giving me the right perspective about both the ministry and myself.

This heart work involved a return to the personal inventory I had used before, two lists with two columns each. The first was "Personal," with a + column and a − column. Some of my pluses were sleeping well, my small group, motorcycle, housing through July, and relatively good health. Some of the personal negatives were not swimming enough, money running out, no worship leading, lethargic, gaining weight, and being controlling. The other list was "Professional," again, with a + and a − column. A few of the professional pluses were Kim doing admin, positive media, eight monthly donors, five houses, Tony's help, and One Winter Night. Some of the negatives were no sustainable funding, revolving volunteer door, little help with property maintenance, and lack of progress for the residents.

In October, I headed north to Kankakee to the One Heart One Soul hermitage on the grounds owned and managed by the Servants of the Holy Heart of Mary. I arrived on Wednesday afternoon and my room was reserved through noon on Tuesday. A friend had paid for this week of spiritual retreat for me. No clock. No phone. No computer. Only the Bible, a few books, and a notebook. I slept well and slept long, until late the next morning. My body was exhausted.

When I did wake up on Thursday, it was raining. I journaled in my notebook, "It's raining and I have no set schedule, nowhere I have to be, no one waiting on me to do anything. I love the sound and smell of rain. I am warm and dry inside my cozy little hermitage. Help me realize and recognize that You are God and I am not. Thank you, Lord for giving me this special time and place to meditate and heal. I need You, Lord. I cannot do this on my own. I have failed and I will fail again. Lord, forgive me for the ways I treated John. I love him. I was so grateful for his help and his partnership. Help me grieve this loss. Help me see Your picture of what C-U at Home looks like without John beside me."

And then I wrote out I Corinthians 13:3-5, from what is commonly known as the "love" chapter in the Bible. Words that stuck out to me were, *Love is patient; love is kind.* I wrote "love is patient" at the top of the next blank page, and "love is kind" on the top of the next page. I then wrote down questions and possible answers.

What does it look like to be patient with Brent? More time in the house with our support to save money.

I developed similar answers for eight different people, the same people in the same order on each list. Some of the responses would require involving other people. If so, I wrote that person's name in parentheses after the response. My hope was to use these two lists as a guideline for me once I got back to Champaign and to mark off those with a definitive solution once they were accomplished.

Later that day I wrote: "Lord, give me Your eyes to see:

- those on the streets,
- our residents,
- staff,
- volunteers,
- friends, and
- leaders.

"I want to feel Your compassion and Your urgency for the gospel. I want to tune in to Your frequency and SLOW DOWN, look and listen, so that I react in Your love, not judgment. Help me be more aware of Your presence all throughout the day."

Once again, this was evidence of God's powerful work in my life on a Thursday, with our band of faithful prayer warriors interceding for me. During my time away, I read and studied three different books, and met twice with one of the sisters for spiritual direction.

The first book that I read, *Success over Stress* by N.T. Wright, caused me to ask some tough questions right away. I journaled, "The higher the level of expectations I have for myself, the more I need to be in control, and the greater my need for perfection, the greater my stress level. Do the ministry activities I am involved in match my gifts? What has God called me to do?" I also noted, "God measures success in the quality of my character and conduct. True success is to satisfy my calling, NOT my ambition. Live as a called woman." I used the personal plan template at the back of the book to implement changes. One was to memorize a scripture to help keep my focus on God. Romans 12:2 says, *Don't let the world around you squeeze you into its own mold.*

Next, as I dug into Bill Hybels book on prayer, *Too Busy Not to Pray*, I was reacquainted with the ACTS format for praying, which I decided to adopt as a strategy to help me pray more effectively.

- A – adoration, tell God the ways I love and worship Him;
- C – confession, tell God where I fall short of His standard;
- T – thanksgiving, tell God what I am grateful for; and
- S – supplication, ask God for others and for myself.

I used this model for my daily morning prayers for the year, and I continue to return to it often. Hybels talked about the importance of listening to promptings from God. So often we ask, is it God? Is it Satan? Is it me? How can I tell? We test to see if the prompting is consistent in three ways Hybels reminded me of – with the Bible, with who God made me to be, and with the spirit and action of servanthood.

Storyline by Donald Miller was the last and by far the most challenging book that I read during my time of retreat. The book served as an exercise to write a life map, identifying all the events from birth until the present that had irrevocably altered my life either positively or negatively. I began recalling and writing down all those key turns throughout my entire life, each with a short description. The next step was to rate the amount of impact each of these events had on my life, on a scale of 1-10. Then I placed them in chronological order on a timeline, with the line length corresponding to the impact score for that event. The positive turns were above the timeline and the negative below.

When I looked at the completed timeline, it was sobering. On the first portion from birth to twenty-five years old, I saw a theme of selfishness, of a focus on physical and personal gratification. The second portion, from twenty-five years old to the present, was focused on God's calling and following Him. The most recent years of my life were filled with powerful, positive turns as well as a couple of very negative turns in the last few years. I recalled wrestling with God about my flat side of control and perfectionism that day in 2010 at Homer Lake, my poor treatment of the volunteers at Salt & Light, and more control carnage from just a few weeks before the retreat, when John left our ministry.

The book also challenged me to look at the various roles I play in life: executive director, friend, teacher, worship leader, bike ministry leader. Then I was encouraged to write out a few action steps to hold myself accountable so that I might go deeper with Christ in each role. One action step was to make a first appointment to see a Christian counselor, as my friend Don Follis had suggested. Another was to pray nightly on the phone with my friend Alicia. Miller challenged me: "We value more that which we have to work to attain, and we devalue almost anything that comes easy." Time to get to work.

On Friday I met again for spiritual direction with one of the sisters, and I was led to talk about John Smith. She encouraged me to sit in John's chair before the Lord, to try to understand his position. What did God want me to learn from this at this time in my life? When I went down to the river with my notebook in hand, I did just that. The Lord let me see a whole list of challenges when I sat in John's chair before the Lord. No wonder my controlling behavior pushed him away. I realized how easily I can become co-dependent and enmesh my life with someone who is trying to help me. I began to see the importance of being very clear with communication and work schedule expectations early in a professional relationship, trying to understand each volunteer or staff member's station in life, their motives and expectations. I also saw the necessity of finding a strong volunteer coordinator for the ministry who would listen to and encourage our volunteers.

That Saturday afternoon I reviewed my personal marked copy of *Radical* in hopes of refreshing God's call on my life and vision for C-U at Home. I noted, "How God works: He puts His people in positions where they are desperate for His power, and then He shows His provision in ways that display His greatness. Yes, we work, we plan, we organize, and we create, but we do it all while we fast, we pray, and we constantly confess our need for the provision of God." If our purpose is to enjoy God's grace and to extend His glory, the danger comes when we assign the obligations of Christianity to a few, while keeping the privileges of Christianity for us all. How often we disconnect God's blessings from His purpose.

I prayed, "Lord, prick my heart. Help me see others through the lens of Your grace. Help my words, my thoughts, and my motives be based on receiving Your grace and extending Your glory. Show me what this looks like at CSPH, with staff, with residents, with my small group, at church, with volunteers, and in the marketplace. Help me take time to see You and hear from You. Thank you, Jesus. Amen."

I wore my "anointed" socks on Sunday morning when I made my way to a little struggling Baptist church in Kankakee. After the service, as I was cruising AM radio stations, I heard Tommy and Mari Anne from Freedom House teaching on the topics of a heart of stone and inner vows. That evening, at a Life Church campus in Kankakee, I was unexpectedly greeted by an old friend, Lynn Metz. He encouraged me and prayed with me.

My prayer before leaving the hermitage was, "Lord, thank you for this time to focus on You at One Heart, One Soul. As I reflect through my journals, I see a strong need to be tethered tightly to You and not ride the waves of highs and lows. Please help me be more stable. Show me how to be the leader that You want me to be. I love You, Lord. Amen."

I had hoped the retreat would be a turning point both for me and for our ministry, guiding me in important decisions about our future direction or about dissolving the ministry. Though it did bring me some peace and healing, clear forward direction about our ministry wouldn't come until a couple of months later, while I happened to be in another country.

On the one year anniversary of Vern's death, many of us took time to reflect and to remember him. The Lord blessed C-U at Home on that day in several ways, and it felt like it was to honor the life of

Vernon Chounard. We closed on the ownership of our first house. Now we could start the rehab work to completely redo the electrical, remodel the bathroom, and raise the roof on the back portion of the house. We received a large financial blessing. We were able to help two more people get off the streets and into a hotel for emergency shelter. And four new volunteers came to an orientation, wanting to join us in helping our friends without an address. Thank you, Jesus!

A few days later, we interviewed a substance abuse counselor from The Prairie Center over his lunch hour. We offered the position to him on the spot and he accepted! Another big event taking place on a Thursday. We FINALLY had a professional who could be our life coach (case manager) for the residents in our Transitional Supportive Housing. Thank you, Jesus!

In August, I hit the road for Kansas City for a five-day getaway. Hopefully I could clear my head a bit and NOT think about C-U at Home at all for a few days. It was time to go re-connect with many seminary and post-seminary friends in the KC area, and to celebrate the marriage of one of my very best friends from seminary, Allen Reger. It was a lovely outdoor ceremony, celebrating two committed believers beginning their covenant marriage, with Christ at the center. At the end of the ceremony, I noticed my phone was ringing. It was Tony. I took a few steps away and quietly answered.

As soon as he started talking, I knew something was terribly wrong. He was on the railroad overpass in downtown where the guys we know would sometimes hang out. The ambulance had just come and taken Richard away. He and Titus (another of our residents) had been using vodka and heroin, and even though he was not a heroin user, Richard had decided to shoot some up. We aren't sure about the amount that he injected, but somehow the mix of the opioid and the alcohol caused him to stop breathing. Titus panicked. He called Tony and tried to tell him, but then hung up. When Tony arrived, he pulled Richard out from behind a mattress and tried to wake him up, but he was not breathing. When Tony called 911, Titus split before the police arrived, as he didn't want to give up their spot.

Here I was at the wedding for one of my best friends, six hours away from Champaign, and Tony was dealing with this tragedy alone. I had a decision to make. Should I start driving back right then? Should I go inside to the reception? What should I do?

I took a few moments alone in my car and cried and prayed. I called Tony back and we talked. He said that I should stay. There's nothing more I could do in Champaign. He was there to take care of

Titus and to deal with everything. I went inside and told Allen what was happening. He and his new bride prayed with me. Then I decided to wish the couple well and leave the wedding reception. I drove to one of my favorite Kansas City restaurants, the Corner Café, and ate alone. I had a lot to try to process. I spent the weekend in Kansas City, but cut the trip short and drove home on Monday.

Tony had proven to be such a blessing to our ministry, and we wanted to add him to our payroll. Though he was initially reluctant because he wanted to remain as a volunteer for us, he did finally agree to accept $100/week from us, plus reimbursement for gas. We now had our third C-U at Home employee.

The next week, a couple we had been working with for several weeks wanted to get married. In just a few days we came up with everything needed – dress, rings, minister, music, photographer, cake, and venue. The ceremony took place in an outdoor pavilion at Crystal Lake Park in Urbana, and we handed the newlyweds keys to their new home. A wedding and a new house (getting off the streets) in the same day – what a whirlwind, and, of course, on a Thursday!

I wish I could say that this couple's story ended happily ever after, but their lives continued to be marked with many challenges. When they moved into the house, Maria was having lots of problems with one of her big toes due to frostbite. Unfortunately, she refused treatment and later ended up having that leg amputated below the knee. A few years later, her other leg was also amputated. She became limited to a wheelchair, while her husband Charlie had to go on oxygen. They have continued to make unhealthy and unwise decisions and are still on and off the streets. Sad, indeed. Almost too much to comprehend. The tangled web of substance abuse, mental illness, trauma, and the freedom of the streets often causes folks to make completely irrational decisions.

Just one week after the wedding, we reserved that same park pavilion for Richard's memorial service. It was almost surreal to plan a wedding for a couple from the streets and a memorial service for another friend a week apart. Another hi/lo time, for sure.

During this time of the wedding, the funeral, the hiring of two new employees, and having a new resident move into our guys' house, we experienced simultaneous emotions of joy and grief. On the lighter side of being pulled in two different directions at once, I went to the first football game of the season on that Saturday, August 31, where the Illini, the local football team, were playing Southern

Illinois University at Carbondale, my alma matre. So, what did I do? I wore a maroon Saluki's t-shirt and an orange and blue Illini ball cap.

Around this time, I sent out an email update, including a request for a volunteer to serve as our volunteer coordinator. It was my prayer that the Lord would bring us someone with organizational ability, as well as a heart and passion for helping volunteers be successful. We needed someone to love and nurture our volunteers, to fill in the gap where my flat side would cause damage.

My prayer became: "Lord, help me trust You more. I want to know in my heart that this is according to Your will. Please give me compassion for the residents. Break the strongholds in their lives and bring Your Spirit's power to their lives. Help us know how to share our faith and the Gospel. Please draw me to Yourself all throughout the day tomorrow. Help me yield control to You and be peaceful with our co-workers. Thank you, Lord. I am grateful for each of them. More of You. Less of me. Thank you, Jesus. Amen."

As the leaves began to fall, I was facing the need to move out of my summer home. I already had a place lined up in Urbana to stay for the winter, but no place to stay until that home was ready. As I waited for God to provide, He used one of our board members who opened his home for me. And there was even room in the garage to store my motorcycle for the entire winter. I was so grateful. God's provision for me and for my bike!

Initially, I honestly thought I would only be doing C-U at Home for the two years remaining in the 100,000 Homes campaign, which ended in 2013. But now here we were, an official organization, an incorporated non-profit ministry. And we owned a house and had our first three paid employees, including myself, as of October. Initially, I had been reluctant to accept any type of salary from the ministry. After all, I had seen God miraculously provide for me for twenty-six months. With no means of income, my bank account never got below $500. The Lord had provided for me in simple and in miraculous ways. That part of this journey has taught me an unquestionable faith in God's personal provision for me. I can NEVER again doubt that if I am being obedient, He WILL take care of me. He will make a way when there seems to be no way! I did agree to take a small part-time income from C-U at Home in October of 2013. I was so grateful for all the ways God was continuing to provide for me and for the ministry.

Early on, during the first One Winter Night, I had been accused publicly of trying to line my pockets with the funds raised. That cut like a knife, but what hurt even more is that the accuser was someone who had stepped up to volunteer with us. I would never consider pocketing a penny from this ministry that the Lord led me to start. That incident was part of why I was so reluctant to receive any type of income from C-U at Home.

I continued my God vision time, spending Thursday afternoon each week praying and brainstorming about how we could change our housing program to make it more effective. I still didn't have a clear direction from the Lord about what He wanted to do with C-U at Home. Were we supposed to re-tool our housing program, do something completely different, or dissolve the ministry and give our resources to another homeless ministry? I was quite frustrated. "God, where are You?" I prayed.

I re-read the book, *When Helping Hurts,* especially since I thought some of what we were doing through our housing ministry might have been hurting or enabling our residents more than helping them. I talked with Mike Kessel, our board president, about having a strategic planning meeting for our board, staff, and key volunteers. We set the date for Saturday, November 23. While I had high expectations to get some tangible direction and unified vision through the process, the meeting was largely a disaster, with more division and indecision. I really had no idea what to do next.

During that same season, I received a phone call offering me a powerful opportunity to get away, far away, and spend time with the Lord processing what He wanted us to do with the ministry. Kevin Coey, my friend who was allowing us to use a house he owned for our residents, was going to Belize in a few days. I said that I sure could use a getaway like that, and he asked if I wanted to go with him. I didn't think he was serious, but he said he could get me a plane ticket and had a place for me to stay in the jungle part of Belize. I was so excited! God's provision, indeed, allowing me to get away, far away, and try to hear His voice. Once again, on a Thursday.

Meeting with our new pastor, Danny, at a coffee shop the next day, I was excited to share more about C-U at Home with him and to hear his heart and get to know him better. While I was waiting for him to arrive, I ran into David Nisbet, a friend from church-league softball. He had been doing both softball and prison ministry in Belize for years. I said, "You'll never guess where I'm going to be over Christmas!" After a couple of hints, he finally said, "Belize?" And then he said something I couldn't believe. He said that they just had someone cancel their reservation for Christmas at the condo that he and his wife owned right on the beach in San Pedro, the island area of Belize. The condo would be empty for a couple of weeks and I was more than welcome to stay there. WOW!!!! Now I would not only be going to the jungle portion of the mainland, but I would also get to spend two weeks right along the beautiful reef on the island of San Pedro. I was very excited and felt totally blessed by this opportunity. I would be leaving for Belize on December 17, with a return date up in the air, but I would be in Belize for at least three weeks.

On the day of my mother's birthday, December 9, I had an appointment with a Christian counselor, Tony Merritt. My ministry coach, Don Follis, had recommended him to me. I'll be honest. I saw counseling as a sign of weakness, only for people who couldn't keep things together. But I was pretty much out of options. So, I went into the meeting as a skeptic, not expecting much real help. I was pleasantly surprised. Tony was not a weirdo talking to me in psychobabble, asking me questions about my childhood. He was insightful and easy to talk to. He did say that I was suffering from burnout, but I didn't want to hear that. I didn't see myself as being in THAT BAD of shape, as burnout to me was a sign of major weakness. After all, I was still functioning (barely). He gave me some good tips on things to do and not to do during my time in Belize, and I looked forward to connecting with him again when I returned from the trip.

I also wrote out a list of C-U at Home positives and negatives. The positives list included: media favor, free office space, Dolores (our volunteer case manager), Canteen Run support, $70,000 in the bank, owning a two-bedroom home, guys that we had gotten to detox and rehab, One Winter Night, and awareness raised. Some of the negatives were: failure of the Housing First model, no real ministry partner, no successor, no sustainable funding, guys going back to the streets, three deaths, and my performance orientation (flat side). I took this with me to Belize.

I journaled, "I want to continue to walk in faith and trust that God is leading my steps and the future direction for CUH. God, help those on the streets come to know and trust You . . . I want to trust You more both personally and professionally. Lord, help me not fear more people walking away from the ministry. Is the opposite of fear trust? Or hope? Or love? . . . Lord, help me change once and for all, with Tony's help. Please help this be the time that I am able to realize YOU are in control. I want to stop hurting people. And especially not even knowing when the offense occurred. I want to be a friend that others enjoy being around, not that they dread. Let Your glory shine through me, Lord. I must decrease . . . He must increase. Help me take the next step in this journey and know that You are leading me. I want to walk on the water, to feel faith and confidence that You are going before me. That I am safe, but not too safe. That I am serving exactly where you want me to serve. Show me Your way, Lord."

Before I left for Belize, a friend told me about a powerful presentation called "Dead Leader Running." I watched it, taking notes and thinking, yep, that's me! Pastor Wayne Cordeiro asked, "What fills and what drains your tank? Who are you with? What are you doing? Where are you doing it?" He encouraged his listeners to find a lightning rod, someone we could verbally vomit on, someone who will ground us, someone "safe." He also warned us NOT to make permanent decisions based on temporary setbacks, and to be ready to disappoint people when you make the needed adjustments.

Soon after I listened to Pastor Cordeiro, we had a very challenging situation through a break-in at one of our transitional houses. Entrance was made through an unlocked back bedroom window. The thief stripped the house of copper, leaving a real mess, with both the furnace and A/C disconnected, and the temperature would soon be below freezing. The house had only been vacant for a few days and only a handful of people knew that. Several of us came to the same conclusion about who the likely culprit was, a resident in one of our other houses with a reputation for scrapping metal. The police investigated, but the thief was never positively identified or charged with the crime.

God's grace and provision was once again evident through this process. When we contacted Dan, the owner of the house, he first wanted to make sure that everyone was ok. Then he asked if we would get some bids for the repairs. He turned it into his home owner's insurance. Dan is the owner of the second house we were able to use. He is the one who had the stove stolen and the house trashed by a previous ministry, yet he allowed us to use the house once again for ministry. Sometimes God's grace through someone else blows me away. He had every right to take his house back and cut his ties with C-U at Home after the break-in, but God's grace was displayed when Dan extended his trust once again to our ministry, a miraculous provision that defies logic. Thank you, Jesus.

Before I left on my trip, we set a new, later date for One Winter Night, so I could have time to get things ready once I got back, assuming there would still be a C-U at Home in 2014. If all went well, OWN would be on Friday, February 21. I was off to Belize!

10

Belize

Following an entire day of travel on December 16, I arrived in San Pedro just before dark. The person who was supposed to meet me at the little island airport was not there, but within a few minutes someone asked if I was Melany Jackson. He had been sent to pick me up and get me to the condo. Driving a golf cart, the preferred mode of motorized transportation on the island, we rumbled along the pot-hole-riddled dirt road across the island, and he gave me the key and helped me get my bags into the room. He also loaned me a flip phone to use, with numbers for a few Belize folks that Dave had told me about. There was a small grocery store right behind the building, so I walked over to try to get some milk, OJ, and cereal for breakfast. Shopping there was an interesting experience. Not much selection and the food was quite expensive, especially American-made products.

A beautiful full moon with a halo, clear skies, and lots of stars greeted me. Feeling another burst of energy, I wasn't ready to sleep yet, so I moved one of the beach chairs underneath a palm tree that was rustling in the cool breeze, right on the ocean. I was somewhat puzzled because there were no waves. I wrote in my journal, "I wish I could sleep right here in this chair tonight. Speak to me, Lord. I want to see You and hear You on this trip. Help me know You more and more. Amen."

I woke up the next morning around 8am to a gentle breeze and a partly cloudy view of the ocean through the palm trees. Peace. Quiet. Then the groundskeeper skimmed the pool and began chopping off the lower palm branches with a machete. At first, I thought it was cruel, hacking apart a tree like that just so tourists could have a better view, but I realized the lower branches would soon be dead anyway. I asked, "Lord, what do You want to prune from my life on this trip? Please do Your work in my life. Thank you."

The next day, I began to read *Changes that Heal* by Henry Cloud, with the goal of reading a chapter a day in San Pedro, making notes of the themes that spoke to me. The book began with the great dichotomy in the Bible between grace and truth. Grace is the unmerited favor of God toward people. It can't be earned. It is unconditional love and acceptance. Grace had been at the center of the original vision for C-U at Home, to reflect the relational part of God's character. Truth is what is real, how things really are, the structural aspect of God's character. Truth is the skeleton that life hangs on. Sin ripped grace and truth apart at the Fall. Truth without grace equals judgment. Grace without truth equals license. Together, they reverse the effects of the Fall. Real intimacy is only available when grace and truth come together.

Thursday was filled with time on the water, sailing and fishing with the Carlson family. Randy and Janice operate a concrete company up in the Yukon, spending the winter for many years on the island of San Pedro. After all, you can't do much concrete business when everything is completely frozen for several months each year. We connected through their son Jason, who knew Dave and Jo Nisbet through their softball ministry. The Carlsons knew exactly where to go and what bait to use to catch barracuda. They encourage their guests to strap on a belt and reel in a very large fish. I was able to "catch" and wrestle a ten pound 'cuda into the boat, and my success was captured in photos. No "big fish" stories here. I had my proof!

Chapter two of Cloud's book focused on time, so necessary to develop grace and truth. There are four seasons of time: planting, nourishing, harvesting, and dying. Fruit grows over time with the proper ingredients, and much of the process is out of our control. This was a keen reminder of Rita's prayers for the seed of C-U at Home that had been planted in the ground back in the beginning. What season of growth were we in now? Was it dying? I recorded a powerful quote, "Worry does not empty tomorrow of sorrows, but it empties today of strength" (Corrie ten Boom).

That evening I journaled, "I really enjoyed the day. Thank you, Jesus. What do You want me to do about CUH? Stay or go? Where? Please let me see Your glory and know Your direction for my life. Thank you. Amen!"

During my time on the island in Belize, God worked in my heart to help me repent and release the ministry of C-U at Home back to

Him. I had a pretty tight grip on the ministry and found most of my identity in being the founder and leader of C-U at Home. The Bible calls this idolatry, when we place more value in someone or something than in God or when we worship anything or anyone other than the one true God. Sometimes idols are abhorrent, sinful things in our lives and other times idols are good, even Godly things. I had to confess that C-U at Home had become an idol for me.

One afternoon on that beautiful sandy beach, with the calm, clear, turquoise water and blue sky and sunshine, I felt the Lord ask me for control of C-U at Home, to release it back to Him. And I did. It was such a freeing feeling to know that God loved me just the same, even if there had never been a C-U at Home. The only way I could move forward with considering how C-U at Home might continue was to first repent and release it, release the dream of it, back to Him. This powerful action of releasing the ministry back to God was key to enabling me to continue leading it successfully, holding it instead with loose, open hands.

Friday morning, I swam laps in the outdoor pool and then rode a bike to the bakery for fresh cinnamon rolls and bread. That day's boat trip with the Carlsons took us to the north part of the reef to practice snorkeling. It was great fun! I got to see different kinds of coral, cool fish, eel, and several stingrays. That night, I fell asleep at home in the condo watching *It's a Wonderful Life.* I prayed, "Lord, are You teaching me something from the movie? Is C-U my Bedford Falls? Please show me the direction You want me to go. I want to go where You want me to go and nowhere else. If You want C-U at Home to head in a new direction, please let me know. Show us how to help those most in need and to help others too. I want to know You more, Lord. I want to see Your glory."

On Saturday, I opened to the next chapter of Cloud's book, "Bonding to Others." Bonding is the ability to establish an emotional attachment to another person. God created us with a hunger for relationship with Him and with people; we are relational beings. God is love. Love is the basic identity of God and therefore our basic identity also. Our sanctification, the process of becoming more like Christ, rests on the working out of our relationships with God and others. God will not call me to something He won't equip me for.

A quiet and relaxing day allowed time for hanging out, shopping, and working. I helped squeeze fresh orange juice at the Carlsons' and got to bring a jug home with me. Yum! I LOVE orange juice. That day's reading explored the topic, "When We Fail to Bond." The three stages in failing to bond are protest, depression and despair, and detachment. Sometimes in depression we desperately try to find meaning in some activity or ministry and we derive our self-worth largely from other people. I was listening. Ouch!

On Sunday morning, I joined the Carlsons at a large non-denominational church on the island called Sagebrush. Dinner out at Estelles Restaurant followed, then softball practice and an evening dip in the pool to cool off concluded the day, and were repeated on Monday as well.

"Learning to Bond" was Cloud's next topic. Often others can't see how emotionally isolated I really am. My friend Kevin saw that and reached out to me in a powerful way, through this trip. The realization of need is the beginning of healing and growth. Both humility and vulnerability are absolutely necessary for bonding at a deep level.

Spending Christmas Eve in the tropics was a new experience for me, with a snorkeling tour on Liza's boat making four of the major snorkel stops along the reef. I actually got to hold a shark in the open water! We saw four beautiful spotted eagle rays, two green sea turtles, an electric green moray eel, and lots of other very interesting fish. I really enjoyed the snorkeling, even though my back got pretty sunburned. I had Christmas Eve dinner with the Carlsons. Then I made the long walk home and watched the end of *It's a Wonderful Life.* I prayed, "Lord, I really don't believe that You want me to quit CUH. Please show me how to really help the most vulnerable and others. Show us Your direction. Give me peace. Amen."

The next evening I wrote: "Christmas day on a tropical beach! Wow! Thank You, Lord for a beautiful, sunny day to celebrate Your birth." I had breakfast and spent the morning relaxing at home. I got morning phone calls from the Cummins while they were opening their presents back in Illinois and from Kevin. Then on to the Carlsons. Jason read Luke 2 in Creole (the native tongue of those on the island). The Carlsons gave me a wrapped gift to open, a nice Belize history book. We had a delectable meal of prime rib, turkey breast, mashed potatoes, and my favorite, turkey gravy, with their friends Henry and Mary at a very nice restaurant on the beach. And I got a very yummy Belize chocolate bar from our lunch hosts. After dinner, Janice, Vanessa, and I had a pleasant walk south down the beach. It was quite a different, but very cool Christmas celebration that year.

Kevin's plan was to come on Sunday afternoon and stay with me on the island through New Year's Day. We would then leave together for the Cayo (mainland) on the first day of the new year. During the in-between days that remained, I read, walked, bicycled, went snorkeling, chatted with a new friend named Harriette, swam, and continued to spend time in prayer.

When Kevin arrived on the island, we rented another bike, and then got him settled in at the condo. We enjoyed each other's company, and that of our hosts, the Carlsons, as well.

The main reason why I was in Belize was to seek the Lord's direction about C-U at Home. Were we supposed to dissolve the ministry and share our assets with another homeless ministry? Or were we supposed to go in a different direction to help the most vulnerable homeless?

When Kim and I had visited Outreach, the homeless ministry for youth in Indianapolis, we learned about their focus on building relationships with the youth and about their day center. I spent some time reflecting on that possibility for our ministry. I made a list, dreaming about what a day center might look like for us. On that list were all kinds of ideas: Tom, Kim, and Tony to help, resource lists, couches, tables, cards, checkers, an address for mail, worship service, coffee and lemonade, a phone set up with private voicemail, and even monthly giveaways. With volunteer support, it could be a haven, a place with no weapons or arguments, even if it was open a limited number of days each week. I felt as though God was encouraging me to pursue this possibility.

As we soaked in the beauty of San Pedro, Kevin and I talked and prayed and brainstormed and dreamed about what it might look like for C-U at Home to open a day center. It seemed like a direction that we could go, both to get the community more directly involved, and to spend time building relationships with the most vulnerable homeless people in our area.

On New Year's Eve, Kevin and I enjoyed a tasty meal together and went down to the dock for the fireworks that were launched from a barge over the reef. The weather was perfect. We joined Randy, Janice, and Jason, and enjoyed the best fireworks show I have ever seen in person. I was so grateful. That night I thanked the Lord for this opportunity and I prayed for His direction for C-U at Home.

New Year's Day. A new day. A new year. A new start. After a tearful good-bye with the Carlsons, Kevin and I boarded the small commuter airplane that took us to the mainland. When we arrived at the Banana Bank Lodge, I was impressed with the simple, beautiful jungle setting. And it was so very nice that I was being treated like a lady. Kevin was opening doors for me and when I got to my room, there was a washcloth and hand towel folded into cute little animals.

Kevin and I walked along the garden path to the cafeteria building, where everyone shared a meal together. I got my first glimpse at Tika Too, a beautiful, young cheetah with a spacious area of the grounds all to herself. The next few days, I spent lots of time hanging out with her, watching and talking to her through the fence. Kevin and I went into the café and he introduced me to several folks, including Nathan, the man helping him with his seed research in Belize, and to John and Carolyn Carr, owners of Banana Bank.

The next morning, I met Festus the monkey, who lived on a long chain leash, attached to a large tree. He showed off his talents to us: walking, hopping, and climbing. Days later, as I helped feed him, I got close enough that he actually climbed up my leg and then my shirt, settling onto my shoulder. I was standing there with a live monkey on my shoulder!

Horseback riding tours were featured at Banana Bank, and Kevin arranged for us to go on a guided tour. It had been many years since I had ridden, and it was fun to be on a horse again, even cantering and then galloping across the open field. Scary, but exhilarating at the same time. We sloshed through mud up to the horses' thighs and made it safely back to the lodge a couple of hours later.

As I reached into my front jeans pocket for the borrowed flip phone, I discovered that it was gone, having disappeared somewhere on the ride. Oh no! I couldn't bear the thought of telling Dave's friend that I had lost his phone. Between the efforts of our guide and his friend, the phone was rather miraculously found where we had galloped the horses across the field, instead of being lost forever in the three feet of mud we had gone through. Back at the lodge, our guide handed me the phone – and there was not a scratch on it! I was so very grateful that the Lord answered our prayer. God's provision in an unlikely circumstance.

Kevin and I visited a prison on the mainland, where we met Mr. Earl Jones, the CEO of the Kolbe Foundation, a ministry that had taken control of the prison several years before. They were in charge of the Belize Central Prison (the only prison in the country). As we toured the prison, we saw first-hand what the Lord had allowed them to do. They even had a state-of-the-art Christian radio station (near and dear to my heart!) right on the prison grounds, located just outside of Belize City. Jones and his staff took several hours to explain their programs and show us their facilities. Wonderful believers doing powerful kingdom ministry.

We also visited some large Mayan ruins, climbing up on a pyramid to see for miles around. That same day we went on to San Ignacio and enjoyed their downtown shops and had lunch at a café there. I had the most delicious mashed potatoes. As a picky eater, I was really missing American food by that point and the real mashed potatoes with butter really hit the spot!

During our remaining time in Belize, Kevin and I continued to talk and pray about what a day center might look like for C-U at Home. It was a blessing to have so much time away from the phone, email, and demands of a full schedule. I asked the Lord to make His way clear to me, so that I could return to Champaign with His vision for His ministry.

On January 8, I began my journey back to Illinois, to discover that a blizzard had just hit the Midwest and both Chicago (where I landed) and Champaign were suffering bone-chilling temperatures. When I had left Belize, the temperature was a balmy 73°. When I landed in Chicago, I was welcomed home to more than one foot of snow on the ground and a temperature of 5°. Such a rude awakening after such a warm, relaxing time in the tropics.

11

A New Direction

Upon my return to Champaign, the clock was counting down for One Winter Night 2014. With only six weeks to get everything planned, I reminded myself daily that God was in control.

I was excited to share the vision for a day center with our staff. Tony, Kim, and Tom were all very interested in the idea and wanted to know more. In the next email update on January 17, I shared, "As we start into this new year, we are looking for a new way to help those who are living on the streets. Plans are still being formulated, but we are excited to think about launching a new initiative that can help us build stronger relationships with residents while they are still on the street. There will be new opportunities for you to get involved with us. Keep watching your email and keep an eye on the news for us to share more details soon." It was my hope that our board and staff would join me in developing a plan for a new day center and publicly sharing that plan through One Winter Night.

In preparation for OWN, we got great news coverage from *The News-Gazette.* In that article, we publicly shared the new vision and direction for the ministry. Deb Pressey wrote, "A local charity that set out to find homes for people living in the streets of Champaign-Urbana is heading in a new direction, looking to open a daytime drop-in center for the homeless and a halfway house for recovering drug addicts. 'There were lots of challenges and many levels of crisis,' Jackson said of C-U at Home's original focus. 'We definitely saw a lot of good things happen, and we were able to bring hope to folks who were pretty hopeless, but overall we have come to realize that that model was not something that makes sense here.' Jackson said two years' experience taught her and the organization that the Housing First philosophy wasn't practical 'as we were trying to implement it.'

'We're hoping to get a place in the downtown-midtown area that is easily accessible with a fairly large room to have some very practical things – couches, a TV in the corner, maybe some computers, just a place for folks to come to congregate,' Jackson said. 'Right now, daytime access is pretty limited.' C-U at Home is looking to lease or buy a space for the drop-in center, or 'it would be wonderful if we find a benevolent owner who would help us out with that,' she said."

Word was now out. We were hopeful to get help from the public in finding a location that would be just right for our new daytime drop-in center, but we also needed to see what other communities were doing as well. Our staff of four took a field trip to a homeless ministry in Northern Illinois to visit their day center, spending time together in the van on the ride up and back just catching up with one another and dreaming about the future. We first visited their powerful transitional program for women and then their men's shelter.

When we got to their day center, it was not quite what I had expected. When Kim and I had visited the day center for youth in Indy, it had a very homey atmosphere, comfortable and inviting. When we walked into this room, it looked kind of like a church. There were rows of chairs and a small stage at the front. There were some bookshelves and a few chairs at the back of the room, with only a couple of people in the center at that time. One desk was located by the door with a staff person, and the folks from the street came in and sat in the rows of chairs to be in a safe place. On the ride home, we all agreed this is NOT what we were hoping to develop in our daytime drop-in center. We wanted it to be a place where folks from the community and folks from the streets came together on equal footing to hang out and build friendships over time.

The next email update laid out our plan: "We are quite excited to reveal the new ways we hope to help our homeless residents this year. Here are the three new areas that we hope to develop soon:

- A new daytime drop-in center.
- A recovery house for those who have graduated from a rehabilitation program.
- A family house for someone with one or more dependents.

Property Search – Can you help us find the right property for our new daytime drop-in center? Our hope is to find a building that is wheelchair accessible with one large room and at least three smaller rooms. Restrooms are also important. A kitchen area would be helpful, but not required. Our strong desire is for this center to be very accessible to those who are living on the street. Here is a map showing the area of downtown/midtown Champaign where we hope to find property."

A week later, I wrote: "What a week! In the last eight days, we have been blessed with the opportunity to be in the right place at the right time to help four different people walk away from life on the streets of Champaign. Together we CAN make a difference! Thank you Tony Comtois, The Prairie Center, Cathy Minor, and Julie Pryde for helping them get the treatment and assistance that they desperately needed:

- 1 woman to residential treatment in Decatur, IL.
- 1 woman to residential treatment in Granite City, IL.
- 1 man a ride back to his home in downstate IL.
- 1 man to residential treatment in Springfield, IL.

Thank you Lord, for allowing us to help people get off the street and take that next step to a new way of life!"

Over the next few weeks, we were blessed to receive the keys to a new transitional rental house for us to use for C-U at Home. And Father Tom invited me to meet Seth Kerlin, one of his friends who worked at the Urbana Free Library. He was serving as a bi-vocational pastor of a relatively new church named Cornerstone Fellowship (add one more "CORNERSTONE" to my list!). We planned to meet after OWN so I could share more with him about C-U at Home, and he could tell me more about his church.

We were also working day and night to recruit new box dwellers for One Winter Night. Even with pushing the event date back by a few weeks, the Belize trip really forced us into crunch time to get things ready for OWN. We were able to successfully round up thirty people to be box dwellers and a handful of business sponsors. We began the event with $24,785 already raised, on the way to our goal of $60,000. We had a LONG WAY to go!

One of the highlights of the event was an eight-year-old boy named Edward Alawelt, who signed up to volunteer with his mom. Holding a Ziploc donation bag, he asked people to give to help people who don't have a place to live. Edward was relentless for our cause and he made many new friends along the way, having a huge impact on city council member and box dweller, Karen Foster.

She wrote in her blog the following Monday, "Edward was there with his mother standing on the corner with his sign, too. Then later he got a big Ziploc bag that the participants were given to collect donations and he and his mom walked up and down the sidewalks along Neil. When I first met Edward, he was so proud to tell me that he had about $40! From then on, any money that I collected I gave to Edward to add to his donations! Eventually, he raised about $100! That was awesome! The pride that he showed was the love that he had inside for those that he was trying to help. It is with Edward's spirit that all of us could bring to life that which can make a difference in anything that we set our sights on. We don't always have to have the most or be the biggest or be the first. It's getting out there and just doing what we can with who we are that will make the difference in the lives of others. And it might just make a change in you, too!"

Edward also made friends that night with three-time box dweller, Don Gerard, the Mayor of Champaign. Mayor Don took Edward up to his desk in the city building and had his picture taken there. It was such a blessing to have someone like Edward Alawelt volunteer for us on behalf of our friends with no place to live.

Another young man had a powerful experience during One Winter Night. On Friday evening, Niko was headed home from seeing a movie with his mom. Their route included driving through downtown on University Avenue. He saw all the people outside and asked his mom if they could stop and check it out. They talked with people who were sleeping in cardboard boxes and holding signs saying, "help the homeless." Once Niko learned that people in our community sleep outside for real every night and that they can get frostbite when it's cold, he decided to donate his Christmas money to help the homeless. Niko got it. He saw a need and he decided to do something about it.

After we closed the books on OWN 2014, we had received $46,787 gross from the event and $44,201 net. Though we did not reach our goal of $60,000, I was quite pleased that we had raised what we did with an event that was basically planned in less than seven weeks. I was grateful for God's financial provision once again.

We continued to get the word out about the new ways our ministry could help folks living on the streets. In our February 27 email update, we shared: "We are so excited to develop three new ways to help our community fight homelessness. Our hope is to open a new daytime drop-in center somewhere in the downtown or midtown area of Champaign. The first step is to find the right property. We hope to have one room large enough to seat at least fifty people and then at least four smaller rooms for offices, counseling, and storage. If you know of any suitable property in the downtown or midtown areas of Champaign, please let us know about it. Thank you. Our other two new developments are a recovery house and a family house. The recovery house is a place where people who have graduated from an addiction rehab program can continue to work together on their recovery in a healthy, supportive environment. It is designed for people who do not have a place to live but have already shown proven success and sincerity in their sobriety. The family house is going to be a place where a small family can live in a supportive environment, while they save money and take steps to get back on their own feet."

It was our hope that by developing a daytime drop-in center to focus on the most vulnerable street homeless and re-vamping our transitional housing model, we would be more effective in helping those who our ministry was dedicated to supporting.

In March, I was contacted about filling in as an assistant teacher for an eight-week Adult Basic Education (ABE) class at Parkland. I was thrilled to once again be teaching, plus this would help me with a bit of additional income. An email to an architect friend, Jeff Johnson, with our rough space request plan for the drop-in center, asked for help with the Champaign city code and zoning requirements for the center to make sure that we were on the right track with our property search.

We were taking practical steps to make the drop-in center a reality, yes, but I also wanted to pray over our city, walking prayerfully around the downtown/midtown area with a notebook and pen in hand. The official search had begun for a location for our drop-in center! For the next few days, I prayed and walked and took notes on any possible property within the boundaries we had determined – Washington Street on the north, Green Street on the south, State Street on the west, and First Street on the east. We wanted to be in the core area where the most vulnerable street homeless folks tend to hang out. That initial notebook list included twenty-six different properties, some of them more feasible than others. One other possibility we were looking at was a property that could also be headquarters for the Canteen Run, housing their truck and supplies.

They were looking for a new home as well and if the Lord provided the right space for us to share together, we would be grateful.

Dan Cothern, a commercial realtor from First Christian, invited us to look at a few possible properties with him. It was exciting to have the help of a believer with lots of experience in commercial property who very much wanted to help us find just the right donated or affordable location for our new drop-in center.

Our March board meeting was a productive one, with a spreadsheet and discussion of two top properties: one on State Street and one on Springfield Avenue. We took time to discuss the pros and cons of each location. My heart was set on the State Street location, but of course, this would all be up to the Lord and His timing.

The News-Gazette did a powerful in-depth article about the details of our new ministry direction and our search for property for the drop-in center. In the article, we received the strong endorsement of Bruce Knight, City Planning and Development Director. He said that, "As far as he's concerned, providing a place for the homeless to go wouldn't be a negative for the city because it's needed. And providing this shelter for homeless people downtown would be appropriate, because that's where the need is." It was very good to have the support from the city for this new initiative.

We had been busy spreading the word throughout the recovery community to find the right man to be our residential recovery house leader. After talking with several different guys, we offered the position to our top candidate. He accepted the offer that day. Of course, it was a Thursday! We would be ready to start moving guys into the new recovery house the next week. The first of our three new initiatives was taking shape!

Early in April, I got a phone call from Mike Royse. Our number one choice for a drop-in center location was a vacant two story and full basement property at 303 S. State Street, a building owned by Mike's family company, Royse & Brinkmeyer. I had been talking with Mike about us using the State Street building for our drop-in center in the basement, C-U at Home offices on the first floor, and possibly start-up ministry incubator spaces on the second floor. Mike told me that after talking with his family, he found out that the building would likely be demolished soon and that we could not use it for C-U at Home, even on a temporary basis.

While I was quite disappointed, I was prompted by the Holy Spirit to ask Mike a question, which I prefaced by acknowledging he was probably one of the busiest people that I knew. I asked if he might be willing to join the C-U at Home board of directors. His response was remarkable. He said yes. Almost immediately. Here, he had just given me some very disappointing news and I, in turn, had asked him to take a leadership role for our ministry. And he said yes. I asked him if he was serious. Had I heard him right? He said that his time was to be guided by God and that God had called him to be obedient. And he felt that saying yes to my request was being obedient. I was in awe of his response, and grateful.

The next week, Dan took me to see 215 S. Neil St. for the first time. I hadn't realized it was available because it still had the bar signs on it. It was a large, open room with a bar on the left, including a small sink. The entire front of the building was ceiling-to-floor plate glass windows for lots of light and visibility. There were handicap-accessible restrooms for men and women and two other rooms in the back. With both a rear and a side entrance, it had the bonus of a full basement. When I walked out of the building, there was a feather on the ground. Wow God! Could You be telling me something? This space quickly became our new number one location choice for our daytime drop-in center, an opportunity to redeem a space that had been a bar, providing healing instead of fueling addiction!

That next Monday, Dan put in an official lease offer on the Neil Street property, giving the owner until Friday to respond. Many of us were praying that this would be God's answer for us. We got word on Thursday, of course, that the owner had agreed to our lease terms and that we would be signing a lease for the property that would take effect on May 1. Hallelujah! We had an ideal drop-in center location!!!

April 28 was also a powerful property day for us. Praise the Lord! Our C-U at Home family house remodel had passed final inspection with flying colors. We hoped to move the first family into the house at the beginning of May. Next up, an HVAC inspection of our drop-in center property. God at work!

But property was only a tool to bring new life to the most vulnerable on our streets. Here is just a snapshot of our experience in the spring of 2014. In terms of property, it was the best of times, but in other ways, it was also the worst of times. Jeff Haynes had befriended one of our residents. In March, they were together at Jeff's place burning stuff outside and there was a horrific accident. Jeff was pouring gasoline and it ignited, causing him third degree burns on 45% of his body. He was life-flighted from his yard directly to the burn unit in Springfield. He was stabilized and treated. Jeff

111

would spend the next five weeks receiving skin grafts and treatment, as he continued to recover in the Springfield hospital.

Another discouraging incident involved one of our friends from the street named Sammy. We had met Sammy on the Canteen Run. He said he was ready for help: it was time to get off the streets, with the first step being detox. I called Tony Comtois, who arrived in just a few minutes, ready to give Sammy that life-changing ride to Peoria for detox, as Champaign-Urbana does not have a detox available for people with no insurance. We helped him into the truck and called to make sure the detox could take him.

Sammy was on a prescription medicine for seizures, and he needed that script filled before he could go. So, he went through his knapsack, and sure enough, he had a paper prescription. A trip to Walgreens got it filled. Tony prepped him about what to expect: three to five days in detox in Peoria, taking with him only a few items, including his meds, the clothes on his back, and four pairs of socks and underwear. Then a trip to The Salvation Army ARC (Adult Rehab Center) in Springfield for six to twelve months of free housing, work, step meetings, and spiritual support.

We assured Sammy that we would store his belongings until he had graduated from the ARC. Sadly, at the Walgreens counter, Sammy decided he was not yet ready to leave his "stuff." And he turned to head back out to the street. So close, yet so far . . . The next time Sammy or any of the other folks on the street who were losing their lives to addiction said that they were ready for help, we would have a vehicle warmed up and waiting, ready to make that life-changing drive.

During these busy months, I made time for self care and spiritual refreshment. I had my follow-up appointment with Tony Merritt, the counselor I had seen before going to Belize. I made the decision right then and there that I would continue to see Tony on a regular basis as long as I was leading C-U at Home. He was able to give me the kind of support I needed to get through the rough times and to stretch me to take a closer look at what God was doing in and through my life. Though I had been quite skeptical about counseling, I now saw it as one of the most valuable tools God had given me to continue in this ministry, and I was grateful.

On this day, he helped me to develop a plan for personal growth (i.e., dealing with my "flat side"). The main theme was that I knew how to treat others with compassion, dignity, and respect. It was the motivation of not doing so that was interfering . . . resentment combined with burnout. We worked together to develop a new daily routine: memorize scripture, listen to worship music, walk and pray in the park, listen to audio teachings, practice gratitude reflection, and be still—let God talk. A weekly goal was to socialize with friends and to grow my relationships outside of CUH. Other parts of the plan were to embrace regular teaching opportunities and allow people to be where they were vs. forcing them to change. Finally, we agreed on weekly counseling sessions with him and that I would complete a comprehensive psychological test to help with self-awareness. I was so grateful for this personal plan and that Tony would be helping me with it in the weeks to come.

On Good Friday, I met with Steve and Kathie Cole at 7:30am, and later accompanied Steve on his walk through the streets, dressed as Jesus and carrying a full-sized cross of wood. It was such a powerful image, a reminder for those driving, walking, and biking by, as well as those in stores, homes, and restaurants along our path. That evening I went to a powerful, reflective Tenebrae service at First United Methodist Church in Champaign. And I followed that experience with my annual tradition of watching *The Passion of the Christ*.

A few days later, I had a nice, long lunch meeting with Seth Kerlin, the pastor of Cornerstone Fellowship. It was such a blessing to share about my journey with him and to hear about his journey as well. He was a strong encourager for me, and I was excited about visiting his church fellowship soon.

That first visit to Cornerstone Fellowship came on April 27. I got there early with my djembe drum and rehearsed with their worship team. Seth gave me the entire message time that evening to share about C-U at Home and how God had led me to start it. While trying to explain the mission of C-U at Home, the Lord gave me a picture to share: "Sometimes, it's like the person living on the streets has no hope; it's gone. He's living in despair, and that's all he can see. We can befriend him, build trust, and hold his hope gently in our hands until he's ready to start taking it back." My message was very well received and several people signed up for our prayer list. It was a blessed service to be a part of. I could very much see myself being a part of this fellowship in the future.

As for my own housing? In April, I moved back into my favorite summer abode, the same home in the lovely Devonshire neighborhood where I had been able to stay the year before. It was great to be back in that part of town, just a couple blocks from my small group meeting at the Coles' home.

12

The Phoenix

On Thursday, May 1, we signed the lease and got the keys to our new daytime drop-in center. We were SO GRATEFUL for this opportunity and couldn't wait to get started on the clean-up and light remodeling that needed to be done on the old bar. It was no coincidence that the Lord did this on the National Day of Prayer, only God-incidence. The Lord was allowing us to redeem the Phoenix bar for His glory! Rising up out of the ashes . . .

There was so much to do to get the new space ready. We started by sorting out all the stuff left over from the bar, deciding what to throw away and what to try to sell. Then the cleaning, lots and lots of cleaning. Painting. Looking for lots of donated office furniture. Hiring our new staff . . . exhausting! And it was our hope to get the drop-in center open in June.

Our administrative assistant left in the beginning of May. Once again, it was my flat side that caused someone close to me to step away. Kim was doing everything she could to help me and our ministry. She prayed for and with me. I bulldozed her tender heart time and time again, and often I was completely unaware. I prayed, "Lord, please help me show more compassion and understanding with those who are helping me and our ministry. Teach me how to be more like You and take away my damaging parts, the drive for perfection and trying to control others."

Needing help in the office, we developed three new job descriptions and shared them far and wide. One option was to hire one full-time person as our managing director to fill two roles, running the daytime drop-in center and serving as the office manager. Another option was to hire two part-time staff, one as the drop-in center coordinator and the other as the office manager. So we decided to put all three job descriptions out there and see what the applicant pool looked like.

I continued feeling the attacks of Satan on our ministry in the middle of May. Our volunteer property coordinator, who had been leading the cleaning, painting, and remodeling efforts at the Phoenix, stepped completely away from our ministry abruptly, with no explanation. Then we were contacted about a potential lawsuit regarding our open staff positions. There were several times throughout the years when the challenges coming against me and against our ministry seemed too much to bear, completely overwhelming. This was one of those times. The man who had stepped away from volunteering with our ministry had been so much help with both remodeling the family house and the work at the drop-in center. It was especially difficult for me to process because I didn't know why he had decided to part ways with us. A couple of years later, I made an effort to reconcile with him, but my effort was met with no response. To this day, I don't know what happened to cause him stop helping us, but I assume it was related to my flat side, my performance orientation. More carnage.

In June, the First Presbyterian Church hosted Courageous Conversations with Bob Lupton, author of *Toxic Charity*. Bob presented some core principles that guide compassionate service toward actually empowering the poor. He shared real life models and methods from his own experience and offered instructive examples of ways to alleviate poverty through partnering with, rather than doing for, those in need. It was exciting to hear from another CCDA practitioner through the eyes of his years of experience. The golden rule in *Toxic Charity* is to "never do for others what they have the capacity to do for themselves." Another guiding principle was the importance of including recipients of the ministry in the decision-making processes. We have partly implemented this philosophy at C-U at Home by having at least one formerly homeless member serving on our board of directors.

We were working tirelessly to get the space at the Phoenix prepared. We'd made the decision to keep the bar name, first suggested by our former volunteer property coordinator. It really seemed to fit: a bird that was dead three days and then rose up out of the ashes. We saw it as an image of new life and hope. In addition to preparing our new building, we were working hard to hire the new staff, sharing the job descriptions everywhere we could think of, narrowing the choice of applicants, and scheduling interviews. In the middle of June, we made the decision to cancel C-U at Home One Summer Day. Trying to put together the grocery cart walk in only a couple of weeks while working to get the center open was just too much to handle.

By then, our new employee had been hired and would be starting as our new managing director at the end of the month. He had personal experience with homelessness, a law degree, and experience with other social service agencies. In the full-time dual role as the Phoenix coordinator and office manager, he would lead the launch of our new drop-in center, and he would take over many of the administrative responsibilities from me. I was also hoping he would be the one to take over the ministry, once it was time for me to leave.

My dear friend Russell Mann took over the drop-in center rehab project, coordinating all the volunteers and purchasing all the materials. What a true blessing! God's provision once again. But on June 17, Russell and his mother Marie were on the way to work at the Phoenix when he began having strong chest pains, sending him to the emergency room. Afraid it was a heart attack, we put out word on lots of prayer chains for him. They finally determined it was not heart-related and he was going to be all right, but he needed to take it easy and cut down his stress level. That meant stepping away from supervising the rehab project. Another blow from Satan, but he could not keep us down! Others stepped up to finish the remaining work at the Phoenix.

We had planned a public open house for the Phoenix in August, with a soft open in mid-June. We had already missed that deadline, so we would open as soon as our offices were moved and everything was ready at the building. Our office supplies were moved in early July, and the internet and phones were operational the next day. This "place of grace," known as The Phoenix Daytime Drop-In Center, would finally open on July 15. The image I hold dear from that first day is Sara Haines (one of our interns) strumming the guitar on the comfy couch, with Tony all laid out in the recliner end next to her taking a nap. The Phoenix was indeed set to be a place where everyone could be comfortable together. Sara helped to develop the mission statement for us: "The Phoenix is a community of hope and grace, rising up from life's ashes as a united Body of Christ." We would open ten hours a week at the Phoenix, Tuesdays and Thursdays from noon-5pm, giving us the opportunity to start nice and easy and let things develop over time.

It was so exciting to see this vision become a reality, born as it was, out of a dark time in my life, when I really thought about ending the ministry. A few weeks before we opened the doors, we did a simple survey of folks living on the streets to see what kinds of things they wanted to have as a part of the drop-in center. We took into consideration as many of these ideas as we could: a bag check to keep their belongings safe, board games, coffee, Bibles, computers, and an address available for people to get mail. We knew that the Phoenix would grow and develop as time went on and take on a personality of its own.

For the August grand opening and open house for the Phoenix, we submitted press releases, flooded social media, and sent out email blasts inviting everyone to come and check out our new digs and see our powerful new direction in ministry to help the most vulnerable homeless in our community. Dear friends from Gifford, IL, had donated a Coachman RV to us, and we were selling $10 raffle tickets to give the portable "home" away to someone at the Open House. One of our recovery house residents was out front cooking his famous Chicago-style hot dogs for everyone. The day was a success.

On the flipside, that summer we had a very frustrating and sadly typical experience with one of our local hospitals. Their patient, one of the most vulnerable of our community, was set to be released on Monday, but that previous Saturday he had an important appointment with a doctor, just two blocks away, for an evaluation to determine his disability status. The hospital refused to allow him to go to the appointment, and the doctors at the hospital were unwilling to do the disability evaluation. The public care of this man had amounted to literally hundreds of thousands of dollars for hospital emergency department and inpatient visits as well as incarceration and court costs. This appointment would have allowed him to begin receiving disability benefits and to move permanently into Eden Supportive Living, a housing community designed for people with disabilities. I was utterly incensed at the lack of willingness on the part doctors and hospitals to cooperate to accomplish the greater good.

It was time for a break from work, so my friend Kevin and I took off on our bikes for a Labor Day weekend adventure cool enough to actually be on my bucket list. I had seen the beauty of the Blue Ridge Parkway several times in a car, but only a few miles of it on two wheels. Our trip took us from the top of Skyline Drive, near Washington, D.C., to the bottom of the Blue Ridge Parkway, including a couple of days on the ocean at Virginia Beach. The ride was everything I had hoped it would be, with beautiful sunny days and warm temperatures for most of the trip. We encountered some nasty rain and fog in the mountains, but on the whole, it was a delightful trip. I was so grateful for the opportunity to once again get my focus off of C-U at Home for a few days, and to be refreshed and renewed in our vision to help our friends without an address.

Fairly early on at the Phoenix, we began talking about what to call the folks who came in. It was Tony's idea to call everyone "friends." Calling people "volunteers" just did not seem to fit, especially since when people volunteer, it usually means a couple of specific things. First, volunteers help people in need, people of lower status who need what you have. And second, volunteers are almost always asked to do a specific task. Part of the goal of the Phoenix was to erase the first idea. It was our hope that both people with a place to live and those without a home would come together in a low barrier environment and over time, build true relationships, friendships. Regarding the second idea, we weren't asking people from the community to come and "do" anything. We wanted them to come and "be," to simply hang out. So, we started calling everyone who came into the center a friend. Over time, we added "without an address" and "with an address" when we needed to make that distinction.

In the fall of 2014, we began taking more and more trips out of town to help people get to detox, rehab, shelter, and transitional supportive housing in other communities. We gave that portion of C-U at Home a new name, calling it our new Transportation Ministry. We also started recruiting volunteer drivers and riders to increase our capacity and ability to assist more people getting where they needed to go to receive the help they were desperately seeking. What a blessing to have a new segment to our ministry!

With everything going on as we worked to develop the Phoenix and to prepare for One Winter Night, I stepped away from being a driver for the Canteen Run. At this point, it was necessary to put my entire focus on C-U at Home.

At the beginning of December, we were excited to start our first church partnership at the Phoenix. Ken Raymond, pastor of Stratford Park Bible Chapel in Champaign, had come to us a couple of months earlier with an idea. What if different churches each adopted a day at the Phoenix and committed to covering that day with at least three people from their church for the five hours of open time? He took the idea back to his church, and they agreed to begin staffing the Phoenix each Tuesday, allowing us to open an additional day. We chose Wednesdays, so we were now open Tuesday-Thursday, from noon-5pm, a total of fifteen hours each week. We hoped to get more churches involved with adopting a day as friends of the Phoenix.

Once again, we were recruiting box dwellers and business sponsors for One Winter Night 2015, scheduled for February 6. We set an ambitious goal of $100,000, about two thirds of our projected annual operating budget for 2015, with our biggest expenses being payroll, rent, utilities, and the costs associated with the Transportation Ministry. To do that, we needed to recruit at least fifty box dwellers, a pretty tall order as we continued to train our new staff and develop our new drop-in center.

We set a time for our new staff member's six-month review in December. He had been doing a nice job with the Phoenix, and we hoped to continue to develop and grow the center under his leadership. But the administrative portion of his position was another story. Things were just not clicking as we had hoped. We discussed this in detail at the review and agreed to work together on the administrative role and to revisit the topic in a month.

I very much needed help getting everything organized and prepared for One Winter Night. Our summer intern, Sara Haines, had been so helpful getting the building ready and developing our Phoenix policies and mission statement, so we asked her to come on board as a temporary contract employee for a few weeks. From running our website to finding boxes to organizing volunteers and making signs, Sara provided us with exceptional help.

During this time, we agreed to open the Phoenix as an emergency warming center any time the temps dropped below 0°, the same guideline that the pop-up winter overnight emergency shelter used. We would be open from 7am-10pm any day that it got below 0°. Vans would come at 9:30pm to begin transporting folks to the pop-up emergency shelter, and from there the folks would be dropped back off at the Phoenix at 7am the next morning. Our first day of being open for emergency warming was Tuesday, January 6. It was truly a blessing to be able to provide this life-saving resource for our friends without an address.

I continued to struggle with our newest staff member, who seemed to have a different scheduling system from the rest of us. As part of my flat side, I have no tolerance for clock-punchers in ministry. We met again and talked about the situation, but unfortunately, it seemed like a band-aid conversation. I was overwhelmed with One Winter Night planning and we needed all-hands-on-deck. I didn't have the time or the patience to deal with anyone unwilling to do that.

One Winter Night 2015 was fueled by a huge amount of energy and excitement, with the audacious financial goal of $100,000. By the time Friday, February 6, rolled around, we had more than fifty box dwellers signed up! It was so wonderful having that many people right in the heart of downtown Champaign living out the loose simulation of life on the streets. The weather really cooperated this year, with a near constant temperature throughout the night of 30°. Many, many people from the community came to hear our slate of speaker presentations about the different aspects of homelessness in the Champaign City Council chambers. We finished the night at just over $94,000, and in the two weeks following OWN, we were able to break through the $100,000 mark. Glory be to God!

13

A Movie and a Move

You never know what God is going to use. Sometimes He even chooses to use a very unexpected sports situation to bless a scrappy little start-up ministry for the homeless. The morning after One Winter Night, Saturday, February 7, the University of Illinois men's basketball team played Michigan State at 11am. During that televised game, there was a very controversial call about a technical foul and Don Gerard, Mayor of Champaign, and a huge supporter of our ministry, got into a twitter war with an ESPN analyst over the call. Jay Mohr, host of a national Fox Sports radio show, picked up on the story and had Mayor Don on the air to talk about it on Monday. Don discussed the lousy call, also mentioning that he was pretty tired because he had slept outside the night before. When Jay asked him why, Don told him about One Winter Night and C-U at Home, and Jay committed on air to a personal donation of $1,000 to C-U at Home on behalf of the mayor's box fund. God's provision for us in a more than unusual way!

As February progressed, we had several more fifteen-hour days of emergency warming at the Phoenix, struggling to recruit friends from the community to host our warming hours. When we opened the Phoenix, we made the commitment to NEVER be open without at least one friend from the community with us. During warming center hours, with our small staff of three, it was impossible for us to be there all the time, so we needed even more friends from the community. But God was faithful to provide people for each shift, sometimes with only minutes to spare.

In March, we were pleased to offer Tony Comtois a full-time position with C-U at Home. Once we knew we had met our OWN goal for 2015, we wanted to get more help, and that's right when Tony needed full-time employment. It was a great match. He was already overseeing our Transitional Supportive Housing, Transportation Ministry, and Street Outreach; now we could make it official and pay him a full-time salary. I was blessed to also start receiving a full-time, regular salary at that time. It took a while for me to get used to this idea and to accept the board's offer, as I still had that accusation of misappropriation of funds ringing in my ears from that first year. I was reluctant to take a salary from donated funds, but at this point God gave me peace in accepting full-time compensation for my service through C-U at Home.

By March 2015, I was again faced with finding new housing for myself. Since I now had the ability to pay rent, I felt that I shouldn't count on God to provide donated housing for me anymore. My initial search for a rental on craigslist was shocking, as I would need at least $800 to rent someplace simple with two bedrooms and a garage for my motorcycle.

I realized that purchasing a house might result in a much lower monthly payment. My realtor friend Carol Meinhart suggested a mortgage banker, who determined I would qualify as a first-time home buyer, with only 2.5% down. Wow! Carol and I looked at various houses, but somehow, I was still unsettled about the decision. After all, I had no idea how long I would still be living in Champaign. And I had one other option: house-sitting for a family, with the possibility of a more permanent space for me to live.

I arranged to spend a trial period of a couple of weekdays and the weekend as a test to see if living there might work. It was great! What a blessing Scott and Martha Harden turned out to be, wonderful empty nesters who love the Lord. Their dog, Henry, was a good fit as well. After prayer, I moved into their home on a year-round basis in April. The Hardens spent a couple of months in Florida each winter, so now I could be there to take care of Henry and watch the house. Not only did I have a beautiful place to live, but the Lord had also given me a family that I didn't know I needed. Scott and Martha became like a big brother and sister to me.

I've been alone the majority of my adult life, quite independent, able to care for myself. I had experienced this sense of family once before, in my first ministry position out of seminary in 2008, when I was the interim associate pastor of worship and outreach at St. Luke Evangelical Free Church in the little Missouri River town of Wellington. Church members there helped me land a paralegal assistant role in a law firm in nearby Lexington, MO, to supplement my part-time salary. During that time, Chuck and Kathy Shroyer and their little dog, Journey, provided housing for me, becoming like family for me during the eighteen months that I lived and served there. I had no idea that I needed a family, but God knew better. At Scott and Martha's, I was grateful for that same sense of family.

In June, I was thrilled to once again serve as an interim worship leader when I was offered a part-time, temporary position at Pennsylvania Avenue Baptist Church in Urbana. Planning weekly worship services again, I felt like I was getting an important piece of myself back. The Lord allowed me to serve there until December.

A personal respite from C-U at Home came through a Cubs/Cardinals game at Busch Stadium in June, with my friend Susie in Cubs blue and me in Cardinal red. We lunched at The Old Spaghetti Factory on Laclede's Landing, knocked around the riverfront, and took in the ball game on a beautiful evening in St. Louis, comparing notes about the challenges of leading a business, and our heartfelt dreams, hers to adopt from China and mine to move to Colorado Springs. I did what I could to encourage Susie to move forward with plans to adopt, telling her that the Lord had put that desire in her heart and He would give her the wisdom and strength that she needed. She also encouraged me with the hope that God would bring C-U at Home the right leader and that God would open the door for me to live in Colorado.

During the summer, I went to Orphan's Treasure Box, a local nonprofit bookstore whose proceeds help children in need, to find a copy of *The Dream Giver* to give to my friend and ministry coach, Don Follis. They didn't have it on the shelf, so I asked if they had it listed online. My friend Elisabeth went to the back to find it. She re-emerged with the book and a look of amazement on her face. There inside the cover of the book was my name! I had purchased this very book eleven years earlier and given it away. Wow! Only God can orchestrate a God-incidence like that.

The next big project that summer was a new transitional housing partnership. Sister Karen Carlson, a social worker at the outreach arm of the local Catholic hospital, had broached the idea of collaborating on new shelter resources for women in our community. In another God-incidence, James Moreland, a friend from my church and fellow brother in Christ who did outreach for those living on the streets, offered us his family home for a small price, knowing his mother would be pleased to have it used for such a good purpose. When he took us to tour the home, it all made sense. Sister Karen and her group of nuns wanted to show hope and love for homeless women through the house that would be named Esther's Place. The Moreland house was within walking distance of the Presence Community Resource Center, where Karen worked to help those in need, AND the home where Karen and several other sisters lived. God was at work each step of the way, and Karen and her group of sisters partnered with C-U at Home in the acquisition plan and program development for this property.

A structural evaluation of the Moreland house by Robby Cekander, a skilled construction professional who loves the Lord and our ministry, indicated that the property had a solid foundation and the walls and floors were in good shape. Robby was willing to help lead the rehab process for Esther's Place, so we began to work on getting the needed permits. The City of Urbana required a special use permit and a zoning change, as no more than four unrelated people could live in an R-2 zoned residence. That process took weeks of meetings, paperwork, door knocking in the neighborhood, an outreach cookout, and more, complete with mixed messages from different departments at the city.

The Urbana City Council meeting to finally vote on the approval for Esther's Place came in September. We were very excited and hopeful that the vote would pass. After twenty-seven additional minutes of discussion, the mayor called for the vote. One by one, the aldermen gave their votes. The result was four to two, against re-zoning. Developing Esther's Place would not be allowed on the Mathews Street property in Urbana. Sister Karen and I were crushed. What seemed so clearly God-ordained had been defeated by a local city government. We were quite disillusioned and discouraged.

Soon, though, another more positive property opportunity came along, as a ministry friend took me on a tour of a home he owned. While we chatted in the living room, he handed me a key and said that he wanted us to use it to help folks get back on their feet. He would keep the property in his name but allow us to use it at no cost – even paying the utilities for us. What a blessing!! After prayer and discussion, we decided to use this new larger house for six men in recovery, and to use the previous recovery house location for four single women. This resulted in a net gain for our ministry of four new transitional beds, two for women who were homeless and two for men in recovery.

Property ownership brought its own challenges, such as when the furnace went out in our transitional family house on a frigid March day. The furnace was beyond repair, but through the help of Chief Bauer, a local heating and air business, the regional Lennox dealer donated a furnace, and Chief Bauer arranged for installation that afternoon! Another God-incidence of provision – a new furnace, up and running within a day at no cost to our ministry. Thank you, Lord.

Earlier that spring, we had continued to expand our knowledge at the two-day Forging a Better Way Conference with Bob Lupton, author of *Toxic Charity*. Once again, he taught us about building empowerment into our ministry. While in Bloomington, we connected with others in Central Illinois involved with empowerment ministries.

Community leaders also joined us on a visit to the living room and detox facility in Peoria, Illinois, as part of our efforts to establish an accessible crisis center and medical detox in Champaign County. We were encouraged to see the resources themselves and meet the staff and volunteers, although the unique funding they had in place in Peoria wouldn't be possible here in Champaign. Still, we would continue throughout the year to attempt to develop these vital crisis resources right here at home.

In another attempt to address the roots of the problem of homelessness, we attended an open meeting sponsored by the sheriff's department on jail diversion models for people with mental illnesses and substance use disorders with Leon Evans, President and CEO of The Center for Health Care Services, Bexar County (San Antonio), Texas. He had been nationally recognized for his jail diversion model which successfully delivered mental health services to four thousand people a year with low-level offenses. Funded by a combination of city, county, and hospital dollars, they had successfully reduced emergency room overuse and greatly reduced jail time. Wanting to jump start our own local efforts for a successful jail diversion program in our community, would we step up with local funds and local organizations to have skin in the game?

We were able to follow up from that meeting with a community dialogue in September. As a key stakeholder, through our Education and Advocacy arm, we invited those interested in medical detox, crisis services, psychiatry, and jail diversion to attend. Our group was pleased to have nearly one hundred interested people show up.

A new step in our story-telling about C-U at Home had begun in 2014, when my friend Phil Gioja, a videographer, signed up to be a box dweller for One Winter Night that year. He had documented it first-hand on film, resulting in a powerful video of his experience in a box: the loud sounds keeping him awake, the bitter cold, the frightening thoughts of not knowing what could happen to him. He wanted to repeat this during OWN 2015, but schedule conflicts had prevented it. Instead, he sent his videographer friend Isaac Musgrave to film some footage during OWN. Later that spring, Phil came down to hang out at the Phoenix and do some more interviews. Every step of the way piqued his curiosity more and more, finally resulting in his offer to create a full-length documentary on our ministry. In June, Phil wrote: "Here's what I'd like to accomplish for July to get this project off the ground. I'm thinking we can knock out this list in two or maybe three days:

- Cool motorcycle footage with Melany. I'll try to bring in a drone for this, gopros, etc.

- Have Melany go back to Restoration Urban Ministries to revisit the room she stayed in. Maybe we can have you arrive on the motorcycle and dress the same to tie this in.

- Interview and b-roll with Tony Comtois, maybe at the place he lives, which would be interesting knowing that he was homeless at one time, or at the shelter where he went, which I think is in Champaign or Urbana? or both?

- Stage a staff meeting so we can get all your faces together in one space."

His memo continued: "Isaac and I want to be present and direct this and do the interviews. I'm setting up a GoFundMe campaign with the initial goal of $3000, but I'm going to do a fairly soft sell, and we'll produce this whether or not we raise the money. If the amount goes over $3000, which would be great, that means we can do more with the documentary. Once these are accomplished, we'll be able to figure out where to go next with this project."

How exciting! We couldn't wait to get started with the filming! We began on two unseasonably hot and humid days in mid-June, with high humidity and temperatures near 100°. Phil and Isaac recorded interviews with me and with Tony, then filmed me where I lived with the Hardens at the time and at Restoration Urban Ministries, where I had lived in the early days of C-U at Home. Saturday was the motorcycle day. The guys got the cameras and the drone camera ready, and we headed to Homer Lake, one of my favorite places to ride and to connect with God. Despite being exhausted from the heat, they got some powerful action footage of me on my bike to use as b-roll for the film. They really didn't know how the bike would fit into the documentary, but Phil just had a sense that it was going to play a part in the film. And we had a whole lot of fun getting the footage. Now the documentary was starting to seem real to us. We could not wait to see how God would use this film as a part of our Education and Advocacy ministry through C-U at Home.

Phil and Isaac kept hard at work, filming more interviews, and Isaac did a detox run with Tony. Phil wrote: "Over and over in the Bible, God gives second chances. Forgiveness and mercy – words like these describe His attitude towards His people. When I watch this video with Tony, I'm reminded that God still gives us second chances today, no matter how far we've fallen. Then, He calls us to extend that mercy to others."

Additional filming for the documentary took place on the steps of the house at 703 N. Mathews, where we had hoped to open Esther's Place. I was not prepared to talk about this on camera, as the pain was still raw, but as I began to talk about what had happened, God helped me see that He did know what was best and that His ways really are higher than our ways. He would provide for Esther's Place in His way, in His time. I had to trust Him.

Isaac spent time with our good friend, Urbana Police Chief Pat Connolly, and did a ride along with C-U at Home board member, Urbana Police Lieutenant Joel Sanders. We had been blessed to have such support and continuing collaboration with local law enforcement. Phil and Isaac filmed an interview with our Phoenix coordinator while riding on a city bus, and another with Dolores Sofranko, case manager for our transitional houses. The guys also did an emotional interview with Dan Denton on campus at the site where he had stayed in an outdoor refrigerator while he was homeless. Phil and Isaac set a goal to have the film ready by the first of February, with the world premiere of our documentary scheduled for One Winter Night, Friday, February 5, 2016, at 6pm, with the title, *The Phoenix: Hope Is Rising*. I really liked the title and couldn't WAIT to see how it turned out and would impact our community, blessing our ministry.

Amidst the excitement of the developing documentary, staffing continued to be a concern in the spring of 2015. I was still struggling with the staff member who wasn't clicking with the rest of our team. I was disappointed to realize that he wasn't the right fit to take over leadership of the ministry, as I had hoped, which would have allowed me to step away at some point. That disappointment spilled into other areas of our relationship, growing over time into resentment. That was not fair to him.

It became difficult for me to go into the office if I knew he was going to be there. The way I saw it, he was simply not the right fit for the dual role we had hired him to fill. Our board president and I discussed this at length, and at one point I said that it was either going to be him or me. We could not both continue to work for C-U at Home. But for some reason, as we continued to try to work through this difficult situation, our board president was not comfortable with letting him go. He wasn't even able to put the reason into words; he could only say that it was not the right thing to do at that time. This proved to be one of the most difficult time periods for me at C-U at Home, comparable only to my struggle with whether or not to dissolve the ministry in the fall of 2013.

At the beginning of July, that staff member handed me a letter of resignation, as he had found a new full-time position with another ministry. I can't even put into words the feeling of relief that came over me. All of the struggle with him not being the right fit for us and the struggle with not being able to let him go and not really even knowing why had come to an end. We wished him all the best.

In the meantime, a young social worker who had been a volunteer photographer for One Winter Night had started spending time with us as a friend of the Phoenix. She was disillusioned with her job, so Tony suggested she might be a fit for the drop-in center. I loved the idea of a licensed social worker, as well as someone who had spent time at the Phoenix as a friend, stepping into the leadership role. She became our interim Phoenix coordinator, as we worked to determine what our next employment roles would be.

On Sunday evening, June 21, we lost another of our friends. Gary Schrader had lived a very tough life on the streets for many years. He was fighting so hard to stay sober and make positive changes, but he was afraid. Like so many folks that we've known through the years, his fear of change was stronger than his desire to be whole. I was honored to work with his family to plan and officiate his memorial service at Douglas Park in Danville. Gary would have liked that his service was outside and at a park. R.I.P. friend.

Often, there are no easy answers in this line of work, but we were glad for the provision we were able to offer in a variety of situations. One such instance began with a call from my former pastor, who had been in contact with a homeless family in Champaign. Since it was the weekend, most offices were not available until Monday. They were staying at a cheap hotel, so C-U at Home was able to extend their stay a bit. The couple who loved the Lord and had five small children were praying for Him to provide for them. Heartbreaking.

We put the word out that they really needed help. On Tuesday, a couple who had allowed us to use one of their homes two years earlier contacted us. They had seen the news story on TV about this family and reached out. If we were willing to do case management and stay involved with the family, they were willing to allow them to live in their vacant rental home for free. What a blessing! With the help of local television coverage, we received donations of furniture, clothes, and toys for the kids – all they needed – in just two and a half days. It was a provision miracle!

At the Phoenix, we continued the search for other churches to sponsor a day each week, and one church did make a commitment to staff a day each week, allowing us to add Fridays to our schedule. Unfortunately, the time slots that the new church had committed to often went unfilled. Our staff spent considerable time covering those shifts, and sometimes we had to close without enough support.

One Thursday, we waited in vain for a friend from the community to come and spend time with us at the Phoenix. Our commitment from the beginning had been to have at least one friend with an address present any time the Phoenix was open. At noon, we let the folks outside know we were waiting for someone else to come so we could open for the day. I put a plea out on Facebook, called and texted several friends, and finally my friend Cheryl Lehman came to save the day. By the time she got there, many of our friends without an address had already left. As this was not the first time this had happened, I wondered if we would EVER get a large enough base of friends from the community who were willing to come and spend time so this would never happen again.

One church came alongside us in an unexpected way. Quest United Methodist Church dedicated their Faith in Action Sunday to helping our organization. This meant that they canceled their Sunday morning service, and their whole congregation spent two hours helping us at C-U at Home, with groups at each of our transitional houses and a group at the Phoenix. A couple of the men even put our vehicles up on ramps and did oil changes for us. It was a lot of work to get everything ready, but a wonderful blessing to have a church break away from regular worship and spend that time serving the least of these through our ministry.

We had known the Phoenix space on Neil Street was temporary, and by May, it seemed that we would need to search for a new location. I wrote to Dan, our commercial realtor: "Looks like our move out of our current location will be sooner than later. The last two days the drilling crew has been here taking soil samples. They had surveyors and building inspectors on the property for the last three weeks. We also got a heads up about the potential purchaser that seems very likely if it is true. That said, I started my walking tour again to find possible properties. This time I came up with nineteen. Most are the same as a year ago. A couple of new possibilities. I'll get you my list of addresses soon. We are pretty much looking for the same as last time around . . . Thank you for any help you can offer in our search. Our lease requires a sixty day notice to vacate. That's not much time, especially depending on the degree of remodel we will have to do to get moved in."

Our prayer email on August 26 was a bit different than usual. Our normal weekly prayer email usually had three or four praises and three or four prayer requests. This time, I wrote, "Tonight's email is going to be a bit different. Just one simple prayer request. Please join us in praying for the Lord to provide a new location for both our Phoenix Daytime Drop-In Center and the C-U at Home office. We are hoping for at least 3,000SF for the drop-in center and at least 750SF for our office. The Phoenix location needs to be in either downtown or midtown. We are also praying for favor from a property owner to offer us reduced or pro-bono rent. *And my God will supply all your needs according to His riches in glory in Christ Jesus* (Philippians 4:19). Thank you for praying."

I felt a new sense of urgency working with Dan to find a new location. The clock was ticking, as our current lease would expire on December 31. We knew it was likely we would have some remodel work to do on any property that we found. Many people were praying for God to provide a new location for our ministry.

In September, we were getting desperate for a new Phoenix location, with our deadline to move out looming only three months away. And disappointment still stung over the zoning decision for our proposed Esther's Place; we were hoping that God would provide another location for it. We scheduled a prayer meeting at the Phoenix on Sunday, September 20. It would be a time to come together in one room and spend time crying out to the Lord for His provision. We developed a list of prayer points for people to use as a guide:

- One location for our Phoenix Drop-In Center and our C-U at Home office to be made clear soon.
- Favor with both the landlord and the neighborhood for our new location.
- Any remodel efforts needed for the new location to be free or at low cost and done quickly.
- Our actual moving process to go well, with plenty of friends to help.
- More friends from the community to join us on a regular basis at the Phoenix.
- Our next leader of the Phoenix to be "Jesus with skin on" for our friends.
- God's grace to be experienced by our Phoenix friends and our staff.

The next day, we had an important meeting with a neighborhood business association in Champaign. One of the top three possible properties for our new location was in their neighborhood, and we needed the business association to embrace our mission and ministry, if we were to succeed there. Sadly, to say the meeting was discouraging would be an understatement. They made it very, very clear that they did not welcome any additional social service agencies to their association and that they wanted only black-owned businesses to move into their neighborhood. So, since I happen to be white and we happen to be a social service agency, this would not be our property solution for the Phoenix.

Finally, on the first day of October, we got some good news. We had been looking at a building at 34 E. Green Street for several weeks, but the owners were only offering a one year lease. It would require a complete build-out, starting with demolition of some walls and plumbing, then the build-out of our new plumbing, walls, and everything else we needed. It did not make sense to go through all that work and expense for space we could only use for one year. However, the owner and his wife had prayed about it and decided to offer us their building for five years instead of one, and at a price we could afford. Of course, this happened on a THURSDAY. Hallelujah!!! We would now have a place to call home for the next five years!

14

Pressure Cooker

By October 2015, we had added two different part-time, temporary employees. One was to help out at the Phoenix and with our houses, and the other with administrative tasks at the office. The second employee was hired through a government program called Experience Works, which pays people over fifty-five to work part-time for non-profits. The next few weeks were a mix of blessings and curses with our two new employees. Sometimes they rubbed each other the wrong way and complained about how they were being treated by the other when I was not around. When I came into the office one morning, a filing cabinet had been pried open, and the petty cash box had been emptied. Since both new employees had access to the building and to that room and there was no sign of forced entry, it was suspicious, especially since this was the first time any funds had been stolen from our ministry.

Then a couple of weeks later, a donation drop box that had been mounted to a wall inside the Phoenix went missing, pried off the wall from behind a locked door, again with no sign of forced entry. We were never able to determine which employee was the culprit, but both ended up leaving of their own volition. There was a great deal of tension during this time period, so we were relieved to get through it and not have any more problems with theft from the ministry.

Another much more positive development during the first week of October was the signing of the five-year lease for 34 E. Green and the beginning of the demolition process. We were anxious to get things done as fast as possible, since we had less than three months to get everything ready for moving day.

Shaping the empty shell into our new drop-in center was exciting, as interior demolition of some concrete block walls and plumbing started the day we signed the lease. Unbeknownst to me, I was taking my first steps into coordinating the whole building project. I had anticipated that a friend would be connecting all the dots and taking care of the details, but that didn't happen. It didn't take long for me to realize I was in way over my head. Even though I've been around a few building projects here and there, I've never been anywhere close to a project manager for everything. On October 29, we got a list from the city with fourteen items that needed to be addressed on the various drawings. It was a tense time, and we had to be out of our current location by December 31, so the clock was ticking.

Every day was filled with meetings, phone calls, errands, and prayer, all connected with our Phoenix build-out. It was all-consuming and filled with one victory and setback after another. There were lots of hi/lo days in November. Each day seemed like an eternity, with only eight weeks remaining until we had to be out of our Neil Street property. Yet work was at a standstill, waiting for the City of Champaign to issue a building permit.

In the midst of the pressure of the building project, I had two precious opportunities for self care. The first was at a cabin in Door County, Wisconsin, called the Sanctuary. A retired ministry couple had built it on their property to give pastors, missionaries, and ministry leaders a beautiful, private place to spend time with the Lord and rejuvenate. I unplugged for a week, enjoying nature with the beautiful change of fall colors. The best parts were the simple sounds of nature, the worship CDs that I had brought with me, and being completely off the digital grid for a few days. Thank you, Lord, for recalibrating my focus and recharging my batteries.

Also, for four days in November, I was blessed with a free registration and hotel room for the annual CCDA (Christian Community Development Association) conference, which was held in Memphis, TN, that year. The weekend was filled with encouragement from others who are involved with Christian empowerment poverty ministries all across the country, including many old friends. A large group of people from Cornerstone Fellowship and New Covenant Fellowship in Champaign were there. We hung out quite a bit and enjoyed a couple of meals together. I was also re-connected with a friend who worked at WBGL with me years ago, Nathaniel Price. He had been doing Christian community development ministry in Tennessee.

During a lunch break from the conference, I had an unsettling interaction on a park bench in downtown Memphis with security officers. It was a beautiful day, about 75°, with a bright sun, a light breeze, and blue skies. I walked to a street vendor to grab a sandwich for lunch and relaxed on a park bench under a tree along the main street. After I ate my sandwich, I still had about half an hour before the next session started. So, I took off my shoes, laid back across the park bench, and closed my eyes. A few minutes later, two men in uniforms came up to me and asked what I was doing. I said that I was enjoying a beautiful day in downtown Memphis, on a break from the CCDA conference. Right at that moment, Jimmy Dorrell, my friend and fellow minister to our friends without an address, walked by. Sitting down on the bench right next to me, he asked what was going on. The two men were downtown security officers, and they said that if they had been city cops, I would have been ticketed, as there was no sleeping allowed on public park benches. Wow! Just when I thought we had de-criminalized homelessness. Jimmy was ready to bail me out, or more likely to go to jail with me!

As I was driving out of Memphis to head home on Saturday, I received an email that took all the wind out of my sails. We had been working with a local construction company to get all the professional drawings needed for the city, and I was under the impression they were going to be able to do much of the work for us for free or for a very low cost. The email detailed their quote for plumbing and HVAC, and it came to over $56,000, which was way out of our price range. We already had another vendor who would be doing all the electrical and lighting, pro bono. By then, it was mid-November, so this was a serious setback. It had taken three and a half weeks to get our building permit, and this setback would require new drawings to be submitted to the city, starting the arduous process all over again. But before that, we had to secure new businesses or individuals to do both our HVAC and our plumbing at a price we could afford (or, we prayed, for free!). "God, what are You up to here?" I wondered. "How are we ever going to get this building ready on time?"

As I returned to Champaign, every day seemed like a challenging mix of recruiting box dwellers and business sponsors and other details for One Winter Night, working on a huge number of different aspects for our Phoenix build-out, and getting everything ready for the documentary, plus all the drama caused by the robberies and the two part-time staff. From the middle of November all the way through One Winter Night, I lived in a continual state of stress and varying levels of chaos. As had happened so often before, I would experience one really good thing and two really bad things all in the same morning. At other times, four positives would be offset by five setbacks, all in the same day. Several hi/lo days in a row. I prayed for God to not only give me the strength I needed, but also the sanity I needed to endure.

We knew that we were going to need additional parking once we got moved in. Once our staff and ministry-owned vehicles were on the lot, only two empty spaces remained. I asked the property owner if we could lay down gravel on the lot next to us to use for parking, but the city would not allow this; this location required either concrete or blacktop. Tony had a friend with a concrete business who offered to pour the concrete we needed for the parking lot for free. What a blessing! A civil engineer friend looked into taking care of those plan drawings for us, but his quote of $5,700 just for the plans wasn't in our budget. I had hoped his company would be willing to help us at little or no cost. Back to the drawing board once again. With the low temperatures, concrete would have to wait until the spring anyway.

We were blessed with plumbers willing to donate their time and get the underground plumbing rough-in started on the day before Thanksgiving, coming back to finish on Friday morning, while the clock just kept on ticking. Our plumbing was approved on Thursday, December 3, requiring the steel framing for the bathroom and shower walls to be complete by Friday – and the concrete hadn't even been poured yet, where the plumbing had been roughed in! When I put out the call far and wide for several skilled framers to come and work for us on that Friday so that the concrete would have time to dry, by God's grace, they came – mostly after work. But by 10pm, the framing was finished for the team of apprentice plumbers coming back to install the above ground plumbing, starting bright and early Saturday morning.

At the beginning of December, we were at our housing capacity for the ministry, with six men in our recovery house, two women in our women's house, and a family of four in our family house. While it felt good to have all our beds filled, it also meant lots of work for Tony, our volunteer case managers, and the others helping our residents.

November's list had been endless: flooring choices, registering new box dwellers, problems with a resident, the need for more footage for the documentary, no one at the Phoenix at noon, website difficulties, disappointing news from the city inspector, reading and writing nearly one hundred emails a day, and a plumber who could no longer help. December was even more frantic and intense than

November, literally one hi/lo day after another. At a couple of points, I actually thought I might end up being hospitalized for a nervous breakdown. There were so many decisions that needed to be made, and our main contractor was headed to Florida for two weeks. Plus, Christmas was coming up right at the end of our time at the old location. "God, how will You get us through this time period?" I prayed. "How will You make a way? And how will You help me keep my sanity for the next two months, through One Winter Night?"

Our board president, Mike Royse, saw the effect this pressure was having on me, knowing how important it was for me to put my focus on One Winter Night instead of the build-out. So he offered to take over leadership of the build-out. I was so very grateful, and even though I knew there would still be lots of people contacting me, at least I could try and let go of as much of it as possible.

On December 9, my mom's birthday, I got an email notifying me of a community honor: "Dear Ms. Jackson, It is our pleasure to notify you that you have been selected by the 2016 MLK Countywide Celebration Committee to receive the 2016 Dr. Martin Luther King, Jr. Outstanding Achievement Award. We would like to honor you at our 15th Annual Rev. Dr. Martin Luther King, Jr. Countywide Celebration. Thank you for your many contributions to our Community. We look forward to seeing you! With respect and gratitude, 2016 MLK Countywide Celebration Committee."

What a difference twenty-four hours can make. The next day, I wrote a desperate note to my counselor: "I have a real sense of dread and failure that continues to loom. Both Tony and I were so very, very busy today. We couldn't even finish one conversation about one demanding challenge before another one started. He gets anxious. Then I get anxious and demanding. Next, our builder gets even more anxious than both of us put together. It is a continual recipe for disaster. Not sure what all is going on, but several things point to a board member trying to take more control and get the board more involved. On the surface that is a good thing. But then tonight, the board wanted to meet again for about ninety minutes without me. I know that they are very opposed to me having a supervisory role over whoever is hired to run the Phoenix. I cannot wrap my head around someone in that position who is not in some way under my leadership. I feel like at that point, it's time for me to exit C-U at Home and pray for God to open a door in Colorado. Also, I'm getting very afraid that OWN is not going to do near what we need it to do this year with fundraising. Like today was my day to work entirely from home. I was pulled away right after noon to pay for insulation and then help deliver it and then . . . finally the board meeting at 5:30pm. And I've been sending box dweller invitation emails since then. I'm so behind on things that need to be done for the event. I am tired and weary. Please pray for me. Thank you."

And then, the very next day was a very good day. Our sheetrock had been delivered the day before and the crew was starting the work on it. Our donated roof-mount HVAC unit was delivered and raised to the roof with a crane. I met with a painter willing to donate her services for us once the drywall was ready. We got some much-needed donated bedding for our family house. And in the afternoon, I had a meeting with a Christian-owned business at the Phoenix. They decided to be $2500 business sponsors for OWN, and two of their employees signed up to be box dwellers and raise funds, in addition to that $2500. That night I went to a madrigal dinner in Bloomington with friends from my old church and had a wonderful time. It seemed as though God was answering my prayers from the night before with hope and encouragement. I was grateful. Once again, a hi/lo experience, from the lowest low to the highest high in a matter of hours.

We had inventoried and evaluated our existing furnishings, and posted pictures online to offer excess items to other organizations. Since we had been blessed so abundantly with donated items when we had first moved into the Phoenix, it was wonderful to share desks, chairs, computers, shelves, tables, and other items with others.

We were so blessed by several people who made donations of thousands of dollars, either directly through cash or with their materials and labor, to help make our Phoenix build-out a reality. Most gave very quietly, not wanting any type of recognition. We saw God's miraculous provision first-hand, through His people, never more evident than throughout the new Phoenix build-out process. Just before Christmas, my former boss at Vet Med offered us an eight-foot, open bed Dodge truck with a trailer hitch and a name – Henry. What a blessing Henry was going to be for our ministry!

Heat and paint arrived on the same December day, as the HVAC unit was donated and installed at no charge. The painting was a collaborative effort. One local business donated the primer, a friend donated the paint, and another local business and volunteers did the painting. Seeing those Phoenix red walls and C-U at Home blue walls for the first time was cause for celebration.

Kelly-Jane (KJ) Monahan stepped back into our ministry the week before Christmas, volunteering to build the OWN box dweller pages and send the links to the participants. We also talked with her about the possibility of working part-time as our administrative assistant. She was excited about the opportunity, but needed to find childcare. KJ was able to come on staff half-time at the first of the year, relieving much of the administrative burden from my shoulders.

On New Year's Day, we were blessed with three guys who worked most of the day, running framing for the drop ceiling in the office and laying vinyl plank flooring in the entire building. Our deadline to exit the old building had been extended to Thursday, January 14, so we planned to move the weekend before, closing Friday at 5pm on Neil Street, moving everything on Saturday, and opening Tuesday, January 12, on Green Street. An e-mail outlined the tasks that needed to be completed before the professional construction clean-up crew arrived. Electrical work, the LAN and IP phones, and the necessary occupancy blessing from the city were all still outstanding, along with hundreds of small details. On Thursday evening, I went to a powerful prayer meeting at Stone Creek Church during their week of prayer, placing everything about this move into the Lord's hands. He was building faith and trust in me.

The sheer number of emails, Facebook posts, and Google calendar entries that January was overwhelming. I averaged just over one hundred emails and several Facebook posts per day for the entire month. I am so grateful for God's strength and energy to make it through the chaos of the documentary development, Phoenix build-out and move, and OWN preparation, in addition to everything else happening with our ministry. We were still providing emergency warming, supporting the residents in our houses, and staffing our Phoenix open hours.

Friday, January 8, was packing day at the old Phoenix and inspection and construction clean-up day at the new Phoenix. We were getting everything ready at both locations for our big move the next morning. With a crew of volunteers and a box truck all lined up, we were able to pack, clean, organize, and transport. With the help of board members and other friends of our ministry, we moved everything a few blocks south and one block east of the current location.

The building inspector arrived on Friday at 1pm, with measuring tape in hand. Two major and unexpected changes would be necessary for our occupancy. Our kitchen counter was the typical height of 36", but they required a height of 34" so that someone in a wheelchair could more easily reach the controls on the sink. We would have to take the counter top off, saw two inches off every cabinet edge, and remount the counter top. Also, measurement of our ADA compliant walk-in shower came back 2" too narrow. The shower surround had been purchased from Illinois Plumbing in Springfield, labeled with a big ADA compliant sticker. But the code enforcement officer for the City of Champaign said that it was 2" too narrow to meet that code.

So, to fix it, we would have to uninstall the shower surround, purchase a new one, take the sheetrock off from the shower walls, trim the metal studs back, by 1" on each side of the room, reinstall sheetrock, mud, tape, and paint, and install the new shower surround. This was all on Friday afternoon and we needed to open to the public on Tuesday at noon. There was NO WAY all of this would happen on that timeline. The city did come back and say that if several other things from their inspection were remedied along with the counter height by a Monday afternoon re-inspection, they would be willing to give us a provisional occupancy with thirty days to solve the shower problem. We would simply have to keep the door to the shower locked and inaccessible.

I simply could not believe they were going to make us go through so much work in the middle of winter, the most critical time for our friends without an address, because of 2". I did some crying and some yelling, and eventually I settled down. Our construction crew said it would be no big deal to get the cabinets trimmed and the counter lowered over the weekend. Our plumbing crew and construction crew committed to changing out the shower units to get the extra 2" needed for the new unit to be installed within thirty days. This last-minute set of challenges with the build-out was par for the course. Each step of the way, we faced one difficult situation after another. And each step of the way, we were witness to how God provided for us.

On Saturday morning, God blessed me with excitement and energy for our big moving day. Papa G, who had prayed over and anointed our first building, joined us at the new location that morning and did the same. It was powerful to have our staff and board members, prayer warriors, and friends without an address all together, hand in hand, encircling the new Phoenix room, dedicating it to the Lord. My mind flashed back to that cold December night outside of the Canteen truck when we had made a circle and joined our hands in prayer. Our plan was to open at our new location

142

according to our regular weekly schedule, at noon on Tuesday. God's plan would not be thwarted by the enemy.

On Monday at 2:30pm, we had our final occupancy inspection. I have never been more relieved than when I picked up our conditional certificate of occupancy at 4:40pm (knowing that their office closed at 5pm). We would officially be able to open to the public the next day. God's provision, and just in a nick of time!

All of this happened with only a month to go before One Winter Night. We were hoping to have at least one hundred box dwellers and we were at sixty-seven at that point. Even though we still had lots of things to figure out at the new building, including phone operation and parking, it was time for me to focus squarely on One Winter Night. Our goal was $150,000 and we desperately needed to raise that amount to provide for our staff, the new location, our houses and transportation.

Dan Denton surprised us with a unique donation for our new Phoenix, a chainsaw-carved bench for the front of the building, inscribed with the phrase, "The Phoenix, Rising Up Out of the Ashes" on the back and "Hope Is Rising" on the seat. A beautiful angel was carved into one arm and a phoenix bird on the other. Phil was there to get some footage of the big reveal for the film. He said that it would likely be the very last footage shot for the documentary. He and Isaac spent the next two weeks in the editing room, preparing for the first public screening of the film at OWN on February 5.

Later that afternoon was the Martin Luther King Day ceremony at Parkland College. They played my acceptance video, and I was given the Dr. Martin Luther King, Jr. Outstanding Achievement Award. Community leaders from all walks of life were present. I was grateful that they allowed me to share my Christian testimony and to give Jesus all the glory for C-U at Home in my video.

That Saturday, Sunday, and Monday, an arctic front was moving in, and that meant more emergency warming hours. And it was even more difficult for us because those are three days that we are not normally open. God did eventually provide a mix of staff, board members, and friends from the community to keep our doors open with a warm, safe place for folks to escape the bitter cold. We had gotten our new location open just in time!

An email to Phil expressed how I was feeling. "Please pray for me. We have a huge parking dilemma at the new location. It's very, very hard for me to deal with on top of everything else. Honestly, I feel like either exploding in a rage or completely shutting down and quitting. The load of the build-out and moving and emergency warming and OWN all at the same time is too much for one person to bear. My stress level is off the charts and I am overwhelmed. Prayers are much appreciated. And I am praying for your final editing phase. Thank you so much for all you have done for us! Mel."

A few days later, Phil sent me a link to view the ninety-minute draft version of the documentary. He still had quite a bit of work to do, but he wanted my input on the editing process. I cried and I laughed and I cried again. Wow! Speechless. I could not wait for people to see this powerful film and learn more about the issues related to homelessness and our ministry's response. Only a week and a half to go until everyone would see what their many hours of labor would bear.

I was somewhat surprised yet encouraged by a couple of Paypal donations that came through in support of box dwellers for One Winter Night. They were from the volunteer who had served as our property coordinator to get our donated house ready and the first Phoenix location ready, and had then stepped completely away and would not communicate with me. I was encouraged that he was willing to financially support our ministry and hopeful that someday our relationship might still be restored.

In the midst of all the construction work, we faced a serious challenge of a different sort. Two members of our small staff of four had gotten into several disagreements over the past few weeks, and they continued to escalate. All of us were under a tremendous amount of stress that just added fuel to any type of argument. As the situation continued to build, I honestly feared losing one or both of them before One Winter Night. This was a very critical HR situation, and I have a huge deficiency when it comes to these kinds of issues. I reached out to a couple of our board members and to my counselor, and their direction served as a band-aid for our employees' relationship for the sake of One Winter Night. We would have to continue to work on a resolution for the situation after we made it through the event.

By the end of January, I sent the following email to our staff and board: "Subject: Box dweller #100!!! Yep, you read that right. God is at work blessing our ministry once again. Several months ago, we set a goal of at least one hundred box dwellers. As God would have it, we also set today as the deadline for both our business sponsors and our box dweller signups. I am pleased to announce that about one hour ago, we posted the webpage for OWN 2016 box dweller #100! I'm blown away. After doing a rough count, I think that thirty-five of the one hundred have been in a box for us before. That means we have sixty-five NEW box dwellers this year. God is so good to bless us in this powerful way. I can't wait to see what downtown looks like with all of these folks in refrigerator boxes! Blessings, Mel."

On February 1, Phil wrote: "Two years ago I spent the night in a box for C-U at Home. That night I heard someone walking by say the ministry gets a lot of attention, raises a lot of money, and does nothing for the homeless. That was the first seed for this film – I had to find out the truth. It's been a long journey since then. I can't wait to share what we've discovered." We were all getting so excited to share the film with everyone at One Winter Night.

Things were very, very hectic the week of OWN. We got our new tri-fold brochure to the printer just in time. A friend came through with a box truck to transport the refrigerator boxes downtown for us in the nick of time. Volunteers failed to show up when they said they would be there. Tony made an impromptu detox run. There were several media interviews of various types. We had lots of problems with the coding on a key spreadsheet for OWN. And we could feel the eyes of the community watching us. What would OWN be like this year? We had just moved to a brand new location three weeks earlier. We had new employees. We were asking for $50,000 more than the year before. And we had a new documentary film to share. Anticipation was building.

Randy Zachary had been working to recruit box dwellers on the air at WBGL. We were all pleased that in only a few weeks he was able to entice fifteen listeners from all across Illinois and Indiana to come and spend the night in a cardboard box for us. It was quite humbling, being supported by Team WBGL, especially after spending almost eight years working for the radio ministry myself.

When I got up on Friday, I was excited to see what God had planned. Arriving at our event headquarters downtown, I could tell we were already behind the eight-ball. We didn't have enough volunteers coming early enough to get everything set up. We worked like madmen to get the registration stations set up, all the banners and signs ready, box dweller backpacks filled, tables and chairs set up, port-a-potties in place, and more. Phil got there just before 5:30pm, as he had been working on the film edit until 2:45 that afternoon! It was 5:50 before we knew it, and the room was starting to fill up with folks ready to see our documentary. Phil and Isaac had just tested the video to make sure everything was ready.

At the strike of 6:00, Isaac was behind the console and Phil took the stage to share about how God had laid it on his heart to tell our story. The three of us were filled with a variety of emotions, even before the film started. Tony was in the back of the room with Phil, and I took a seat in the middle of the room. I was nervous and excited all at the same time, since this would be the first time I got to see the completed version. A couple of minutes later, my ministry coach, Don Follis, came to sit in the empty seat beside me. Thank you, Jesus, for bringing Don to experience this powerful life moment with me.

Watching the film was very emotional for me. It had changed significantly since the draft version I had seen a couple of weeks earlier. One thing that absolutely blew me away was the quality of the cinematography. The music score and the camera shots were as good as anything you see on the small screen or even the big screen. Watching it made me so proud of Tony. He had become such a good friend and had already done so much for our ministry. The film did a great job of capturing his story and his personality.

There were a couple of spots that really humbled me. At one point Rick was talking about me being focused on how I want things to be done a specific way, resulting in sometimes rubbing people the wrong way. Ouch! The truth hurts, my flat side exposed for all the world to see. And Tony said that when he first met me he thought I was nuts. Thanks, Tony. But it did get a good chuckle out of the crowd.

When the film finished, I took the stage to answer questions. It was almost a full minute before I could speak, and I wasn't sure what to say. The Q&A time was like a blur, and I really don't remember much of what was asked or what I said. I do remember Phil's dad, Les, asking a couple of good questions. I was so glad that Phil's folks could be there to support him. We continued to show the film every two hours throughout the night. And either Phil or Isaac or both of them introduced the film each time. After each showing, either Tony or I or the two of us together led the Q&A. What a blessing to share this film with our community, including our staff, volunteers, box dwellers, and some of our friends without an address.

After leading that first Q&A, around 8pm, it was time for me to load up a hand cart and distribute two crates of *Radical* books, one for each box dweller. This was a very special annual tradition for me, to touch base in person with each box dweller and tell them how this book had impacted my life and influenced the start of C-U at Home. Wanting a friend to go with me, I asked Meridith Foster, who was volunteering with her husband and kids. Meridith had been my co-worker at WBGL, and she was the one who had given that first $100 to help with the first survey in 2011. With so many box dwellers, the process took almost two hours. This was my sweet spot. I really loved getting *Radical* into people's hands to see how God would use it in their lives, as well as sharing the way God had given me the vision for C-U at Home.

In the middle of the night, Phil wrote this about his experience: "We just met the original goal for our film. When we originally set the vision for this film, we talked a lot about our goals. We wanted to make something really good – the best thing either of us had ever made. We wanted to win awards. We wanted it to be financially successful. We decided, though, that our first and only goal would be to motivate one person's heart to turn towards helping and loving others, and we focused everything we had on that one goal. I just received a message that someone brought their teenager to the film viewing, and he was so moved by the film that he has decided to volunteer to help the homeless. We can officially say now that our film is a success – we met our original goal."

That Sunday right after OWN, reflecting on the success of the event, I journaled: "Lounging at home enjoying going through the box dweller debriefing comments. This is one of my favorites. 'A somewhat unexpected byproduct of C-U at Home One Winter Night is the true community that is formed for a few hours on the streets of Champaign each year on the first Friday in February.' It really resonates with me and reminds me of the special community I was a part of for seventeen years at the Cornerstone Music Festival with my friends Chuck and Cheryl Conway. And a remnant of that community has continued through the passion and vision of my friends Jim and Jennifer Eisenmenger, called AudioFeed. Thank you, Jesus for wiring us humans to yearn for true community."

On Tuesday, just three days after OWN, the temps dropped drastically once again and we were back to emergency warming for fourteen hours a day, five of the next six days! I prayed, "Lord, thank you for giving us the opportunity to keep our friends safe. But could you please give us all a break and some time to recover and recuperate?"

That same day I received an email from Urbana Alderman Eric Jakobsson with great news. "On February 1, we passed a revision to the zoning ordinance that provides for transitional housing in neighborhoods zoned for single family (R2). I regret that we did not move fast enough to provide for the house on North Mathews, but I believe as a city that we have moved in a good direction in providing a better environment to meet the needs of the people you are helping." What a blessing! Our film had played a part in this powerful change in direction for a city government. Isaac had interviewed both Eric and Alderwoman Diane Marlin for the film in November, which had helped to kick-start the discussion again to find a solution for us and other agencies with similar plans for transitional housing in the City of Urbana.

The pressure cooker of OWN had yielded tangible results, as well. We finished the night with just over $128,000 raised. It was our hope to get to our goal of at least $150,000 by February 18, the day we closed the books on OWN 2016. That date turned out to be worthy of celebration: when all was said and done, we had raised a net of $156,615. We were right in the middle of emergency warming hours, so our board president Mike came to staff the Phoenix while all of our staff went out to the new Black Dog in Champaign for some of the best barbeque in town. We had met our goal. Thank you, Jesus!

15

Self-Care

Vacation! I was so very ready to get away and clear my mind of all things C-U at Home. The week was going to be full: time with seminary friends in Kansas City, skiing and snowmobiling in Colorado, time in my favorite place on earth, Colorado Springs, and then back for a weekend in Wellington, MO, with my St. Luke church family. After updating the new OWN total on our website, I made it on the road around 1:30pm, my destination set to my former pastor's home in Kansas City, KS, where I was staying that night. I even got to sneak in a quick visit that evening in Independence, MO, with my dear friends Jack and Louise Taylor from Blue Ridge Baptist Church.

Lunch on Saturday was with Dr. B and Mama Jo Butler at my most favorite Kansas City restaurant, the Corner Café. This dear man and woman had been powerful music mentors for me during my time in Kansas City. Dr. B was the one who had started the church music program at Midwestern Seminary. During my second year at seminary, Mama Jo and I had struck up a deal. I would come over to their home for a couple hours each week, where she would teach me basic piano chords and I would help her with the computer, a beautiful barter system. When lesson time was over, the three of us enjoyed a homemade dessert treat together, a sweet time of fellowship. They believed in me, and God had used them both as strong encouragers in my life.

Dinner was with my dear friends Chris and Lori Lancaster, a wonderful meal of homemade pizza. Chris and I had attended seminary at the same time, and we were both involved with our evangelism teams. When I had moved back to Illinois from Wellington, MO, in 2009, Chris had ridden my motorcycle back home more than six hours from KC to Champaign, so I wouldn't have to trailer it. And it was COLD! Such a trooper. The Lancasters were my only seminary friends who regularly supported C-U at Home.

Morning worship with my Haven Baptist family was wonderful! I played the congas with the worship team, and Pastor Don gave me a few minutes to share what God had been doing in my life through CUH. Lunch with church friends was followed by a coffee shop visit with another seminary friend, John Mills. It was so good to see him and hear what God was up to in his life. John had been my ministry buddy, leading that powerful seminary mission trip post-Katrina.

That evening, I met Allen and Kelsey Reger at the Kansas City classic, Gates BBQ. Allen had been my best friend through seminary and I hadn't seen him since his wedding, when my time there was cut short by the phone call about Richard's death. Allen had served as pastor for a couple of different small, rural churches, and now he was serving as a ministry intern, being mentored by a man of God with years of successful experience as a pastor.

Monday morning, I met Dr. Rod Harrison at the small café on the seminary campus. An encourager for me during my seminary days, he had brought the Faith Riders motorcycle chapter to Midwestern. In 2009, he led the trip to Sturgis to do evangelism and give away a Harley, when I had that second experience of weeping, of God breaking my heart for those in poverty.

The trip to Colorado was long but good, complete with some white-knuckle snowstorm driving after dark in the mountains – fresh powder on the slopes and perfect conditions for skiing the next morning. My friend Josh McGarvey and his friend Terrill took me skiing on a buddy pass, on a beautiful day, with sunshine, blue skies, temperatures in the upper 20s, and low winds.

I skied alone the next day and had a meaningful experience with God on the overcast mountain that afternoon. I heard the Lord say, "Hire believers." He had been convicting me to move our paid staff in the direction of everyone being Christ-followers. I could not deny His clear direction. Our original leadership team and every board member C-U at Home has ever had (twenty-nine, and counting), has been a believer, and that had been my intention for paid staff as well. But over the years some people had gotten involved who were respectful of our Christian beliefs but not yet Christ-followers themselves. And then at some point we had started paying them. It was now crystal clear to me that we would not be hiring any additional staff who were not dedicated Jesus followers.

Thursday morning, I took an extreme adventure three-hour snowmobile tour. I was the only one signed up, which meant I was assigned to my own personal guide, named Ryan. I could tell when he looked at me he was thinking, "Here we go, some woman who has no idea what she's doing." And then we started riding the trails. Ryan saw that I knew how to handle the machine and that I was ready to do more, so he led us to a back portion of their property with fresh powder, sweeping slopes, and no one else around. It was the first time that year he had been back to that part of the property.

After snowmobiling, I took the back way to Colorado Springs. It was like going home. Maybe someday God would bring the right person to take over leadership of C-U at Home and I would be able to move there. I checked out the Olympic Village and spent the entire afternoon hiking and being a rock lizard at the Garden of the Gods. There's no place quite like the Garden of the Gods at sunset.

Driving back to Wellington, MO, on Saturday, I had an unexpected detour. After I stopped to get gas in WaKeeney, a little town in western Kansas, I began losing acceleration going uphill on I-70. Had I gotten some bad gas? BAM! There was a loud noise and the car died. I coasted downhill to the side of the interstate. I tried to start the car again and got nothing. I popped the hood and quickly realized that oil was spattered everywhere, on the hood and in a trail behind the car. My car was towed to a small garage in WaKeeney. It was Saturday afternoon and the garage was closed, but the trooper showed me three places where I could get a room for the night.

That night I wrote: "The good news is, I am safe. It was 76° for my drive today, and I spent time with a wonderful good Samaritan named Henry from Alabama, an undersheriff named Jim, and a garage owner named Steve. When he got the car up on a lift, we saw a hole in my engine block where my Vibe threw a rod, lost all the oil, and seized the engine. Please pray for many decisions I will need to make in the next couple of days – buy a rebuilt engine or scrap the car, how and when to get back to Illinois, and what God wants me to learn from this experience. He already gave me a feather, so I know that He's up to something. Just not sure what. Thank you."

I really did not know what to do. There were no good options. Tow the car home – I couldn't get any kind of rental truck until Monday. Have a friend or relative from Illinois come get me and tow it home – again, this would take time, and after reaching out to several different people, I couldn't find anyone. Scrap the car – I really didn't want to do that since I loved it and it had lots of life left in it. Get the

151

engine repaired or replaced – a possibility, but that would take weeks, and we could not find out about anything until Monday, at the earliest. And I would still have to find some way back home.

I was bummed that it didn't look like I was going to get to see any of my friends in Wellington, MO. I went to sleep in the little, not-so-clean, hotel that night, having no idea what God was up to.

The day before, the officer had also driven me by the three Protestant churches in town. One of them was a small storefront Baptist church called Crosspoint, and I walked there to worship the next morning. I met Ed Hughes and his wife Beverly at Crosspoint Church, a sweet retired couple who asked me what I was doing in WaKeeney. God's people to the rescue!

Ed hooked up a friend's borrowed trailer to his truck and transported me and my car to Champaign that very night! Ed was a retired Greyhound driver and was determined to get me and my car safely home on that windy, ten-hour drive. Fortified by the snacks Beverly had provided, we made it to Champaign just before 3am. Ed slept for about three hours, and then we unloaded the Vibe and he hopped back in his truck to head home. I thanked the Lord for His incredible provision through this lovely couple.

I located a certified used engine for my Vibe and a Christian mechanic to do the swap for a very reasonable price. I finally got to pick up my little blue Vibe with her new engine in mid-April. It was so good to have my car back again! I was so grateful for all of the folks who had made it possible.

We chose not to have a March board meeting, but I was able to catch up with Mike Royse and share my God-directed vision for our staffing with him. This included:

- The equivalent of four full-time employees, either four full-time or three full-time and two half-time.

- Both new employees to be Christ followers, willing to pray with others and to share the gospel with compassion and discernment.

- Roles: an executive director (Mel), a mentor (Tony), a Phoenix coordinator (full-time?), a Phoenix assistant (half-time?), and an office manager (half-time?).

- Phoenix coordinator and Phoenix assistant should be opposite genders, one male, one female.

152

- Phoenix coordinator and Phoenix assistant should be of opposite general backgrounds: one clinically trained and experienced, the other with personal experience dealing with homelessness and/or addiction. At least one of these employees should be an LCSW (social work license).
- Phoenix coordinator to spend morning and Monday hours doing individual friend case management and developing future plans and programs related to the Phoenix.
- Phoenix assistant to work during all open Phoenix hours (including emergency warming, as needed).
- Mentor to oversee Transitional Supportive Housing (residents and property), Transportation Ministry, and Street Outreach. Mentor to assist with the Phoenix (including emergency warming) and Education and Advocacy ministry.
- Office manager to lead in both a clerical and administrative role for C-U at Home.
- Executive director to lead in an administrative role, overseeing all staff, fund raising, building community relationships, and offering vision and direction to all areas of C-U at Home, while assisting in all areas of the ministry, as needed.

Our focus on staff at that time was crucial because we continued to experience tension between various staff members. Unfortunately, our Phoenix friends paid the highest price for the stressful staff relationship situations. We've learned over time that some of our friends without an address are more keenly discerning about motive than we will ever be. The tension between staff members negatively affected the atmosphere at the Phoenix. I deeply regret that part of what happened, and I pray to God that nothing like that will ever happen again at C-U at Home.

In March, we had to decide who the next leader of the Phoenix would be. Kelly-Jane had her social work degree, and she was still working for us part-time as an administrative assistant. I talked with her to see if she had interest in being an interim Phoenix coordinator through the summer, even though that would mean I would once again have no administrative help. She talked with her husband and was very excited to serve in that role for us. And we were grateful to have someone who we already knew was a loyal worker, dedicated to our ministry and who already had a good relationship with many of our Phoenix friends. She was able to overlap for two weeks and shadow our Phoenix leader, very valuable sponge time for her.

In March and April, we went through the painstaking process of figuring out what was best for our future staffing needs. I came to agreement with our board that we needed to hire an executive, someone to be my partner in leading the ministry. This person would take over leadership for both the operations of the ministry and the supervision and development of the staff. Where we continued to disagree was to whom this new staff person would report. Some on the board thought that this operations manager should report directly to the board. I simply could not wrap my mind around our ministry having a leader that did not in some way report to me as long as I was still around. It was my prayer that this new leader would be someone who could eventually take over the ministry once the Lord gave me permission to step away.

By the middle of April, this position evolved into a managing director job description to lead operations and staff and to be supervised jointly by myself and the board. The board had formed an executive team for the purpose of developing the staffing plan and job descriptions, as well as managing the hiring process by vetting applications and conducting interviews. We hoped to have the right person hired by the end of the summer.

In the meantime, our documentary was growing in its impact. Dawn Broers, a social work instructor at Olivet Nazarene University in Bourbonnais, IL, called Phil to express interest in developing a college curriculum to go along with various video segments of our documentary. Our film was accepted to compete for best documentary in an International Christian Film Festival and two different National Christian Film Festivals. Subsequently, we received this announcement: "Congratulations. *The Phoenix: Hope is Rising* by Philip Gioja, a 2016 Christian Film Festival Award Winner for 'Best Documentary' and the CFF 'Good Samaritan Award'! The documentary shows some really amazing Christians giving up time, money, and some even their livelihoods, to help the homeless and those in real need!"

That spring, we scheduled public film screenings, followed by open conversations. The first was at St. Paul Lutheran Church and School in Milford, Illinois, where Phil's kids went to school. It was so powerful to see the film once again and to have folks who know Phil share their thankfulness for him and to congratulate him on the film.

16

Gray Hair

On Tuesday, April 19, 2016, we hosted a lovely, well-attended open house and ribbon cutting for our new Phoenix and C-U at Home office location, as many old and new friends came together to celebrate what God had done. The Chamber of Commerce did an official ribbon cutting, and I was blessed with beautiful flowers from Papa G and a lovely schefflera plant from Don Follis, a reminder to me of Rita's prophetic prayer about seeds and plants.

By early May, work began on the grading for our new, expanded parking lot – nine new parking spaces for the Phoenix. We couldn't get those new spaces quick enough, as neighbors were threatening to tow our friends if they parked in their lots without permission.

Throughout 2016, we continued to strengthen our staff. During the spring semester, we were blessed with four interns from the Psychology Department at the University of Illinois. After his internship, Kyle Gomez was hired as our part-time hourly Phoenix assistant for the summer. The hire made sense, as he already had a strong relationship with quite a few of our Phoenix friends, and was a nice complement to KJ, our female Phoenix coordinator.

In July, I met with one of our recovery house residents, Terry Andrews. He had been to church that morning and had been deeply affected by the sermon. God had spoken to him and called him to help us with our ministry. We had a powerful time of prayer and encouragement together that afternoon. "What are you up to Lord?" I asked, "Could this be our new Phoenix assistant? Someone who would be a graduate of our own recovery house?"

And in August, my friend Michelle agreed to join our team part-time as our administrative assistant. She had been a part of every One Winter Night, helping us with registration and other tasks, and was a founding board member. Her organizational skills and love for our ministry made her a great fit, and she agreed to start in the office on August 8. What a relief to FINALLY be getting some administrative help again!

Unfortunately, Michelle had been going through a challenging time with a family situation, plus a serious medical situation. In the end, she decided to stay with her current full-time job and the insurance benefits it offered. I was happy for her to be getting the support she needed, but quite sad and discouraged that we still did not have anyone to help with administrative needs for the ministry.

I had a significant meeting with Mike Royse and Jenny Eisenmenger at the end of April. We'd come to respect Jenny's gracious way of interacting with our friends and staff in her weekly Friday visits, and we valued her perspective on both future leadership and the culture of the Phoenix. Though we had flipped our model to an empowerment-focused ministry, she reminded us of the role of grace as the filter to make decisions and guide our conversations. After this meeting, I added a signature to every text message I sent: "Lead with grace." Using the grace filter for our decisions and conversations can change our world. I was grateful to Jenny for helping us recalibrate our ministry compass.

We also adapted Bill Hybel's three C's for our staff hiring process: character, competence, and chemistry, and added one of own as well: culture. Character is Christian character, displaying the qualities of Jesus in all types of challenging situations. Competence is the mix of gifts and abilities in various areas needed for the role. Chemistry is the "fit" with other team members. And culture is the ability to connect with our Phoenix friends and other friends without an address.

Starting in the spring, our primary staffing goal was to hire a managing director. Joel's wife, Loren Sanders, who has years of HR experience with a major company, helped us design an interview guide to use during the hiring process, with a scorecard to rank the applications that came pouring in. Loren developed a variety of questions and scenarios to help measure our four C's, as we wanted to place a higher emphasis on character rather than on specific education, ability, or skills, and knowing how difficult it is to measure character through a resume and cover letter. Working in teams, we utilized the categories of competence (self motivation, management ability, HR experience, financial experience, and leading through others), chemistry (working under stress, empowerment), culture (team building), and Christian character (integrity, moral compass, grace, Christian viewpoint) to determine the top few candidates to interview.

Although it wasn't listed, I was convinced our managing director should have some gray hair, with practical life experience in addition to valuable education, skills, and gifts. After we went through the first set of interviews and we discussed them, we all decided that none of the applicants was the right candidate for us. So, back to the drawing board. We kept fishing for the person God wanted as my partner in leading the ministry.

We recruited candidates nationally for managing director, and we had some promising applicants from California, Indiana, and Michigan. We ended up bringing two of them into town for interviews and doing a third interview via Skype. We also had a couple of new local candidates to interview. Another part of the interview process was asking the applicants to come and spend some time at the Phoenix during open hours and to take a ride with Tony and see our transitional houses. We wanted them to meet and interact with our other staff and to experience the environment at the Phoenix and see how they might fit or not fit. With fifty applicants and more than a dozen interviews, the whole process took a tremendous amount of both time and energy. Yet we learned so much from this five-month process, both about the interview process itself, and through the life stories of so many interesting applicants.

After ranking the third round of interviews, as well as lots and lots of prayer, we finally found our managing director, Rob Dalhaus III, on August 9. And he was right here in our own back yard, working for Community Elements/Rosecrance in three different roles, his last being the director for the TIMES Center men's shelter and transitional housing. I'm not sure who was more excited, us or him. While he was not yet thirty years old, for the record, he did already have a bit of gray hair, so I was ok with hiring him. He had to give a long notice to his employer and had a vacation that was already planned, so he was not able to start with us until Monday, September 19. That five-week waiting period was grueling, as we had hoped to have our new managing director on the field with us by the end of the summer, before school started. Rob couldn't get here fast enough!

There had been some changes happening that spring and summer regarding the services available for those without an address in our community. The TIMES Center announced it was eliminating its last transitional shelter beds in June, the only shelter beds remaining in our community, as The Salvation Army had closed their transitional shelter program in March. One year earlier, there had been ninety-five transitional shelter beds for men in our community. Now, there would be zero. Both programs were more than a quarter million dollars in debt, due to issues with the State of Illinois budget and to changes in federal funding for transitional housing and shelter. What a travesty!

When Mike and I met for lunch the day after hearing the news about the TIMES Center, I told him about the last shelter beds going away and he said, "So, what are we going to do about it?" I suggested that since we were going to have a large screening of our documentary at the Carle Forum on June 21, we could focus the public discussion time on the need for shelter beds in our community.

The documentary continued to impact our community throughout 2016. That first showing welcomed more than 125 stakeholders and other community members in attendance to The Forum, a large auditorium on the campus of Carle Foundation Hospital in Urbana. After the film, a panel of experts led a discussion on the development of new shelter beds in our community. It was a good dialogue and the beginning of three public community forums focused on developing shelter. We were grateful for the platform and for the encouragement we received. That was the beginning of a long and arduous public campaign led by the Council of Service Providers to the Homeless to re-establish emergency shelter beds, at least for the winter.

On Monday, we hosted Illinois State Senator Scott Bennett and his assistant Michelle Gonzales at the Phoenix where we shared about our drop-in center, gave them a tour, and introduced them to our staff. After that, we took them in our ministry van to tour each of our transitional houses and told them more about our ministry. It was our hope that this would open Senator Bennett's eyes more to the plight of our friends without an address and hopefully gain his future support for our ministry.

At the July meeting of the Council of Service Providers to the Homeless, we discussed shelter needs and formed a shelter development team as a subgroup of the CSPH, another positive step towards getting shelter beds in place for the winter.

A few days later, God brought me just what I needed. I journaled, "What a GREAT day! Got to meet two University of Illinois students, Luke and Grant, who are starting a new homeless ministry on campus called 'The Dollar Club.' Then we got to host our documentary, *The Phoenix: Hope Is Rising*, at my home church. And at the screening, I got to meet a nice couple, Kobert and Trenda from Springfield, who were doing lots to help their friends without an address there and were hoping to do more. I got to bring them back and show them around the Phoenix and pray with them. What a privilege! Thank you, Jesus, for bringing me this encouragement at a time when it's most needed. I am excited to be leading C-U at Home and all that God is doing through our ministry."

It was time for my annual respite at AudioFeed. This year was very, very special for two reasons. One, The Asylum agreed to host our C-U at Home documentary and discussion during the festival. What a privilege to share about our ministry and about my livelihood for the last five years with my Cornerstone remnant family at AudioFeed. I also had the opportunity to sing and play on one of the stages. The worship team from my church (appropriately named CORNERSTONE Fellowship) had the privilege of leading a worship set at the Anchor worship tent. What a blessing to be a part of leading others to the throne of grace with my brothers and sisters at this festival that is such an important part of who I am. "Thank you, Jesus," I prayed, "for opening these doors of opportunity for me this year."

That summer we met and talked with station manager Jeff Scott about WBGL hosting a screening tour for our documentary across their listening area. Jeff was supportive of our idea, so we brainstormed what it might look like and decided to do it the week before Thanksgiving. I would reach out to churches and theatres across the listening area to see which five cities and venues we would use, including possibly the Virginia Theatre for the Champaign screening. I left the meeting VERY excited. WBGL, where I had served in ministry for seven and a half years, was getting firmly behind C-U at Home, and I was grateful. Thank you, Jesus.

In mid-July, Phil completed a DVD version of our documentary so people could order them online or we could purchase them from Phil at a discounted price and then sell them at the Phoenix and at screenings and other events.

Our second public forum to discuss the development of emergency shelter was hosted at The Salvation Army in July, with more than seventy-five people in attendance. Some parts of the discussion were positive, while other parts were confusing, at best. The leader of one organization clearly shared bits of misinformation and several mixed messages. We did what we could to keep kicking the can down the road to advance the cause.

While facing these challenges in our community, I was in the midst of my own family challenge. On the last day of May, I received word that my brother-in-law, Steve Jackson, had been in a horrific motorcycle accident in Southern Illinois. On his way home from a Memorial Day ride with friends, a car had run off the road and overcorrected, crossing the center line and hitting two motorcycles head-on. The couple on the other motorcycle had both died, the husband on impact and the wife a short time later at the hospital. Steve had been badly injured, with internal bleeding, fractures, and other damage, so he was life-flighted to the trauma unit at St. Louis University Hospital (SLUH), where they did their best to save his life and stabilize him.

I immediately canceled appointments and hit the road for the three hour drive to St. Louis to be with my family, by Steve's side. When I finally arrived, Steve was waiting for an operating room to open up for back-to-back surgeries to repair a tear in his aorta and to stabilize his crushed pelvis. It was a miracle that he was still breathing and that his heart was pumping. The aorta repair and pelvis stabilization surgeries were both successful! Steve would remain sedated and intubated for several days. We had requested prayers through networks all over the world for Steve, and we claimed the success of these two surgeries as a major victory. Thank you, Jesus! He had casts on both legs and one arm and a hard neck collar, and he was sedated to help him heal. We gave God the glory and continued to cry out in prayer.

I was able to get back to St. Louis about ten days after the accident. That week I shared this prayer request: "Steve is scheduled for four hours of spine surgery. Please join me in prayer. Lord, You are mighty and we know that You are in total control of our comings and goings. You gave us the very breath that we breathe. We cannot thank you enough for preserving Steve's life. Please be with the surgical team today who are operating on his back. Protect his spinal cord from injury. Give him the ability to regain total mobility. We say no to any form of permanent paralysis. Steve loves You and we love Steve. Be his Daddy and his healer. Thank you, Jesus. Amen."

Each day seemed like a new battle for Steve with challenges like a high temperature, frustration with the ventilator, the finding of yet another broken bone, and a high white blood cell count. I cried out with this note to my counselor and to my mentor: "For the last few days I've been feeling various levels of discouragement on many fronts:

- my all-day Saturday visit to see Steve in the hospital;
- the disappointment of the hiring process taking longer than we had hoped, as our top contender to be my ministry partner has just dropped out of contention;
- the closing of the last shelter beds for men in our community;
- our screening last night in a venue that was 90° without AC, with less than twenty in attendance;
- my increasing desire to be in Colorado;
- my waning passion to lead CUH;
- one of our recovery house guys making a couple of very bad decisions and moving out of the house; and
- the family in our house being very close to being asked to leave.

"I am asking for your prayers. I really don't want to do this anymore and I'm not even sure why. I'm getting enough sleep and exercise. Enough sunshine and social time. Enough motorcycle riding. I'm feeling fine and eating OK. I just don't want to keep doing this. It kind of feels like I can't do anything right."

On June 14, Steve's daughter Stacy shared the following note: "FLASH UPDATE: Dad is totally off the ventilator and breathing on his own! He does not need a trach! What a huge surprise and blessing! We didn't know they were going to try this and were surprised when his doctor came and got us from the waiting room. We expected to walk in and see the trach, but he's only on oxygen! We just cried with joy. He's very hoarse, but talks a little bit. He knew his name, but thought he was at the bank. With all of these medications he's on, this is going to be very entertaining! Thank you Jesus! And thank you guys for your continued prayers! Please keep them coming, we all make a great team with God as our leader!"

Steve's ongoing recovery was slow but steady. We got a good update in mid-July. "Tonight's update: dad has been weaned off the oxygen and even flossed (with an adapter) and brushed his own teeth today! He should get the dialysis catheter out by the end of the week. He got pretty worked up and agitated this evening because he is just so sick of being in that same position in the bed and his tushy hurts. Even though they use wedges to rotate him, it's just not enough. Please pray for patience and physical comfort until they can get him into a chair. They are calling it an early night because dad finally calmed down and is working on relaxing, so we have no prayer requests or words of wisdom tonight. Hope you all have a great night!"

By the beginning of August, the news continued to be positive. "More improvement today . . . all the glory to God! Dad got to sit on the edge of the bed for about fifteen minutes while he ate lunch. Dad was also able to perform resisted hip extension! Yay for muscle function! The physical therapist was really excited! He can contract his hip extensors and adductors on both of the lower extremities, the right being stronger than the left. Still no lower leg (knee or ankle region) muscle activity yet, but we remain hopeful! Speech therapy also worked with him on his cognition, and while they will still work with him, they are happy with his improvements! One day at a time!" My brother-in-law was making progress.

On Saturday, August 6, friends put on a huge benefit dinner and auction in Centralia to help the Jackson family with their medical expenses. Both Steve and Mary Ann had been without work or income since before Memorial Day and the bills were piling up. But they were also continually seeing God's provision for Steve's health and for their finances and other areas of need. I sold raffle tickets as folks came in and Kathy, Gayla, and Callie all helped get folks registered and welcomed. We were blown away by the more than $15,000 donated through everything that happened that evening. God's provision for Steve and his family. Thank you, Jesus!

October 11 was a tear-filled, exciting day for the Jackson family. Nineteen weeks and one day after the horrific motorcycle accident, Steve was able to GO HOME! His family built a wonderful, integrated ramp onto their home and even decorated it for fall. There were lots of tears and prayers thanking the Lord for all He had done to save Steve's life, heal him, and allow him to return home.

17

Hope Keeps Rising

The documentary continued to open doors for C-U at Home. The Global Leadership Summit (GLS) sponsored by the Willow Creek Association is a powerful time of connecting with other leaders and drinking in great leadership training, one speaker after another, as if through a fire hose. In 2016, C-U at Home had a display table at the summit simulcasts in Urbana and Danville, and the documentary trailer was shown at both locations, extending an invitation to upcoming documentary film screenings in those communities.

A few weeks later, as part of our Education and Advocacy ministry, Dawn Broers, a social work instructor from Olivet Nazarene University, invited me to guest-lecture for her two classes. The next day, she had arranged for two different screenings and public discussions about our film. The first, screening #13, was at Kankakee Community College, and offered CEU's for professionals, with a panel of knowledgeable stakeholders for the discussion. The evening screening (#14) at Olivet's auditorium included Tony's participation in the ensuing discussion. It was a tiring but very rewarding two days for our ministry. Seeing stereotypes broken and hearts softened invigorates me to the core.

In anticipation of Rob's start date of September 19, I asked him to review applications for our two part-time roles of Phoenix assistant and office manager. He provided support in the vetting of our applications and the interview process to follow. What a blessing to share that responsibility!

Kelly-Jane (KJ) had approached us about the possibility of a permanent position as our Phoenix coordinator starting in the fall, since she had served in that role on an interim basis through the summer. After reviewing her resume, job performance, and other intangibles, we decided to offer her the permanent position as of August 15. It was good to have a key staff position filled with someone who was already a part of our team. What a relief!

Terry Andrews was also hired to serve as our Phoenix assistant. How special it was to have a God-called graduate of our own transitional housing program now serving as a C-U at Home staff member! He began on August 23. It was a typical busy day in the ministry that included coordinating shelter for a man and woman in Bloomington, detox for a man in Decatur, and the acceptance of a donated car. Thank you, Jesus, for your blessings for our ministry!

It was disappointing when Michelle couldn't join our staff, as we had not had any administrative help since KJ had taken over leading the Phoenix in March. After what felt like waiting forever, our staff reached full strength when Rob finally started his new position as our managing director on September 19 and Bailie Porter started as our office manager the very next day.

We had four new staff members in addition to Tony and me, all during a single month. It was almost too good to be true. I prayed that God would use this new team of six to love others with the right mix of grace and empowerment.

We continued to advocate for the development of emergency shelter, with an August meeting at the Champaign Public Library. The discussion took an interesting direction as one organizational leader spoke out of turn several times at this meeting, trying to change the focus of the conversation, causing some tense moments. The general consensus of the previous two public forums had been that we desperately needed shelter for the most vulnerable, those who were repeat customers at the emergency departments and familiar to law enforcement. Despite the bump in the road, we continued our efforts to develop a pilot men's winter emergency shelter that would be designated as "damp," providing a place to stay for those who were under the influence of drugs or alcohol, without allowing drugs or alcohol on the property.

In September, the plan for a new damp shelter was put down on paper. It would have a budget of $150,000, would offer between thirty and fifty shelter beds 365 days per year, and would operate with a full-time staff of four, including the shelter director. Costs included materials, insurance, utilities, and possible rent. We were continuing to do everything we could to get folks behind our efforts to open shelter beds, at least for the winter months.

On September 1, we had a powerful opportunity to have a lasting impact on a nearby community by sharing what we had learned in our years of operation. New friends in Danville, IL, were interested in developing a daytime drop-in center, modeled on the Phoenix. The folks at Second Church of God, who had hosted the Global Leadership Summit back in August, were hosting a screening of our documentary and public panel discussion of community leaders to follow. The screening and discussion was very well attended by a cross-section of Vermilion County stakeholders and community members, and we collected many names for their email list of people interested in developing more resources for their friends without an address. Another powerful Thursday, God at work!

I spent the next day with groups of friends from my previous church. I journaled: *"There is a time for everything, and a reason for every purpose under heaven; a time to be born, and a time to die . . . This morning I said goodbye to a dear saint, Eileen Warner, who was ninety-nine years young. Eileen was my partner in launching the USA Café ministry to international students when she was ninety-five. A few minutes later, I held the newborn Clara Rife Frericks while she slept, so aware that each of us has numbered days on this celestial ball we call earth. Will you live for Jesus today? Is Jesus worth it? God used this experience to help me with a much healthier perspective on life."*

That fall, I was blessed to put a pack on my Magna and head to the hills of North Carolina to meet nearly one hundred friends for a spiritual retreat, a weekend of camping, music, worship, fellowship, meals, campfires, and connecting with God. I had learned about this event from my musical friends, Reckless Mercy, and discovered a handful of longtime Cornerstone Festival friends there as well. I was blessed to disconnect from all things C-U at Home, to have riding time on the bike to and from the fest, and to play djembe with the worship team on Sunday morning. A highlight of my weekend was two hundred miles on the Blue Ridge Parkway, my most favorite riding road in the whole country!

After I got back from my trip, I was privileged to deliver a sermon at Faith United Methodist Church in Champaign as part of their local missions focus, integrating the story of C-U at Home with the liturgical scripture for the day, the story of the good Samaritan. I brought the same message to the pulpit of Central Christian Church in Danville two weeks later, returning to the church God had used to call me to transitional worship ministry in the spring of 2005. In the economy of God's grace, I was able to recycle, revamp, and share the same message with my own church family the following Sunday at Cornerstone Fellowship. Thank you, Jesus!

Ministry is not for the faint of heart, and at times, I felt like the walls were crushing in on me. I shared with my counselor: "I've not been doing well at all and hope that you can help me. Here's what's on my mind, not in any particular order.

"Emergency shelter: I have such a mix of emotions and thoughts about this. Too much to type. It ranges from completely walking away from the issue to CUH taking on both male and female shelter for both dry and damp guests. A new friend who has been helping with our shelter development efforts talked through things with me and suggested that I need to let it go, other than developing emergency shelter for six to eight women with Sister Karen. Or to use our current location for emergency shelter for twelve to fifteen men. I have NO IDEA what it would take for our property to be approved by the city for overnight shelter.

"Miscommunication: There have been probably a dozen things happen in the last few days at work that point to miscommunication. It's been very frustrating. It's like none of our employees know what I mean and what I want.

"Physical Health: Ten pounds more than I want to weigh or have ever weighed before, pretty much for the last year. No summer softball. Not much physical activity at all except for the lap swimming. I do NOT want to stay at this weight or gain more weight. Also, starting yesterday I had a new physical symptom that is very weird. It feels like an internal buzz, much like a cell phone vibration, in the middle of the bottom of my left heel. Did some online research and it could be some kind of neuropathy attributed to stress. Goes for two or three seconds, off for a few seconds and then on again. I wonder if this is a random way that my body is responding to stress.

"Housing: Last week the folks I stay with told me their timeline so that I could plan ahead. They asked that I plan to move out by mid-April of 2017, at the latest. They will likely be putting this house on the market. I think this news hit me harder than I realize. The plan that I've had in my head and my heart is that I would stay here, living with them, until it's time for me to move to Colorado Springs. Now I don't know what to think. I cringe at the thought of moving all my stuff into some apartment to rent here in Champaign. I DO NOT want to feel trapped here!

"Relationships: Several are strained right now. Especially at work. Partly because of the miscommunication. And partly because right now I really do not want to be there anymore.

"Colorado: I find myself thinking more and more about being there. About the mountains. About being able to breathe much better. About having a 'normal' job. About no longer being a supervisor of people. About no longer working with the homeless, addicted, and mentally ill. About hiking, biking, motorcycling, about finding a new church and being a part of the worship team, about skiing and snowmobiling and learning to snowboard. About watching people train at the Olympic training center. Starting over. It's weird because I look around me and I literally have every material thing I could want right now. A car and a motorcycle running well, and I really like both of them. A top-notch laptop. A great home to live in with people who care about me. A job where I am my own boss and create my own flexible schedule. Part of a worship team at a small growing church that I really like. Even more money in the bank and a higher salary than I have ever earned.

"Whatever I do, I want to have a kingdom purpose to my life. I want to be in full-time ministry, but that could be Christian radio or worship ministry at a church or lots of other things. Why am I so restless and unhappy? I really do not want to be leading a homeless ministry anymore. Everything in me wants to get through the documentary screenings, put everything I have into a big OWN 2017, and start looking for a job and a place to live in Colorado Springs in April of 2017. But I will not go unless I believe God has released me from this appointment. Tomorrow I'm taking a day off the grid completely—no phone, computer, or TV. In the evening, I'm hoping to get with my good friend John and work on my bike – oil change and new rear tire."

Life continued to be intense. At the end of the month, I wrote: "Well, sometimes when it rains, it pours. Even when it's good stuff happening. On Wednesday night, I sent out one prayer request to our prayer email list, for emergency shelter for this winter. And on Thursday morning, God started working through several meetings, calls and emails. And by the time we got to Friday afternoon, we now have a plan for a three-month winter emergency shelter. Still lots to organize and determine, but the basic plan is in place and I am SO grateful!" That evening I started to make a simple list of all the things I was trying to juggle over the next few weeks/months; several things demanding undivided attention.

"Stuff to do:

- OWN 2017 with a $200k goal
- three-month pilot plan for men's winter emergency shelter
- our week-long BGL documentary tour in two weeks
- women's shelter development with the sisters and maybe Teen Challenge
- statement of faith and becoming a religious c3
- Decatur Agape House development
- upcoming emergency warming extended hours at the Phoenix (fourteen hour days)
- new place to live for myself by mid-April at the latest
- training and developing our new staff.

"Mixed in with quite a few other speaking, preaching, and other special events in the next four weeks, I pray to keep my focus on the Lord and rely on His strength to get me through. Also, that I will be able to prioritize and be efficient and focused on each of these, as needed."

18

A Tour, a Van, and a Shelter

As the end of 2016 approached, our Education and Advocacy focus was quite active in the community. Our ministry was invited to the All-Campus Worship event at the University of Illinois, sponsored by the Evangelical Christian Union to talk about what we do and how students can get involved. They even gave us the love offering received that evening.

I was blessed to be asked to preach at First Presbyterian Church in Danville on a Saturday night and Sunday morning, again using the good Samaritan scripture passage. I also shared about their own community's interest in developing a drop-in center there, modeled after the Phoenix. That Sunday evening, we had a documentary screening at Wesley United Methodist Church on campus.

The next night was the start of the WBGL Screening Tour for *The Phoenix: Hope Is Rising,* with five consecutive evenings of film and discussion, four across the state of Illinois and one in Indiana. The first three nights of the tour included the Stone Creek Church Campus in Rantoul, IL; the Family Worship Center in Mattoon, IL; and the Calumet Street Christian Church in my hometown of Centralia, IL (complete with a mandatory visit to the Burger Haven). I was so glad that my brother Mike could be there to see what God had been doing in my life for the last five years, and Mary Ann was able to get Steve in the car and to the church. I shed tears as I saw him again, for the first time since the hospital in St. Louis. Thank you, Jehovah Rapha, our Healer!

Thursday was our longest trip, as Tony and I hit the road early to get to the Chicago suburb of Wheaton in time to get everything set up for the screening. This screening had a strange vibe from the moment we walked in the door. It was in a wealthy, white Chicago suburb in a large church auditorium. Only a handful of people showed up for the film and there was an eerie silence in the room before it began. Those in attendance weren't talking to one another, not even people who had come together. Our film did not play correctly; for some reason, the audio and the video were out of synch, distracting viewers the entire length of the film. During the discussion panel, one ministry representative was quite forceful in his insistence that people accept Christ as Savior at the front door of their ministry before receiving services. Tony did a great job of diffusing the tension in the air, as some believers were embarrassed for the man and others were put off by him. We got everything packed up for the long journey home and arrived just after midnight. We had known this was going to be draining, both physically and emotionally, but we weren't quite prepared for the sense of spiritual confusion we felt that night.

We ended the week at the Next Step Recovery ministry in Terre Haute, IN. Rob and I rode over together, comforted by a visit to Chick-fil-A for dinner. Tony and Terry drove separately and stopped at a couple of recovery ministries there before the screening. As we arrived, the rain began, buckets and cats and dogs and everything! We sat in the car until it eased up, and as soon as we walked in, we were home. The room looked a lot like the Phoenix. They had been using it as a coffee shop, with little tables and chairs and artwork all around the room. Dana and Ron gave us a tour of their whole facility, and we were glad to share notes and encourage each other. The screening and panel discussion were filled with energy and excitement for what could be done for folks there in Terre Haute. Dana shared that they were praying about converting the space we were sitting in from a coffeehouse into a drop-in center. What a great and meaningful experience to end our WBGL Screening Tour.

Sunday morning, I presented for a few minutes at New Covenant Fellowship in Champaign about our needs for C-U at Home. They would be having a discussion that afternoon about the possibility of their church becoming the single location for a men's emergency winter shelter. The speaking engagements continued the next day at the Champaign Rotary. My main topic was the need for the development of emergency shelter beds, and I also got to talk a bit about C-U at Home. We were hopeful that this and several other Rotaries would donate significantly to help with the cost of the winter shelter. That was the tenth public speaking event in ten days for me. I remember going home that Monday afternoon in somewhat of a comatose state. Nap time for me!

Thursday was Thanksgiving, a break in my schedule that brought the usual trip downstate to have the lunch meal with the Jackson family, the early evening meal with my cousins, the Rollinsons, and the late evening meal with the family of my best friend from high school, the Reynolds. The lunch in Mt. Vernon with the Jackson family was really something special, since we were able to have Steve and Mary Ann at the table with us. We had so much to be thankful for. At dinner, I learned that they were still borrowing their daughter Stacy's compact car because both of their vehicles were too tall for Steve to get into and out of. Mary Ann mentioned what a blessing it would be for them to have a wheelchair van. The Lord pricked my heart and triggered my desire to help. That night, I began searching craigslist in a three-state area for wheelchair vans. I decided to reach out to every single one of them, sharing Steve's story and asking if they would consider donating a van to help him. The other option would be to ask for a greatly reduced price and then look for folks to donate money towards the cost of a van.

I sent many emails and texts to the owners of wheelchair accessible vans within a five-hundred-mile radius over several days. After a rough day in December, filled with staff misunderstandings, bad news on the shelter front, and controversy at the Phoenix, I received a phone call and was vulgarly cussed out and accused of being a scammer for asking a van owner about donating the van to Steve. My heart hurt from his accusation; I went down to my bedroom, buried my head in my pillow, and spent some time crying. All I was trying to do was help a loved one get the transportation he needed to go to therapy and to the doctor. Some people are downright mean!

A couple of people with wheelchair vans were hopeful possibilities, but both fell through, though I didn't let that slow me down. On December 14, I was in contact with the owner of a van in Chicagoland who was working with Lutheran Church Charities to find someone in need of the lift van. Five days later, he confirmed that his family would donate the van to the Jackson family at no charge! I was on cloud nine, calling Steve's brother Greg and swearing him to secrecy. It was a beautiful 1999 Chevy Econoline Van with chair lift and electric controlled driver's seat that could eventually be used with driver controls so that Steve could drive again. My hope was to be able to pick it up on or before Christmas day and deliver it as a very special Christmas gift for the family.

In the end, Scott and I picked up the donated van on December 29, a Thursday, an exhausting yet very rewarding day. We arrived in Chicago mid-morning, but it took a while to get everything squared away before we got back on the road with it.

The donor had to keep the seatbelts that anchored the wheelchair for his new van, and I was concerned about how Steve could use it right away. Googling "wheelchair anchor straps for van" and the brand name during a pit stop for gas, I located a place that had them in Champaign, and that was right on the way downstate to Centralia. When I arrived, it took some time and some finagling, but they got a set of straps to work and only charged me only a small amount. What a blessing! Then it was back south on I-57 to Steve and Mary Ann's house. Sister Karen followed me in her car so that she could give me a ride back to Champaign. I was disappointed that we were not able to get there before sunset, as I really wanted them to be able to see the van in the daylight. Greg called the rest of the family out of the house under a ruse, and we totally pulled off the surprise.

When Steve and Mary Ann saw the van, they were both absolutely blown away, glad for the improved mobility and additional options. Stacy could have her car back, and it would be much easier for Steve to get to his physical therapy, doctor, and other ordinary activities. Lots of tears of joy were shed that night, and although I was completely exhausted from all that driving and from the emotions at the house, it helped to get me out of my funk. I was so grateful for God's provision for Steve on a Thursday. Thank you, Jesus!

Stacy wrote the next day: "Yesterday was a pretty amazing day! I went to therapy and the pain management appointment with mom and dad. Most of the time when mom and dad get out of the house, they can only make about two-three stops before they are exhausted from getting dad in and out of the car and have to go back home. For the past two and a half months they have been using my car for transportation because mom's truck is too tall, and so is the SUV Dad got right before his accident. Every day they have talked about how they need to go look at wheelchair accessible vans, but they knew how expensive they would be. Little did we know that Melany would surprise them with exactly what they needed! Since Thanksgiving, she has searched craigslist in three different states for vans. Who knows how many emails she sent out to those van owners telling them of dad's journey and asking if they'd be willing to donate their van. One incredible man and his family responded with their blessing in the form of a FREE wheelchair accessible van! Once dad is ready to drive sometime in the future, they will just need to purchase and install the hand controls. The owner of the van was a man who was in a motorcycle accident in 2003. He even recorded a sweet video message to dad. So Miss Melany and her friend drove up to Chicago to pick it up and drove all the way down to Centralia to surprise mom and dad! Wish you all could have been there . . . lots of smiles and tears! God works in wondrous ways!"

It was a long time between Memorial Day and Christmas, but I was glad that Steve was on a healing path. In the meantime, in the midst of my search for a van, C-U at Home's work had continued. I spent Cyber-Monday sending email invitations to all our previous box dwellers. Once again, I was quite late getting these out, as they should have been sent in September. It seemed like every year I got behind the eight-ball with One Winter Night invitations. But the Lord is gracious, and He has blessed our ministry in spite of my shortcomings.

That December, we had many days of emergency warming, bringing fourteen hour days and the need for extra friends from the community to help keep our doors open morning, noon, and night. Necessary as they were, they also put an extra burden on our small staff. Through the media coverage about the cold temps, we were able to continue to get the word out about the need for emergency winter shelter and to ask for donations to support the desperately needed shelter beds.

Also that December, I made an important decision. After prayerful consideration, I submitted my written resignation as the chairperson for the Council of Service Providers to the Homeless on December 12, 2016. I had served in that volunteer capacity since April of 2011, and God had used that platform to advance the cause of assisting our friends without an address, raising awareness in the community to educate and advocate on their behalf. I had been through many ups and downs, not the least of which was this six-month long campaign to develop emergency shelter. It was time for me to step away and allow someone else to lead.

I had been feeling the weight of securing a location for the shelter, as well as gathering enough donations, hiring staff, establishing policies, and getting the cots or mats, in addition to the guilt of getting such a late start once again on One Winter Night. Something had to give. Yet it proved difficult to pull away from leadership of the emergency shelter development team, even though I knew it was the right decision, because people kept asking me questions and expecting me to have the answers. I had been the voice of the effort since that first meeting at the Carle Forum in June, but now it was up to Bev (from United Way), Pastor Sheryl, and the rest of the team to get everything finalized and the shelter up and running.

On December 16, our first ever staff and board Christmas party brought an evening of well-deserved respite for our crew. Bailie and KJ planned all the delicious food we enjoyed in a lovely space at Meadowbrook Church, which was already nicely decorated for Christmas. All of our staff and board and most of their spouses and significant others were able to take part in the low key gathering with no agenda. We kept each other entertained with conversation and fellowship on a night of freezing rain. Doors and windshields were frozen over when we got out, but our hearts were warmed and our bellies were full. Thankfully, everyone made it home safely.

On December 22, everything caught up with me again. I journaled: "I feel kind of like I'm spiraling downward. Discouragement about the shelter situation. January is now ten days away and there still is no clear location solution. God touched my heart through that conversation in the car with Mike to start this effort more than six months ago, and now I'm trying to pull out and let others handle it. In many ways, I'm between a rock and a hard place. Things with one of our new staff members have continued to be difficult. We had to realign responsibilities, and things still aren't getting any better."

The six weeks leading up to OWN are always the most stressful time of the year for me. I journaled, "In the past, it has been exciting and stressful combined, but there isn't much of the excitement part in preparing for 2017. I am really struggling with even wanting to do this event again. With wanting to do CUH anymore. With wanting to be in Colorado and not here. I have no joy. I feel like the situation with our new employee is a lose-lose situation. My old controlling and demanding tendencies are alive and well again and I'm not even aware of it. I do NOT want to hurt any more co-workers or employees or volunteers because of this. I don't feel like my heart is in it anymore, just wearing a mask and going through the motions. I can't help but think maybe it's best if I step away from C-U at Home right now rather than later. There is a solid team of four people leading things now, plus Bailie, and a steady board of directors, especially with Mike at the helm. I really hoped to go out on top, and that's now. I don't want to hang on too long and make things worse again, especially relating to the work environment."

I was unable to arrange to see either Tony or Don and I really needed some help, so I asked to pray with my pastor, Seth, the next afternoon. It helped on one level, just to get everything out to another human being, one who happens to care about me. But I was still quite discouraged and unsure how to proceed with the challenges in our staff, with the shelter situation, and with C-U at Home in general.

Christmas Eve was spent with my adopted family, the Kauffmans, spending time with the kids and glad for a good meal, the Christmas story read from Luke 2, and presents to unwrap. I was trying to find joy, but it really wasn't there for me. On Christmas Day, my church did not have any services, so I stayed at home in my pj's, napped, and exchanged a few presents with the Hardens. Very low key. I actually spent part of the day online looking at housing in Colorado Springs, dreaming . . .

The next day, I wrote: "Had a nice day yesterday here at home with the Hardens. Kept my phone off the entire day. Today and tomorrow trying to work from home. I'm fighting what feels a lot like apathy. I just want OWN to be over and Rob to be set to lead CUH. I really do not want to be here anymore. Not sure if my energy or passion will be coming back any time soon. Went by myself to see the new Will Smith film this evening, 'Collateral Beauty.' Good film. But I don't think it helped how I am feeling. Planned my Colorado vacation for after OWN today. Been thinking about saying goodbye to certain people and how they will react when I tell them I am moving, that is, if God gives me the green light to move next year. Also been thinking about loneliness and being alone."

My New Year's Eve tradition always involves hanging out with friends from my old church. This year I invited Sister Karen to be my "date." We enjoyed a prime rib buffet dinner at Silver Creek, followed by a visit to the Kessels' new home in Mahomet for games, lava cake, and fake champagne at midnight. It was very nice to just relax and spend time with friends.

After lots of high hopes and crushing disappointments, the Men's Pilot Winter Emergency Shelter was set to open a few days into the new year, on Friday, January 6. The shelter would be at First Presbyterian Church in downtown Champaign on weeknights and at Faith United Methodist Church on the weekends, staffed by two paid employees each night, open to their guests for nine hours each evening. They had bed space for up to thirty men each night. I was so grateful that God finally made a way for this to happen in our community!

As I reflected on C-U at Home through the year 2016, I thought of it as the year of hiring and training staff. We had four new employee hires during the year. For the second year in a row, I had written the development of an employment program into our budget, and for the second year in a row, I had to give up the idea of developing that new employment program. But I did have the privilege, through the CSPH, of leading the charge to develop new emergency shelter beds in our community. I hoped that eventually C-U at Home would have that damp shelter for men under its ministry umbrella.

19

Peace for My Heart

By the beginning of January, recruitment for One Winter Night 2017 was in full swing, with commitments for seventy-five box stations, halfway to our goal of 150. Camp WBGL was starting to develop, as they were on track to double their seventeen box dwellers from 2016.

During the months of January and February, C-U at Home was the mission focus organization for Windsor Road Christian Church. Bailie handled all our professional display designs and I got to share from the pulpit one Sunday each month – about CUH, OWN, emergency shelter, and the documentary screening that the church was hosting.

On Sunday, January 15, our team of six split in half between the girls and the guys: with KJ, Bailie, and me at Windsor Road, and Rob, Tony, and Terry at First Christian. I had pre-recorded a video to play at the First Christian services much like the "I am second" interviews that had become popular, in which famous believers share their stories about being second to Christ. I was simultaneously on the screen at First Christian sharing and live at Windsor Road, with staff at our information tables at both locations, signing up several new box dwellers.

The weather was really crazy that year, alternating between extremely cold days and a few really warm days all throughout December, January and February. On January 21, just thirteen days before One Winter Night, it was sunny, with temps in the 60s. So, I got a Casey's pizza and headed to Crystal Lake Park for a picnic lunch. Then I got my motorcycle off the trickle charger and took it out for a ride. We had no idea what the weather would be like for OWN, but I was determined to enjoy the mid-January spring day.

Every day brought a new list of OWN tasks to complete, and as usual many of them revolved around email – recruiting new box dwellers, giving current box dwellers their weekly reports, recruiting business sponsors, recruiting event volunteers, and more correspondence. I have a love/hate relationship with the administrative details behind such a huge community event with so many moving parts. Administration is one of my primary gifts and I love the behind-the-scenes tasks that go into a successful event. But the time comes when it can feel overwhelming, and generally that happened for me at least two or three times each year in preparation for OWN. Maybe this happens to everyone who plans big events, I don't know. But there was always some type of encouragement or a good night's rest that got me back on track. And for that, I'm grateful.

One week before One Winter Night, on Friday, January 27, Jenny Eisenmenger asked if we had ever done anything for the kids during OWN. So we took a few minutes to brainstorm, and the OWN Children's Corner idea was born. Jenny offered to organize and lead it with her friends and family, so we could have a special area where kids could play games, do activities and hear stories to help them learn more about our friends without an address.

Camp WBGL took on a life of its own, and by February 3, they had forty-four box stations consisting of sixty-seven box dwellers signed up. We had told them that if they recruited at least fifty-one box dwellers, they could have the primo location in front of the city building, with heated sidewalks (can you believe that!). They met and surpassed that challenge. So many folks from all over Illinois and Indiana sacrificing one night of comfort to come and experience life outside in a cardboard box and, on top of that, to raise at least $1,000 each for our ministry. Wow!

Friday, February 3, began with a good all-staff breakfast at Merry Ann's Diner in downtown Champaign, as we prepared for our adventure together, and reading *The News-Gazette* with a photo and story about OWN at the top of A-1 that morning. Their profile story was on Scott Swann, a retired Champaign police officer who was participating in OWN in honor of his fallen officer friend, Michael Swaney.

This year, something was different for me. Around 5:30pm, thirty minutes before the event would officially begin, I got this strange yet fulfilling sensation that I was not needed. Literally every area had leadership and volunteers ready to make things happen. Everything was in motion, and it was a beautiful thing. This gave me peace in my heart that OWN would not suffer from my absence in the future, as there were enough people invested who had been through the event multiple times that they would do just great without me. I was so grateful for this sense of affirmation, hopeful that my move to Colorado would be possible later in the year.

Kelly-Jane had the great idea to have one massive joint prayer sometime during the event, perhaps praying from the top of one of the buildings with a bullhorn, but our boxes were covering too many blocks for that to work. Prayer from a helicopter would be too expensive and noisy. So instead, we asked Papa G to lead the prayer from our stage at 8pm, using Facebook live so that everyone with a phone or digital device could log in and join in the prayer as we dedicated the evening to the Lord, thanking Him for all He was doing in our hearts through One Winter Night. It was all for His glory!

Our goal was to have at least one hundred fundraising box stations and at least two hundred human box dwellers. We ended up with 153 box stations and at least 247 box dwellers, including at least eighteen children, who slept outside in a cardboard box on behalf of our ministry – and three hundred volunteers.

Financially, we started the night at $142,638, on the way to hopefully at least $200,000 net from the event. When we closed down the donation processing team around 3:30am, our new total was $195,638. We were ALMOST there! Each year we keep the accounting books open for two weeks following the event to give folks time to get their donations in. I was sure that God would provide and we would meet our goal.

Rob's wife, Jess, was nine months pregnant and several days overdue at One Winter Night. Rob wanted so very much to have the experience as a box dweller and be there for the whole event, and it turned out his baby girl was quite cooperative. His wife was even able to come by One Winter Night for awhile with her family. Early that morning, as Rob was trying to get just a bit of sleep before the breakfast, hosted by The Daily Bread Soup kitchen at 6am, Jess called. She asked how he was doing and when he told her he was good but very tired, she told him he that wasn't going to be getting sleep any time soon—the baby was on its way!

Jess arrived at hospital around 6:30am and their healthy baby was born at 7:30am. We teased Rob that they should name the baby Owen if it was a boy, since it had turned out to be an OWN baby. Instead, they were blessed with a beautiful baby girl and named her

Bridget Lauren Dalhaus. I was able to get some sleep that Saturday afternoon and then go to the hospital to see and hold her that evening. What a blessing!

That day, we once again had a photo and blurb about OWN on A-1, above the fold in *The News-Gazette*, symbolic of the tremendous community support behind C-U at Home One Winter Night. Our ministry would simply not be in existence without funding and volunteer support from Champaign-Urbana. We were so grateful for the Lord's provision in this tangible, experiential, educational manner.

At our February board meeting, we gave a powerful summary of One Winter Night. When we closed the books on OWN 2017, we had received more than 2,300 donations from almost 2,000 different donors. Our goal was to raise at least $200,000 during OWN 2017, and God allowed us to raise a total of $229,614. Praise the Lord! The expenses for One Winter Night were about $7,000, leaving us a net amount raised of approximately $222,000. Since the budget for C-U at Home for 2017 was around $325,000, One Winter Night once again had raised approximately two-thirds of our annual budget. To God be the glory!!!

While Rob was on paternity leave for a couple of weeks, Bailie and I had planned staff supervision time. As the snow, which we both loved, fell all around us, we decided to spend our time sledding on the hill at Orchard Downs, giving us a chance to connect and have some fun away from the office.

The men's shelter was up and running and we were so grateful, but with it came some challenges. The person hired to lead the shelter had a strong military background, and a rather black-and-white way of looking at life. His way of relating to others was not very compatible with the most vulnerable street homeless population, who needed to be met with grace and patience. Night after night there were unfortunate situations between shelter staff and the shelter guests. C-U at Home has had a no-ban policy since day one, but the shelter began to ban various men from their property. In contrast, we advocated for tolerance and a willingness to give second chances and third and fourth and fifth chances, in providing simple shelter space, a mat on the floor, for the most vulnerable men with no place to go.

Tensions between the shelter staff and our Phoenix staff rose all throughout the months of January and February, as this important community resource seemed to be moving away from grace. If we had been able to operate the shelter through C-U at Home, it would have been managed differently. Hopefully in the next few years, C-U at Home will have the building and staff to be able to open a men's damp shelter 365 days a year. Until then, we will be praying for a more grace-centered environment each winter for the groups willing to offer the shelter space to our friends without an address.

On the home front, I got an email at the beginning of February from the family I was living with that brought me huge relief. Earlier, they had asked me to move out by mid-April prior to their own move. This email indicated a change of plans for them. Scott said they were not likely to be moving in 2017, and if I still wanted to, I could stay with them until I moved to Colorado, hopefully sometime later in 2017. What a relief! I had arranged an alternative housing plan for the summer if necessary, but this would be so much easier. For the last year, I had felt I would be moving straight from their house to Colorado, with no other points in between. I was so grateful to have this concern off my plate and out of my thoughts. More powerful provision from our Lord.

Ready for a break from the work of the last month, I made my last check of the ten-day forecast for Kansas City, Colorado Springs, and Copper Mountain. I hit the road for my vacation, looking forward to seeing friends on both weekends in the Kansas City metro area, including a weekend with my Wellington, MO, church family. I was especially looking forward to spending my time during the week in Colorado with my heart and ears turned toward the Lord.

I left for Colorado with a mind to moving there sometime in 2017. I was going with a green light in my heart about moving and a desire to spend time with the Lord and have Him clearly stop me if it was not yet His timing for me to leave CUH. Don Follis and his wife Jennifer were my biggest cheerleaders to make this move, to go for it. But I was determined NOT to go unless the Lord made it clear that He was releasing me from C-U at Home and opening the door for me to move. I had tried to move to Colorado in 2005 and again in 2009, but God had closed the door both times. But now, I really felt my time at C-U at Home was drawing to a close and that Rob was the man God was calling to lead it into the future.

As I approached Kansas City, I realized I had enough time before my dinner appointment to run by and catch up a few minutes with my friend Chris Lancaster. He and his wife had been so supportive of me and our ministry over the years, and I wanted him to have his own copy of our documentary. As I shared my dream of Colorado with him, he became excited for me and said to just let him know where to start sending a check to in Colorado because he had confidence that God was preparing to do great things through me there. What an encouragement!

It's a long drive from Kansas City to Colorado Springs, so I didn't arrive at the Stones' apartment until after 9pm on Saturday night. Rebecca was home with their young Judah cub and Evan was gone, leading their church's junior high retreat that weekend. It was great to finally get to see their little Judah in person, as I had been watching his first few months of life on Facebook. I was quite excited to once again be in the Springs and to be on the cusp of hearing from the Lord about His direction for my life at this point.

The next day, I prepared for worship at Mountain Springs Church, where Evan serves at the student pastor. Since Rebecca and Judah were not able to go with me, I went to church solo. Evan had sent a note to several of the church staff that I would be there that morning, and to introduce themselves to me. He told them that I might be moving to the Springs and was seeking the Lord's direction.

The surroundings were peaceful, and the music and worship powerful that morning. People were really engaged and singing out loud, which is something that I love, when a church truly has corporate worship through song. A man with a British accent announced the topic for the message: solitude. He explained his own type A workaholic tendencies and shared how difficult this particular spiritual discipline was for him to carry out. Now, this really had my attention.

After the service, I prayed with the pastor who had preached that morning in the meet-n-greet area. He offered to help me to seek the Lord that week in any way possible. Then Pastor Rick spent some time talking with me and said, "You know, maybe the Lord wants you to rest." I heard that with my ears and with my heart. Rest. Probably the single most difficult thing for me to do. Yep, sounds like something God would ask me to do!

That afternoon, I drove up around the mountain to Cripple Creek, where a huge ice carving festival was in full swing in the cool little mountain mining town. Incredible carving talent was on display, including a solid ice slide set up for the kids. One by one, the kids, perched on sheets of cardboard, made their way down the slide.

I spent some time on the internet looking for possible places to live, hopefully for something like my current situation, living with an empty nest couple with extra space. On Monday, I went to see an apartment in the basement of a home in NE Colorado Springs that was a possibility, but there was no stove or access to a full stove, only a small toaster oven and a two-burner hot plate. With several unrelated people living upstairs, this one was not going to be for me.

Next was a quick stop at the Christian bookstore that turned out to be absolutely huge and was very well stocked with books and music. Then lunch at my favorite, Chick-fil-A. When I pulled up at noon, the parking lot was packed, but I was game. I really wanted to satisfy my chicken and lemonade fix. Once I got inside, I saw that the restaurant was full of kids; moms and dads with school-aged kids. And then I realized school was out for President's Day. Ugh! The last thing I wanted to do was have my lunch in a room full of squirming, squealing children.

My sandwich came with pickle, contrary to my request, so I returned it to the counter. They gave me a new sandwich, but the attendant refused to take the original one back, as they would just have to throw it away. She said, "If there is any way you can use it, please keep it." I returned to my seat and looked around. Who could I give the sandwich to? There were a couple of guys sitting at a table that was at an angle to my right, with no food on their table, but they each had an open Bible in front of them. I offered them the sandwich, but one of them couldn't eat gluten and the other didn't want it. So, I looked around again and offered the sandwich to a family sitting next to me. They were finishing up their meal, but they were grateful to take the sandwich home for another meal later.

Grumpy, and facing the prospect of my now-cold waffle fries, I just wanted to eat and get out of that noisy restaurant. As the men doing their Bible study got up to leave, one of them came over to me and put out his hand for me to shake. Introducing himself, he asked my name. When I answered, "Melany," he held onto my hand and held my gaze, telling me, "You are about to go through some really big changes in your life. All kinds of things have been blocking your way and they are all being removed." I was in awe. I replied, "Thank you, I receive that." And then they left. When I tell others about this powerful prophetic encounter, I like to say that I think his name might have been Clarence.

I thought to myself, yep, sounds just like God to bring someone to prophesy to me right in the middle of a Chick-fil-A. He had my full attention once again. Could this encounter mean what I thought it meant? I quietly prayed for a fleece, that God would do something else to let me know if this was indeed His green light for me to move to Colorado.

From the restaurant, I headed southwest to the Cheyenne Mountain Zoo to spend the beautiful afternoon hanging out with all the neat animals. There was an old ski lift just inside the gate and you could ride it up to a platform and have a beautiful view of the foothills, Colorado Springs, and beyond. So, I did that first. There was a bit of a line, and then I got a lift seat alone and rode to the observation area at the top. A couple of yurts were set up there, displaying some Colorado historical displays, but I wasn't really interested. I took in the nice view from the platform for a few moments and then got in the line to go back down.

About halfway down the lift, I saw something remarkable. A feather. But not just any feather. It was about twelve-fifteen feet long, on the roof of one of the buildings, a perfect off-white feather sculpture that looked incredibly real. God opened the floodgates, and out came the tears. Thank you, Jesus! Now I knew that I knew that I knew He was speaking to me. I was finally going to live out my dream of being in Colorado Springs. I was so grateful. I enjoyed the afternoon at the zoo and could relax the rest of the week, knowing that God had already made Himself clear to me. I had my green light for the move.

On Tuesday, Evan gave me the full tour of the church, including their food pantry and hydroponics greenhouse. It was a very cool setup where they were growing lettuce and then were able to get it to folks who needed it through their food pantry; both were right there on the church property. There at Mountain Springs, I also met with Natalie Schauer, their new hospitality and connect coordinator. I shared about God's clear direction for me to move to the Springs in September, telling her all about my housing and vehicle needs. She was very encouraging and said she would get word out far and wide and do what she could to help me find both a place to live and the right vehicle for the right price. What a blessing!

A weekday visit to the Garden of the Gods brought me to a remote location, a rock on a cliff, as God provided just the right spot. I only saw three humans from afar and no cars the entire two and a half hours unplugged. My perch had a stunning view of Pikes Peak on that beautiful, sunny, clear, 78° day – on February 21! I took off my shoes and socks and rolled up my jeans, at peace in my "happy place." I felt the peace of God, glimpsing just a snapshot of the rest He was calling me to in September, captured in the beauty of the giant red rocks and the Peak at sunset.

Checking out another housing possibility, I noticed a dozen wooden crosses on the owner's coffee table. She was carving the words "amazing grace" out of them for her church, to be sent to missionaries across the globe. Pretty neat. We sat and chatted a bit and she asked me what I was doing in Illinois and what was bringing me to Colorado. I told her about C-U at Home and she got this interesting look in her eyes. She said that she and some of her friends from church had been making sandwiches for a few weeks and taking them to folks in this one area of town where they are camped out, living on the streets. A God-incidence, for sure.

That evening, I drove to the little town of Frisco in the mountains for skiing and snowmobiling. My Garden Hills Church friend, Josh, met me and joined me on the slopes for a day, again allowing me to use his buddy pass. While there was plenty of fresh powder and low middle-of-the week numbers on the slopes, it was COLD and quite windy at the top. I still had a great day. We headed back to town and went into Breckenridge for a nice dinner together.

It was forecast to be -2° the next morning for my snowmobiling adventure on White Mountain. Brrrrrrrr! Bundled up in my long johns and layers, I headed to their base camp for excitement on the sled. There were a lot more people signed up for the two-hour ride than had been there the year before. There were at least forty sleds out on the warm-up track, all at once. It was quite crowded. I wanted to get my sled legs under me, so I kind of tested the limits with speed and lean. Too much hot dogging on my part. As I was getting ready to go between two sleds, the space closed up and I didn't brake fast enough. Crunch! I rear-ended another rider at about thirty-five mph. We were both thrown from our sleds, him to the infield and me to the track. I hit my right shoulder and my helmet on the ice, and I was scared. Scared of getting run over by another sled. Scared of my own injuries. Scared about how badly the other rider might be hurt.

The instructors shut everyone down immediately. I got up, checked out my arm and my head. I was ok. Next I turned my attention to the other rider, who was holding his lower back. That really scared me. I told him that I was so very sorry and I began praying for him. They took him back to the base shack to check him out and watch him, but he said that he still wanted to go on the ride. When the other rider and his wife came back out to get a new sled, I went over to talk with them, and they said they forgave me and that he was doing fine. It was an accident. I was so humbled. It had been totally my fault for trying to show off. One of us could have been seriously injured or even killed. How could I have been so careless, Lord? This experience humbled me and it slowed me down. It caused me to think about how fragile life really is for all of us.

The rest of the snow mobiling went well, and I had a peaceful, reflective drive back to Colorado Springs that afternoon on the remote 24 East highway. There were a couple of times when I went more than twenty minutes without seeing another vehicle or human being.

That evening I experienced the opening session of the senior high retreat for Mountain Springs, being co-led by Evan and his brother-in-law, Adam Blackman, from First Christian in Champaign. Both guys had been disciple and mentored by an incredible pastor friend of mine, Jason Epperson. It was so cool to see both young men carrying on the anointed mantle of effectively sharing the gospel.

I had really enjoyed my time in the Springs, driving around different neighborhoods and seeing where different stores and businesses were located. I tested out swimming laps at three different YMCA facilities to see which one I liked best. And I got to look at two different rooms where I could possibly live.

Though I wasn't certain about the length of time, I took "rest" to mean specifically NOT working and NOT looking for work or a ministry position, not carrying a resume, not searching online for jobs. Planning to move on September 11 gave Rob and me one entire year together to transition the leadership of C-U at Home. I decided that this "rest" would be at least through the end of October and maybe longer.

Saturday morning, it was time to say good-bye, or really just so-long, to Colorado Springs. It had snowed the day before and roads were mucked up with a dirty slush. As I glanced at Pikes Peak in the rearview mirror, I was grateful for what God was doing in my life and the knowledge that if it was His will, I would be returning in September to stay.

I had an encouraging stop on the way back across on I-70 in WaKeeney, KS. My guardian angels, Ed and Bev Hughes, met me at the restaurant for a late lunch. It was so nice to see them again and to catch up with everything happening in our lives. I hadn't said anything about a move to Colorado, but Bev asked me, "So, when are you going to get yourself on out to Colorado to stay?" Then I was able to tell them of all the ways God had spoken to me on the trip and that I would, indeed, be moving later that year to Colorado. They were so happy for me to be seeing my dreams come true. Even more affirmation for me.

I hit Kansas City around 8:30pm and knew there was only one place for me to have my late dinner, the Corner Café. A turkey manhattan and some lemonade hit the spot. Comfort food was so good after a long day of interstate driving. I made it to the Shroyers in Wellington, MO, just before 10pm. What a sight for sore eyes! It was so good to see them and stay in my room again at their home. I worshiped on Sunday with my St. Luke Church family. We had a wonderful time sharing and re-connecting, eating BBQ on the square together after church. When I had lived in Wellington, I had spent lots and lots of time walking downtown around the little town square and right down the middle of the quiet streets. It felt comfortable to be there again.

Sunday afternoon was cool and beautiful. It was almost 50° and calm, with a clear blue sky. I drove down the river road to the next little town of Napoleon. They have a park with access to the river. This is another place where I had spent a lot of time when I lived there. I felt close to God there on the bank of the Missouri, experiencing quiet, peaceful moments overlooking the river. Now God reminded me of my previous time in Wellington, a time of rest, a slow, easy life that I had desperately needed after the high stress of seminary. Once again, He affirmed this call for me to rest in the Rockies, after what had certainly been the most intense six years of my life, developing C-U at Home from scratch and leading it through all kinds of challenges and victories. Thank you, Lord, for speaking to my heart.

20

Transition Time

My trip back to Champaign was on the last Monday in February, 2017. I set up a meeting the next day with Rob and Mike to share the news with both of them in person. At this point, the only people in Champaign who knew of my plans to move were the Hardens and Don and Jennifer Follis. Mike was sick that day, so he was on a conference call with us, as Rob and I met in person at the Urbana Library. From the moment I told them I was planning to move, Rob had peace. I was watching his body language, and while he had every reason on earth to be anxious, to be afraid about what this would mean for him, instead, there was peace, for Rob and for me. Thank you, Jesus!

We had just entered into the delicate dance of who to tell in what order about the news of my move, being intentional about the public announcement, as we knew we couldn't keep it under wraps for very long. I needed to talk with Tony before the rest of the staff, so I asked if he could come to the office for a few minutes that afternoon. It was hard to tell him, and I wasn't sure that he believed me at first. Tony and I had been through so much together, the highs and the lows. It would be hard for me to say good-bye to him.

Wednesday morning at our staff meeting, I shared the news with the rest of our staff. There was a certain amount of shock, and disbelief. We didn't really take time right then to process the news, and I regret that, but we did plan a special staff time on Monday afternoon to talk things through. In retrospect, I should have taken time during our staff meeting to let them talk, cry, ask questions— whatever they needed to do. We did take time over the next few weeks to continue to talk things through, each one coming to grips with the news in their own way in their own time.

That Wednesday afternoon, I met with Mike. He said that he would get in touch with each board member with the news and ask them to keep it quiet until we made a public announcement soon. I was grateful for his willingness to do this on my behalf.

On Thursday, I met with Don Follis. He was so happy for me, and proud of me for having the courage to take this step. He helped me think through how and when to go about our public announcement of the leadership transition, and suggested an outline for a six-month transition plan with Rob.

Over the weekend, I called both of my brothers and other friends and family to let them know about my upcoming move. Saturday and Sunday also meant it was time to get back to writing. I was newly inspired now to get this story on paper before my move. I was bummed that I would not be here in Champaign with the book available to help C-U at Home, but I had to leave the publication plans up to the Lord. At the end of Sunday, I was up to ten thousand words, feeling pretty good about the progress.

On Monday evening, Susie Rapp and I headed to the nearest Chick-fil-A, in Bloomington, for a celebration dinner. This would be the year when both of our dreams would be realized, for her to welcome her new son Noah home from China and for me to finally move to Colorado Springs. We had so much fun bragging on God and all that He was doing in both of our lives.

Our whole CUH team felt uncertain about what the leadership of C-U at Home would look like in the future. Would it be Rob alone as the executive director, or Rob and another new staff person to be ED or MD or maybe a new role, such as development director or donor relations specialist? Consequently, we wanted to handle our public transition announcements with great care, giving Rob our full confidence, while not specifically naming him as the next executive director.

We needed to inform our C-U at Home case management team, our OWN volunteer leadership team, our friends from the community who spend time at the Phoenix on a regular basis, our faithful donors, the churches who support us, and local law enforcement leaders. They all received a note with the request to keep the news under wraps until we could make the announcement public on Wednesday.

I had not planned to go to the March meetings of the Continuum of Care and the Council of Service Providers to the Homeless on Tuesday. Since I had stepped away as the chair for the CSPH, I wanted to give them some space. But now I had an important announcement to share with all the other organizations that help our friends without an address, so I went to the meeting. The news was greeted by multiple friends offering their encouragement.

The previous weekend, Mike, Rob, and I had worked on our transition announcement. We followed Don's advice, presenting a united front and emphasizing the planning that had already taken place. We shared this announcement at our lunch board meeting on Wednesday to get their approval and then publicly released it later that afternoon.

"I am excited to announce that I will be moving to Colorado Springs, Colorado, in early September. Yep, pull yourself up off the floor. This is a God thing! One of the most rewarding accomplishments in my life has been following the Lord's lead in launching and growing the ministry of C-U at Home. God has done more than I could have ever imagined.

"Since the first time I set foot in Colorado Springs in 2005, it has been my heart's desire to move there. On a recent trip to the Springs, God opened that door for me. Please see the messages below from Mike and Rob. Our ministry is in EXCELLENT hands, as we grow into the future. Please pray for me and for all of us at C-U at Home during this exciting time of transition. –Melany Jackson, Executive Director."

"Melany Jackson has let the Lord use her as an instrument in drawing the CU community together to focus efforts towards our most vulnerable friends, the homeless. Her inspiration and leadership have resulted in the creation of a sustaining ministry in C-U at Home. It's a blessing and a joy for me to walk with Melany in facilitating the loving service our community now continuously provides to these friends.

"Over the next six months, I look forward to helping Mel hand the reigns over to the team we've built together. I imagine her impact on our community will not end once she relocates to lovely Colorado in September, as we will still have her prayers and her legacy. –Mike Royse, Board President."

"I was excited to follow God's call to join the ministry of C-U at Home back in September 2016. What a great encouragement to learn from Melany Jackson these last six months, culminating for me in seeing the outstanding community support for One Winter Night 2017 on February 3rd. Now I share in her excitement as she follows the call of Christ to move to Colorado this fall. I wish her a multitude of blessings as she continues to do the work of Christ wherever the Lord leads her next.

"More than ever, I am committed to this ministry, and doing all I can to carry on the vision that God gave Melany for our community. I will spend the coming months learning everything I can from Melany and making sure C-U at Home remains a strong, passionate and grace-centered ministry in the Champaign-Urbana community, as we advocate for the homeless and serve the most vulnerable. –Rob Dalhaus III, Managing Director."

This announcement was shared with our entire email list and across several platforms of social media. It also included a photo of each of us with our portion of the announcement. Once this note was released, it opened the floodgates of people emailing, calling, texting, and contacting me in person with congratulations and sadness that I would be leaving. This part of the process was very humbling.

Deb Pressey from *The News-Gazette* was one of the first callers, hoping to be the one to break the story of my upcoming move. She had been covering C-U at Home since that first year, and she wanted to ask me some questions about my upcoming move. By 6pm that night, she had a story posted online, and it ran in the newspaper the following morning. It was kind of amazing that even though the very first sentence of the article said that I would be moving to Colorado Springs in September, person after person asked me when I would be moving, and others said they were surprised to still see me, because they thought I had already moved.

One thing that a lot of folks did not realize is that I was choosing to leave C-U at Home at the top of my game. The ministry had never been in better shape; the staff was the strongest it had ever been, the board of directors was the best suited and most involved they had ever been, and we had more funds in the bank than we had ever had at any other time. Any time a founder leaves a church or ministry, there are always critics who focus on the negative. Did he have a moral failure? Did she have a mental breakdown? Were there any illegal activities? Did he walk away from his faith? Will the ministry fail when she walks away?

With a grateful heart, I can see that the Lord finally ended my season of waiting to move to Colorado at just the right time. Nothing can compare to launching a new ministry and then having God call me in a new direction when that ministry was thriving, with the very best team to keep C-U at Home not only afloat, but poised for great success in the years to come.

I am blessed to know that He was calling me specifically to a time of rest and NOT to a new position. That would come in time, but only after a period of rest and focus on the Lord, allowing Him to do a work *in* me, rather than *through* me. This would likely be one of the most difficult periods of my life, to "be," and NOT to "do."

That next Saturday evening, I had the privilege to preach again, this time with a translator. To honor The International Day of Women, the French-speaking Congolese congregation at First Presbyterian Church in Champaign had invited female leaders in the area to speak at their services the entire month of March. I wasn't sure what to talk about that would inspire Congolese women to develop their leadership potential. In general, I'm never really comfortable in situations that focus on women as leaders. I've honestly not ever thought of myself in those terms. I am a follower of Christ who is a leader, and I happen to be female. But I don't see that my gender has much of anything specifically to do with my leadership. Fortunately, the Lord led me to the story of Esther and all that she did to stand up for her people. I was grateful that my friend Kevin showed up to encourage me.

On Monday afternoon, we had a staff development time planned. It had started snowing that morning, so I came up with a different idea. What if we ditched the video training and discussion and instead spent that time as a staff on the hill enjoying the snow and sledding together? It was unanimous, so each person went home to get their boots and winter gear and head to the hill. It was so much fun! Thank you, Lord, for giving us a lovely white blanket of snow as a platform for our staff to connect, especially at this time, on the heels of my announcement about moving.

The pilot Emergency Shelter was able to move to one new location in mid-March. New Covenant Fellowship had been doing all the work needed on their downtown building to satisfy the city codes for shelter. So for the last two weeks of the season, they were able to have the shelter in one location rather than moving the bedding back and forth each week between the two locations. Plus, it gave everyone involved a snapshot of what it would look like to have the winter shelter located at New Covenant in the future.

Our staff and several of the guests continued to face challenges with the emergency shelter all the way up until its close on March 31. It was our hope that those leading the shelter would find employees who could host a grace-centered, no-ban environment for our friends without an address next year.

In March, we were blessed by a local ministry and a local business with new siding for the transitional house that we owned.

Illini Life Christian Ministry, a University of Illinois campus organization, decided to take their spring break locally and help us. Several students and staff helped with cleaning up the yard, doing some painting, and installing the new vinyl siding. They also took turns spending time with us by being friends at the Phoenix. Caleb and the guys at SK Exteriors blessed our socks off, not only with the donated vinyl siding, but also by assisting with the installation.

Rob and I began having weekly, scheduled transition time, putting together a list of things to go through – everything from passwords to selecting our new donor software to meeting several key volunteers. We scheduled a minimum of seven hours of transition time for the two of us together each week all the way through August, when my employment for C-U at Home would officially end. It was good to have this focused time for the two of us to go over as much as we could and do as much as possible together before my move.

Our first-ever board retreat took place in April, in a cabin at Lake of the Woods Park in Mahomet. It was our hope to spend time connecting with one another, building our relationships, and focusing on strategic planning for several aspects of the ministry in the months and years to come.

We invited the staff to join us for breakfast and the first ninety minutes of the retreat sharing time so that the staff and board could get to know each other better. We had a powerful, emotional time of sharing important life memories with one another. Lots of laughing and quite a few tears were shed together. The retreat was filled with many powerful brainstorming sessions and many flipchart pages filled with strategic planning notes. We spent some time focused on staffing and what staff would be needed once I was gone. The decision was made to keep all five staff members and see how they did alone, without hiring anyone else, at least through OWN 2018. That also meant Rob would become the next leader, the next executive director for C-U at Home. The board voted unanimously to offer Rob the position. He wanted some time to talk and pray with his wife about the decision, but we could all see his excitement.

Rob, Bailie, and I had a meeting with Stacey, our webmaster, about developing our new ministry website over the summer. Four new things needed to be developed that summer – a new website from the ground up, new donor software, new online donation software, and new email marketing software; a huge undertaking at any time, but even more challenging during this transition period.

A lunch meeting with my friend and author, Doug Peterson, informed me that a normal timeframe for book publication is two to three years. I really wanted to get this book finished by the end of May and have a printed copy of the book in my hands by the end of August, before my move to Colorado. He put me in contact with a woman who had started a new publishing business out of her home in, of all places, Colorado Springs! I sent her an email the next day.

In April, we had two upcoming staff reviews to do and two new job roles to develop. We met with both Kelly-Jane, our Phoenix coordinator, and with Bailie, offering her a new full-time position as communications manager. We were going to need her help with all the software changes and our new website. Finally, we met with Terry to offer him a new full-time position as our Phoenix and outreach assistant, beginning at the end of August.

Tony Comtois, our housing and outreach coordinator, had begun by doing outreach and transportation as a volunteer, long before he was ever employed by C-U at Home. After a while, we had been able to start paying him some gas money and then moved him into part-time employment. For the last two years Tony had served as a full-time, salaried employee for C-U at Home. We are so proud of everything God has done to help him turn his life completely around, a real 180.

Over the last few months, our ministry had been blessed to develop strong relationships with our local law enforcement. Our Phoenix and Street Outreach staff had the privilege of meeting the street beat officers during roll call at the following police departments: Urbana, Champaign, and University of Illinois, and also with many of the Champaign County deputies.

On April 27, Tony was given a special community service award by the Urbana Police Department for all that he had done to assist them with calls for people wanting to get to detox or to shelter. We were also pleased to have the addition of Terry Andrews to our outreach team. Terry had become Tony's right-hand man and was also willing to help officers with calls when the person needed shelter or detox.

I got a phone call from our bookkeeper, Donna, around 9:30pm on Sunday, April 30. She had been at her office for a couple of hours that afternoon, and when she came home, she discovered that her husband had died. I was really in shock. He had been in good health, but she found him slumped over in his recliner, and he had already been gone for a while. I love Donna. She had done so much to support this ministry and others over the years. I simply could not imagine how she was feeling. The sudden loss of her husband really threw me off kilter for the next two days. I couldn't write. All I could do was think on the brevity of life and the idea of carpe diem, to live every day like it is my last. I was going to be preaching that following Sunday at Central Christian in Danville, and this became the inspiration for the sermon. On May 21, I preached that same message at my church, praying that the Lord would use me as a vessel to point others to His Truth.

On the second Thursday in May, C-U at Home was blessed with an incredible day of volunteering from the members of Keller Williams Real Estate. Every year, all their affiliates across the country take one day off work to help by volunteering in their community. They call it RED (renew, energize, donate) Day. More than seventy employees, working two different shifts, helped at all three of our transitional houses, at the Phoenix, and with our vehicles. What a blessing to have so much community support from one business. And it took place on a Thursday!

Once I had shared the news about my upcoming move to Colorado, I did face one big disappointment. A University of Illinois student who had helped our ministry over the years had wanted to do his year-long School of Social Work internship with us, beginning in the fall. For him to do so, I would need to be his supervisor. Now that I was leaving, he would no longer be able to intern with us. He would have been our first ever social work intern, a fine young man who wanted to learn about developing and leading a non-profit ministry. I was sad that this was not going to happen now for him or for us.

Also in May, we made the public announcement that Rob would be the new executive director:

"We are excited to announce that beginning on August 1, 2017, Rob Dalhaus III will become the new executive director for C-U at Home.

"Mike Royse, Board President for C-U at Home: It's been such a privilege for me to be present for the unfolding of God's plan for C-U at Home. God has used Melany to create a powerful movement in our community. Then he placed Rob Dalhaus into that movement, and is leading Mel onto her long-time dream of serving the Lord in Colorado Springs. I sure look forward to what God has in mind for us next! For me, and the board team, I know we just want to keep an obedient humble heart, and be ready to serve.

"Melany Jackson, founder and Executive Director of C-U at Home: The last two months have been an emotional rollercoaster for me. As God is calling me to Colorado Springs this fall, Rob, Mike, and I are spending focused time each week on the leadership transition for C-U at Home. From the first birth pangs of C-U at Home in the winter of 2010, until this moment in time, I am so grateful for all that God has done and is doing through this ministry. And I couldn't be more pleased with the man God has brought us to continue leading C-U at Home into the future. Rob brings with him a heart of compassion and a quiet maturity beyond his years. We appreciate your prayers for each of us as we continue to work through this period of transition.

"Rob Dalhaus III, Managing Director of C-U at Home: Watching God open new doors and present us with new opportunities is a breathtaking experience but can also teach us a healthy amount of patience. I know Melany has had Colorado on her heart for quite some time and now God has opened that door! I praise her for the incredible work she has done in this community and her willingness to heed God's call on her life and head West. I can hardly put into words my appreciation for Melany, our board of directors, and this community. I welcome this new opportunity with enthusiasm and a humble heart. God has blessed me and the ministry of C-U at Home so abundantly. I ask for your prayers as we begin a new chapter and that we be obedient to the will of our Heavenly Father.

"If you have not yet had the opportunity to meet Rob in person, we invite you to contact him today to set up a time for coffee or to meet with him at our offices on Green Street. Rob can be reached at rob@cuathome.us."

This was Rob's reaction to the public announcement of his new role: "There are no words to describe how excited I am about this next step in my life! Overjoyed, ecstatic, humbled, blessed, empowered, jubilant . . . okay maybe there are some words to describe how I'm feeling!

"A special thanks goes out to Melany Jackson, Mike Royse, our entire board of directors and the community for helping C-U at Home be a blessing to those around us.

"Please continue to pray for the ministry and me as we move forward with our transition. And I will give our Father all the praise and honor and glory for what He has done and what He is going to do through the ministry of C-U at Home."

It was good to have everything be decided and out in the open. Many people brought their congratulations to both Rob and to me. We were all excited for what God had in store for C-U at Home.

On Palm Sunday, I preached on John Wesley's "worship as a means of grace" for my friend Rob Adams at the two rural United Methodist Churches he pastors. Developing the message was much more challenging than I had anticipated, as the terms "worship" and "grace" have so many nuances and layers of meaning and both are such key elements of our faith. I spent about twenty hours that week preparing the sermon. I was able to take a biblical topic, pray through it, do the research, and write a solid message to share, a delightful and empowering experience. What a blessing!

The next day, Monday, I got a video from Mary Ann Jackson that brought me literal tears of joy. They had been working with Steve a lot in physical therapy. This video showed him in a harness that looked a little bit like a cherry picker for an engine. And he was actually taking steps under his own power!!! Hallelujah! This brought us all hope that he would, indeed, eventually be able to walk again. Thank you, Jesus.

At the end of AudioFeed 2015, God had used an author, Frank Viola, to encourage me to tell this story of miraculous provision. I'm not sure what took me so long to start writing, but I did finally get a good boilerplate timeline to work from, and Sunday, July 24, 2016, was the day I began with narrative. I got about twenty pages written over the next few months and didn't pick it up again until March of 2017. Then it was finally time to start writing the chronicle of God's provision for me and for C-U at Home over the last six plus years. I had already selected the title *More Than Enough* by that point.

In early April, I had my first phone call with that publishing contact from my friend Doug about getting her help with the book. She said that she would be more than willing to help me with the book and said if I met my May 28 manuscript deadline, it would even be possible for me to have a book in my hands by the end of August, before leaving Champaign!!! How cool would that be? She wanted me to send her a small sample of what I had done so far. I sent her a sample from the book, and on April 19, she wrote, "Hi, Melany! I have just finished reading through your writing sample and I'm excited. You are a great writer and the story really draws you in. I didn't want it to end so quickly! Can't wait to read the whole thing." I continued to ask her to get me an estimate of what this would cost. She had told me about her ministry and that she started doing this to help people like me get their kingdom-focused works out to the public. She also said that she sometimes used a sliding scale for the fees.

The first Sunday in May, I spent the lovely afternoon on the back porch writing. I had made it up to 48,865 words chronicling my journey through September 2014 at that point. I was making good progress, but still had a long way to go. The next week, I finally got the first quote of what the costs might be to print this book, and I was quite disappointed. It was more than three times the amount I had been hoping for, and the quote was only for 48,000 words. The book was looking like it would be around 90,000 words. So, I found myself asking a few friends, "Would you please pray for my wisdom and discernment? Also for God's provision if He wants this book about His provision to be produced and distributed. I know that sounds rather ironic, but that's where I'm at."

In the first couple weeks of May, I started re-reading my copy of *The Dream Giver*. It was remarkable to see some of my hand-written notes in the margin from when I had first read it in April of 2004. Right at the beginning of the book, Ordinary spent most of his time thinking about his Big Dream and "how wonderful it would be to do what he loved to do instead of just dreaming about it." In the margin, I had written, "What is this for me? Is it really leading worship or is it leading/planning/organizing a ministry?" Little did I know that God had the development and leadership of C-U at Home in my future. I also made notes about God's provision, where there seems to be no possible way. It was powerful, re-reading about the process that Ordinary experienced to break through his comfort zone, journey through the wasteland, be asked by the Dream Giver to give back his dream and let it go, to finally get to the land where his dream was realized, and then, in time, to receive a new dream to pursue. "Here I am again, Lord," I prayed, "One dream realized, and You have opened the door for me to follow after You into a new dream. Thank you, Jesus. May I have the faith and strength needed to follow You."

I finished writing this book draft on May 19, 2017. The draft manuscript came in at 89,395 words on 264 pages. Even if nothing ever happens with getting this published and into people's hands, I felt a sense of great accomplishment. What a cathartic experience, once again living the highs and lows of everything that God had done in and through me and in and through the ministry of C-U at Home. I'm convinced that my procrastination in writing the book was "for such a time as this," to help me bring closure to this C-U at Home chapter in my life. And for that, I am grateful.

As of my concluding words on that date, I did not know:

- how this book would be paid for or published;
- where I would live in Colorado or how I would pay for it if it cost something; or
- what my next vocation would be in Colorado.

On the surface, all of that looks pretty crazy. But, then again, this is a book about God's miraculous provision. How ironic for me to let fear and worry overcome me at this point. He WILL provide in His way, in His time. I prayed, "I believe; Lord, help my unbelief. Grow my faith. I want to trust You for today, tomorrow, and the day after tomorrow. My life is Yours. Amen."

That same afternoon, I had something pretty cool happen. Brandon was one of our friends without an address, a real hard-core street guy. We had been friends since the very beginning of C-U at Home. Earlier, I had written about how we were prepared to house him and instead, he went to prison for a time. Our friends at the Phoenix had been talking with him about getting under a roof and he decided to take us up on it and go to a shelter in Peoria. It was a privilege to be the one to take him to the terminal downtown, purchase the Greyhound ticket, walk him to the bus, and get and give that tearful hug. As he held me tight, he said, "You take care of yourself in Colorado and don't forget about us." What had started on the street for me came right back to the street again. A fitting end to this journey of obedience called C-U at Home.

REFERENCES

Blackaby, Henry T., et al. *Experiencing God: Knowing and Doing the Will of God.* Broadman & Holman Publishers, 1990.

Capra, Frank, and James Stewart. *It's a Wonderful Life.* Liberty Films, 1946.

Cloud, Henry, *Changes that Heal: the Four Shifts that Make Everything Better... and that Anyone Can Do.* Zondervan, 1992.

Corbett, Steve, et al. *When Helping Hurts: How to Alleviate Poverty Without Hurting the Poor... and Yourself.* Moody Publishers, 2009.

Cordeiro, Wayne. "Dead Man Running." Online video clip. YouTube. Samuel Yi, 31 January 2013. 5 November 2013.

Foster, K. (2014, February 24). One Winter Night [Web log post]. Retrieved from http://insidekarenscity.blogspot.com/2014/02/

Gibson, Mel. *The Passion of the Christ.* Twentieth Century Fox, 2004.

Gioja, Phil and Isaac Musgrave. *The Phoenix: Hope Is Rising.* Independent, 2016.

Harker, Gene, and Curt Smith. *Pause Points: The Mindful Pursuit of Health and Well-Being.* WestBow Press, 2011.

Hybels, Bill, and LaVonne Neff. *Too Busy Not to Pray: Slowing Down to Be with God.* InterVarsity Press, 1998.

Lupton, Robert D. *Toxic Charity: How Churches and Charities Hurt Those They Help (and How to Reverse It)*. HarperCollins, 2011.

Miller, Donald. *Storyline 2.0: Finding Your Subplot in God's Story*. The author, 2012.

Platt, David. *Radical: Taking Back Your Faith from the American Dream*. Multnomah, 2010.

Pressey, D. (2014, January 22). Charity for homeless switching tactics. *The News-Gazette*, pp. A1, A4.

Pressey, D. (2014, March 25). C-U at Home moves forward on projects. *The News-Gazette*, pp. A1, A6.

Warren, Rick. *The Purpose Driven Life*. Zondervan, 2002.

Wilkinson, Bruce, and David Kopp. *The Prayer of Jabez: Breaking Through to the Blessed Life*. Thorndike Press, 2000.

Wilkinson, Bruce, et al. *The Dream Giver*. Multnomah Publishers, 2003.

Wright, H. Norman. *Success Over Stress*. Harvest House Publishers, 2013.

More about the book:
www.morethanenoughthebook.com

Contact the author:
melany@morethanenoughthebook.com

More about C-U at Home:
www.cuathome.us

View the Phoenix documentary:
www.thephoenixhopeisrising.com

Paperback and Kindle copies:
www.amazon.com

Please take a few moments and give this memoir a positive online review at amazon.com. Positive reviews help with getting the book to a larger audience.

And please, share about this book with your friends. It's my prayer for this book to have a widespread impact, encouraging others to step out of the boat, onto the water, and to trust God to guide and provide.

49725226R00117

Made in the USA
Columbia, SC
27 January 2019